Charlie Brown's America

Charlie Brown's America

The Popular Politics of Peanuts

Blake Scott Ball

OXFORD
UNIVERSITY PRESS

OXFORD
UNIVERSITY PRESS

Oxford University Press is a department of the University of Oxford. It furthers the University's objective of excellence in research, scholarship, and education by publishing worldwide. Oxford is a registered trade mark of Oxford University Press in the UK and certain other countries.

Published in the United States of America by Oxford University Press
198 Madison Avenue, New York, NY 10016, United States of America.

Library of Congress Cataloging-in-Publication Data
Names: Ball, Blake Scott, author.
Title: Charlie Brown's America : the popular politics of *Peanuts* / Blake Scott Ball.
Description: New York, NY : Oxford University Press, [2021] |
Includes bibliographical references and index.
Identifiers: LCCN 2020048676 (print) | LCCN 2020048677 (ebook) |
ISBN 9780190090463 (hardback) | ISBN 9780190090487 (epub) |
ISBN 9780190090494
Subjects: LCSH: Schulz, Charles M. (Charles Monroe),
1922–2000—Criticism and interpretation. |
Schulz, Charles M. (Charles Monroe), 1922-2000.
Peanuts. | Peanuts (Comic strip) | Comic books, strips, etc.—United States—Political aspects.
Classification: LCC PN6727.S3 Z624 2021 (print) | LCC PN6727.S3 (ebook) |
DDC 741.5/973—dc23
LC record available at https://lccn.loc.gov/2020048676
LC ebook record available at https://lccn.loc.gov/2020048677

DOI: 10.1093/oso/9780190090463.001.0001

3 5 7 9 8 6 4 2

Printed by Sheridan Books, Inc., United States of America

To Nana, who taught me to love reading,
and to Dr. Nelson, who taught me to love history.

Contents

Acknowledgments

Like most kids, I grew up reading comics and cartoons. My family did not subscribe to the newspaper, but my grandmother would save the Sunday funny pages for when we came to visit. I loved to read *Garfield*, *Blondie*, *Beetle Bailey*, *Hagar the Horrible*, and the long-running action serial *The Phantom*. And I genuinely loved *Peanuts*, which often appeared at the top of the front page. Charles Schulz's work, however, was not like the others. Snoopy was always entertaining. But something was different.

For starters, *Peanuts* was not always funny. A comic strip was supposed to be funny, wasn't it? While characters like Lucy might have strong, clear opinions, Charlie Brown could be frustratingly indecisive. In most cases, it was downright confusing to a kid. This is why many of my most vivid memories of reading *Peanuts* involved asking my grandmother to explain what it meant and how that was supposed to be funny. As often as not she struggled to translate the subtleties and melancholy of the strip to me. The holiday television specials were just as perplexing. They were nothing like the animated superhero shows that I loved. There were no vibrant colors, no professional voice actors, and very little action. In short, *Peanuts* was an anomaly.

This book has been my journey to try and figure out *Peanuts*, and so many people have helped me along the way. I did not know who Andrew Huebner was when I arrived for a campus visit at the University of Alabama in the spring of 2009. After an engaging conversation about his ideas concerning cultural history, though, I knew I had found my path. Over the years, Andrew was both a mentor and a friend, enduring countless meetings to discuss some new trouble that plagued my thinking. He knew when to give me space and when to give me a push. He relentlessly critiqued my footnotes and marked every typo, and yet always left me feeling encouraged about the progress I was making. Getting to work with him was a supreme pleasure and I am thankful for all the time he spared for me. Bart Elmore was another mentor who had just come out of graduate school and knew exactly what I was going through. He took time to show me the ropes of academic life and public scholarship. His boundless energy and enthusiasm always lifted my spirits and gave me the courage to step out of my comfort zone and pursue higher goals. Kari Frederickson, who was department chair for much of my graduate school career, was always looking out for me and helped me in so many ways. She was also the first person to tell me I had a chance as a writer, which meant the world to me.

Many others were instrumental in making my years at the University of Alabama fruitful and enjoyable. Holly Grout, George McClure, Sarah Steinbock-Pratt, David Beito, Larry Kohl, Margaret Peacock, Jenny Shaw, and Heather Kopelson all took an interest in my work and advised me in their fields of expertise at various stages in the project. Sharony Green was and continues to be a dear friend and encourager. John Giggie introduced me to my editor. Grad school friends made the experience worthwhile when the studying got tough. Allison Huntley, Daniel Burge, Mark Johnson, David McRae, Joseph Pearson, and Johnathan Merritt all listened to me endlessly talk about comic strips and read chapter drafts along the way. Aaron Phillips graciously helped me access resources I needed during my manuscript revisions, especially during the pandemic. Katie Deale was a constant confidante who listened to me complain about research frustrations when no one else would have listened. Marcus Witcher became a pacesetter for me as I was nearing my defense. Had it not been for working with him every day in the summer of 2016, I am not sure that I could have finished on time.

Outside of the University of Alabama, others helped guide this project along. Michael Stewart Foley worked with me on edits for my first journal article. His patience, kindness, and mentorship were exemplary and went far beyond what I would have ever expected of an editor. Kevin Kruse was equally gracious with his time when I reached out to him for advice on a Masters seminar. He eventually became a reader for my dissertation and has been an advocate for me and my work. Ben Saunders offered extensive comments on my original manuscript and this book is far better for it. Stephen Lind, a fellow *Peanuts* scholar, listened to my ideas and helped me make sense of the pieces that were holding me back. Charles Hatfield and Jared Gardner both offered encouragement, advice, and a warm welcome to a newbie to the comic studies field.

I am so thankful for all the incredible people at Oxford University Press who made this book possible. I could not have asked for a better editor than Susan Ferber. She is thorough, thoughtful, and kind. At one crucial juncture in production, she went to bat to save the book as it now appears. So much of what is good about this book has her fingerprints on it. I would also like to thank Theo Calderara, Jeremy Toynbee, and my copy editors for their contributions to the finished project.

I have been fortunate to find colleagues in my young career who have become like old friends. John Morgan, my department chair at my first position at Miles College, looked for every opportunity he could to give me time and space to work on this book. Donna Manson, my chair once I moved to Huntingdon College, was equally supportive. My first provost, Anna McEwan, celebrated my achievements and helped guide me through a low personal season. I am forever grateful to her for that. Tom Perrin and Elizabeth Hutcheon talked me into sending the draft of my manuscript off when I was still too terrified to let my editor read it. Nordis Smith helped me get copies of books and resources not readily available. Kyle Christensen helped connect me with a new *Peanuts* scholar with whom to exchange ideas.

Numerous archives were instrumental in making this book possible. The archives at Anderson University, Duke University, Syracuse University, Harvard University, NASA, the National Archives, and the presidential libraries of Johnson, Nixon, Ford, Carter, and Reagan were all tremendously helpful in locating relevant sources.

I could not have written this book without the amazing folks at the Charles M. Schulz Museum, Creative Associates, and Peanuts Worldwide. Lisa Monhoff was the archivist at the Schulz Museum when I first walked through the doors. She showed me around the collections, and her intimate knowledge from having helped create the archive was vital. Cesar Gallegos was indispensable in completing my research. He also got me a ride on the Zamboni at Snoopy's Home Ice, the ice rink Schulz built for the Santa Rosa community. Sarah Breaux was so helpful in the production phase of the book as I was navigating permissions. Paige Craddock at Creative Associates took an afternoon to show me around Schulz's old studio, which is a memory I will never forget. Craig Herman, Paul Gagliardi, and Caitlin Kelley at Peanuts Worldwide were a delight to work with during the permissions negotiations, make a difficult process much easier. Jeannie Schulz, Schulz's wife, was so gracious in taking the time to discuss the project with me and suggesting sources to consider.

So many good friends brightened my life as I went through the years of writing this book. Justin and Allison Ingram and Nick and Jaimie Sewell forced me to put the work down and have some fun now and again. Nick, in particular, discovered that the best way to motivate me was to question whether I was really ever going to finish and he used this strategy often and to great effect. Since I have moved to the Montgomery area, Carter Reeves and Keith Chandler have become the very best of friends and some of my biggest supporters. Bill Youngblood and Wes Cahoon got me excited about this project all over again with their interest in my manuscript. Currin and Kristen Clonch did the author photo for this book and helped me on a lot of home projects when I was writing or teaching. Faye Mize, my childhood neighbor, granted me an extended interview about his time in Vietnam. Unfortunately, he passed away before the book could be completed. Pleas Davis shared his own personal experiences and kept me laughing with his wonderful sense of humor.

This book is dedicated to Dr. Larry Nelson, my undergraduate advisor and mentor, who set my mind and soul ablaze with his love for history and for God. I regret that he did not live to see this fruit of his personal investment. Everyone who ever knew him was changed by the experience and I carry his memory into the classroom with me each day. It is also dedicated to Nana, my grandmother, who helped raise me and taught me to love reading and asking questions. She believed I would write a book long before I even enjoyed reading them.

Everything I am and the existence of this book I owe to my family. Mom and Dad have believed in me, supported me, and encouraged me at every stage of my life. Ashley, Lauren, and Madison, my younger siblings, gave me the motivation to try and be the best big brother I could be. Gammaw and Aunt Kerri have the gift of encouragement and always made me feel a special part of the family. Aunt Charlie and my cousin Jordan taught me that just because there were dark spots in my ancestors' past, it did not have to define me. Mary Kathryn is the best mother-in-law in the world and such a tremendous help at home. My daughters, Maleah, Macey, and Madelyn, taught me love like I never knew possible. And Katie, my beautiful bride, has been my rock through every battle of this book. She knew when to kick me into gear and when to give me a hug. Her patience, support, and commitment are far beyond what I ever deserved and I love her so much for it.

My deepest apologies to anyone I may have omitted from this list and, of course, all errors contained in this book are solely my own.

Charlie Brown's America

Introduction

Charlie Brown had a hard time choosing sides. This was always part of the humor of his character. It was also one of the many things he hated about himself.

One New Year's Eve he decided to change it once and for all: in 1965, he would be decisive, clear-cut, and well-grounded, and resolved to be "strong and firm." Ever the realist and always happy to burst Charlie Brown's bubble, Lucy would not let the boy deceive himself with such an impossible resolution. "Forget it," she blurted. "You'll always be wishy-washy."[1]

Charles M. Schulz, the creator behind the comic strip *Peanuts*, often described his work the same way. "One of the remarkable things about the strip," stated one interviewer in 1987, "is that there are no perceivable ideologies." Schulz agreed. "Sort of a wishy-washiness," he chuckled. Often the humble, Midwestern cartoonist seemed to deploy such statements as a defense mechanism to avoid staking a definite position on a controversial topic. But it was more than that. "Wishy-washiness" *was* his ideology. In practice Schulz was a sort of political chameleon, shifting left and right within the bounds of the broad middle of American political culture during the Cold War era. He was adept at creating scenes that acted as Rorschach tests for readers, broaching a controversial issue but leaving enough ambiguity for readers to see whatever excited or disgusted them. Between 1950 and 2000 Schulz reflected and amplified a complex range of popular feelings on issues from civil religion, racial integration, and women's rights to fears of capitalism's decline, environmental degradation, and the Vietnam War through his cartoons.[2]

A number of commentators, however, accused *Peanuts* of being too aloof from the most serious national and global events of its time. Social ethics professor Roger Shinn of Union Theological Seminary faulted *Peanuts* for being too "detached" from real-world problems. The *Boston Post* asserted that "in the midst of wars, rumors of wars, clamor and controversy," *Peanuts* was an "escape hatch into a 'make believe' world of serenity and laughter." Even at the end of the strip's fifty-year run in national syndication, as Americans mourned Schulz's retirement announcement and attempted to interpret his

Figure I.1 Lucy sinks Charlie Brown's New Year's resolution, insisting that he will "always be wishy-washy." Charles Schulz, *Peanuts*, December 31, 1965. © 1965 Peanuts Worldwide LLC.

legacy, journalists still viewed *Peanuts* as largely apolitical. "Inflation . . . and other current events," wrote *Newsweek*'s Mary Voboril in late 1999, "seldom invade the gentle provinces of the strip." In her reading of the series, the most pressing issues in postwar American politics were missing from the period's most-read newspaper comic strip. "Hippies, Vietnam, Watergate, Iran-Contra, CIA spy scandals, impeachments, elections," she listed to prove her point, "never found a topical home here."[3]

Schulz often seemed to confirm this line of reasoning. A personally conservative man, he always thought of himself as a businessman first and foremost. His primary job, he believed, was to help sell newspapers. Controversial political positions were the quickest way to undermine a comic strip's popular appeal, he believed. "You're being hired by a newspaper editor and he buys your strip because he wants to sell his newspaper," Schulz explained to one interviewer. "So why should you double-cross him by putting in things that will aggravate him? That's not my job." In his mind, he went to great lengths to avoid controversial issues. "I lean over backwards to keep from offending anybody," he told a reporter for the *Milwaukee Journal*.[4]

Yet Schulz regularly addressed controversial issues in his comic strip, animated television programs, and feature films. At the peak of *Peanuts*' popularity, Schulz's thoughts on such issues reached over 100 million readers each day. It is possible to pinpoint exactly how some readers interpreted *Peanuts*, because they told Schulz. By 1971, Schulz was receiving as many as a hundred new fan letters every day. While not all of this correspondence survived years of spring cleaning and storage, as well as a fire that claimed his first California studio in 1966, a sizable collection of letters has survived and are maintained in the Charles M. Schulz Museum and Research Center in Santa Rosa, California, just down the road from the artist's second studio. This book relies heavily on those collections to uncover readers' thoughts about *Peanuts* and how they saw it interacting with the Cold War world. This book also draws from numerous interviews, articles, speeches, private letters, and oral histories to try and understand what Schulz was thinking, both when he produced the art and when he encountered others' interpretations of his work. Finally, it investigates various public appropriations, both legal and extralegal, of Schulz's characters and concepts to see how his work took on a cultural life far beyond the newspaper page or television screen. In many cases, the *Peanuts* characters became repositories for and expressions of Americans' dreams, hopes, fears, and worries.[5]

In doing so, *Charlie Brown's America* demonstrates that *Peanuts* was never simply an escapist endeavor, but regularly touched on the lived experience of socially- and politically-conscious Americans in the postwar era. While *Peanuts* readers of differing political stripes regularly wrote in to argue with Schulz about the ideas they saw in his work, what is most revealing is how often people of opposing viewpoints loved the same comic strip but for contradictory reasons. Walt Kelly, a former Disney cartoonist who became famous in the 1950s for his political satire comic strip *Pogo*, has been credited by one scholar with "providing in his strip . . . a rallying point around which like-minded people could gather." Schulz provided the opposite: a rallying point around which people of diverse opinions could gather and debate.[6]

This book is not a biography, at least not one of Charles Schulz. If anything, it is a biography of *Peanuts*' cultural life, both in the minds of the creator and his audience, as well as in the world outside the close-knit community of fan and idol. In this way, the characters are treated as both the creation of the cartoonist and also as public symbols who took on a life of their own after leaving the printing press.

While *Peanuts* may be the most successful example of the comic strip medium, it was deeply rooted and inseparable from the history of the art. Comic strips evolved from the raucous visual world of 1890s advertising, as newspaper moguls sought to expand their readership, and burgeoning corporations searched for a means to capture public attention and private dollars through recognizable characters. In the rapidly urbanized and industrialized nineteenth-century United States, comic strips and illustrated advertising served as an indispensable visual guide to life in the multicultural, multilingual melting pot of American cities. In this context, the symbols of comic arts became a sort of linguistic mediary between the wide range of peoples in turn-of-the-century America. It is no coincidence, then, that comic strip characters like Buster Brown easily danced between the funny pages and mass advertising. The approval of a recognizable cultural figure could often be just the impetus a wary consumer needed to try out a new product.[7]

Integral to the success of the American comic strip was a characteristic comic scholars call polysemy. This meant that the same character or scene could be reasonably read in multiple ways by a diverse audience. The more people could relate to a comic strip, the more successful that comic strip could be in sales and marketing. Sometimes this meant using racial, ethnic, or gendered stereotypes to calcify the boundaries of American cultural citizenship. But in the most transcendent works of the comic strip medium, even these exclusionary boundaries could be bridged or dismantled to broaden the audience. Comic strips like *Katzenjammer Kids*, *Little Nemo in Slumberland*, and *Krazy Kat* all found ways to broaden audiences, whether through including ethnic characters in the American citizenry, traveling through universal dream worlds, or abandoning the world of direct social discourse for the allegories of anthropomorphized animals.

Peanuts represents the ultimate perfection of the comic strip medium. Charles Schulz created a comic world so successfully polysemic that it attracted the largest audience in the history of the medium, counting every other American as a daily reader at its height. The comic strip sold newspapers like no other in a time of considerable consolidation and decline in the industry. There are countless stories in the Schulz archive of editors being barraged by complaints when *Peanuts* was accidentally left out of the final copy of local newspapers, or fans who carried a second newspaper subscription because their local paper did not carry *Peanuts*. But Schulz's work also sold much more than newspapers. By the 1970s *Peanuts* was a multimillion dollar licensing franchise, more visible than any property not owned by Disney. In fact, in *Forbes* magazine's 2019 report of the top-earning past celebrity estates in the world, Charles Schulz finished third behind only Michael Jackson and Elvis Presly. While many critics over the years lamented Schulz's licensing decisions as a commercial sellout, the truth is that *Peanuts* actually succeeded more than any other comic strip at doing what comic strips were invented to do: sell. For his part, Schulz always insisted that he kept the comic strip foremost, never allowing the quality to slide. The proof of his commitment was the fact that unlike most successful cartoonists in the industry, he refused to outsource any part of the comic strip to an assistant, whether drafting, inking, or lettering. For nearly fifty years, everything readers saw in the *Peanuts* comic strip came from the mind and hands of Charles Schulz.[8]

Central to Charles Schulz's success was his adept usage of both ambiguity and allegory to create space for multiple interpretations. Ambiguity, or a sort of intentional vagueness on the part of the cartoonist, was key in the way that he often handled religious and philosophical issues. In the foremost examples, such as the October 20, 1963 *Peanuts* strip where Schulz used only eight words across eleven panels to comment on the controversy over school prayer, the cartoonist's ambiguity was so successful that readers could not agree among themselves where the artist stood on the issue of school prayer. Ambiguity allowed the cartoonist to virtually disappear and leave the readers with a sort of mirror through which they could evaluate their own opinions of the issue at hand. Allegory in *Peanuts*, on the other hand, utilized readily recognizable symbols and stories, like the World War I flying ace's dog fights with the historic Red Baron, to enable Schulz to broach enormously sensitive contemporary issues like the Vietnam War. Schulz's innate sense and skill for employing ambiguity and allegory set him apart from his contemporaries, and his mastery of polysemy enabled readers to see the world they wanted to see. And for decades, readers got what they were looking for with the delivery of every daily newspaper.

There are at least three reasons why a study of *Peanuts* provides new insights into Cold War America. First, the need for fifty years of daily content required Schulz to be remarkably responsive to the social, political, and cultural changes in American life as he attempted to deliver his unique voice to an audience that could be a rapidly moving target. Second, the comic strip was capable of eliciting emotional connections to politics that did not always appear in more traditional mediums of debate, providing scholars with a way to think more deeply about the role of emotional lives of Cold War Americans. Third, while the cartoonist tried to be responsive to his audience, his audience was also very responsive to him. The decades of fan mail to Schulz includes voices that likely would have never ended up in the archive of a congressman or senator. Many of these people, like Schulz himself, did not consider themselves highly educated or of tremendous importance, yet they felt comfortable to share their deep concerns about their country and the world with their favorite newspaper cartoonist.

Peanuts has been woefully understudied for an artifact of such incredible cultural significance. Still, there have been a handful of important studies of Charles Schulz and his work. In 1989, Rheta Grimsley Johnson published an authorized biography of Schulz titled *Good Grief: The Story of Charles M. Schulz*, a popular memoir that had the benefit of extensive interviews with Schulz himself, though Schulz obviously played a considerable role in determining its boundaries. In 2007, David Michaelis was able to delve into some of the darker elements of Schulz's life with his bestselling *Schulz and Peanuts*. His considerable work in digging up early syndicate correspondence in Manhattan—a collection of documents that became an important part of the opening of the Schulz Museum archive—was essential in opening the door for studies such as this one. While Michaelis discussed the cultural influence of *Peanuts*, however, his book tended to focus on the most unseemly and sensational elements of Schulz's relatively tame life and did little to address the later decades of Schulz's career. Two other recent books have been significant contributions to the study of *Peanuts*. Stephen Lind's *A Charlie Brown Religion* offers a religious biography of the cartoonist, while Jared Gardner and Ian Gordon's edited volume *The Comics of Charles Schulz: The Good Grief of Modern Life* was the first concerted effort among critical scholars to analyze the meaning and significance of the comic strips. Still, none of these volumes provided an all-encompassing study of *Peanuts*'s immense place in Cold War American life.[9]

The chapters in this book are organized chronologically, each one highlighting an important theme that defined the direction of the *Peanuts* property in those years. This means that at times, chapters will backtrack to focus on the development of a theme earlier in Schulz's career.

Chapter 1 introduces the man behind *Peanuts*. Beginning with his childhood, this biographical chapter follows Charles Schulz through school and his art education. It then delves into the unexpected passing of his mother, his draft orders for the Army, and service in World War II. Following the war, Schulz returned home searching for meaning in life. He found it in evangelical Christianity and in the pursuit of his dream of becoming a nationally known cartoonist. The remainder of the chapter follows Schulz through his surprisingly rapid rise to a nationally syndicated comic strip.

Chapter 2 investigates the Cold War origins of *Peanuts*. The strip in the early 1950s was quite different from what later generations would come to recognize and cherish. During these years Schulz became a sort of cult hero of existentialism, drawing a strip that could be quite bleak in its meditations about modern life. Issues of social alienation, atomic anxiety, and emotional conflict were common themes of this period during which Schulz's artistic and literary styles were developing. From early in his career, Schulz attracted considerable attention for some of the deep subjects addressed in his works. Linus's security blanket in particular became a massive hit with both young parents raising the baby boomer generation and psychologists looking for relatable ways to express the unique psychological issues they were observing in modern life. Schulz's work also ascended to the heights of both his profession and national influence during the 1950s, winning him top accolades among his peers and admiration in the White House.

Chapter 3 explores *Peanuts*' religious commentary. By the end of the 1950s, Cold War America was deep in the throes of a third Great Awakening. This mid-century revivalism had its origins in the nuclear anxieties of the decade and was fueled by a number of middle-class social worries from racial integration and urban decay to fears of juvenile delinquency and the decline of American culture. These were the same issues addressed in *Peanuts* as the comic strip made its rapid climb to national prominence. It is not surprising, then, that Schulz's work became overtly evangelical by the end of the decade. And by the middle of the 1960s, Schulz and a growing religious subset in his audience would come to see *Peanuts* as a lone bastion of evangelical Christianity in American popular culture. This change showed up most drastically in the character Linus Van Pelt, who became America's best-known pop theologian. Linus regularly rebuked, counseled, and corrected his friends with direct quotations from the Bible and his meditations on Christian theology. This new direction in *Peanuts* increasingly singled Schulz out as a Christian cartoonist and pop thinker.

While religion was becoming a central part of *Peanuts* by the 1960s, racial diversity was not. Schulz had pushed back against gender norms of the mid-twentieth century, but like all other national syndicated cartoonists in the 1960s, largely avoided the minefield of race and civil rights. By 1968, however, Schulz would become a somewhat reluctant reformer when he introduced the first black regular cast member in a national comic strip. Yet while Schulz was the first to take that step, he would struggle in subsequent years to find an authentic voice and role for his new cast member. Chapter 4 tells this story of the integration of *Peanuts*.

In the late 1960s, there was only one issue that could ultimately overtake civil rights as the leading concern for Americans: the Vietnam War. Chapter 5 analyzes Charles Schulz's commentary on the divisive conflict that came to define three presidencies and a generation of young Americans. By the end of the decade, Snoopy had blossomed into a central character in the comic strip. His characteristic daydreams and regular role-playing increasingly set him apart from the other characters in *Peanuts* as he imagined a world far larger than theirs. Schulz would openly come to worry that Snoopy might come to overshadow the children—and in many cases in the 1960s, he did. Nowhere was this more true than in Snoopy's Vietnam era dreams of endless combat and defeat. This chapter tells the story of how Snoopy's war in *Peanuts* during the 1960s and 1970s became a voice for the desperate anguish many

Americans felt as they tried to maintain support for individual soldiers while simultaneously hating the draft and despising the Vietnam War.

Chapter 6 delves into the ways that Schulz's personal disenchantment with the role of the federal government was displayed in *Peanuts* in the 1970s and 1980s. Like much of his audience, Schulz increasingly characterized his understanding of American values in individualistic terms and found subtle ways to vilify government expansion, on issues such as environmental protection and abortion rights. This chapter also analyzes three different federal ad campaigns involving *Peanuts* characters during the Nixon, Ford, and Carter administrations. Dealing with issues of energy consumption, the American economic system, and air pollution, these three campaigns carried a central message of personal responsibility, decentralization, and the power of the individual to shape a better future. There was also a clear emphasis on free-market capitalism as the solution to the national problems of consumer waste, stagnation, and environmental degradation. This chapter examines previously unpublished correspondence of the friendship between Charles Schulz and Ronald Reagan, from the latter's governorship to the presidency. Reagan joked with Schulz on the eve of his election in 1980 that Snoopy might be able to undercut his appeal to his base. Reagan even offered the famous beagle a cabinet position in his administration in exchange for not entering the presidential race. As this chapter demonstrates, *Peanuts* had close but subtle ties to the rightward shift in American politics. *Peanuts*, of course, was far from a rightwing, ideological publication. But in the 1970s and 1980s, there was a decided shift in tone in Schulz's work that mirrored growing public skepticism of government management and the rising culture wars. As the center moved, so did *Peanuts*.

Chapter 7 turns to feminism, sexuality, and gender identity in the work of Charles Schulz. *Peanuts* had always been about the battle of the sexes. On October 3, 1950, the second day of the strip, the little girl Patty had skipped down the sidewalk gleefully reciting the children's rhyme, "Sugar and spice and everything nice, that's what little girls are made of," stopping only to emphasize her point by giving Charlie Brown a black eye. Yet it was Lucy Van Pelt who most embodied the characteristics of the powerful female in *Peanuts*, refusing to accept her prescribed place in society. But with all of her strength, Lucy also embodied many negative stereotypes of women in postwar America. As the 1960s progressed, so did Schulz's handling of his female characters, and by the 1970s *Peanuts* became intertwined with the feminist movement in 1970s. Still some of the most prominent connections between *Peanuts* and social movements came not from the artist, but from fans who employed the characters to reflect their own feelings and ideas about the changing times. This chapter will conclude with an in-depth look into how Peppermint Patty and Marcie became important symbols in lesbian publications, against Schulz's wishes.

In the fall of 1970, as Schulz celebrated the thirtieth anniversary of *Peanuts*, a young artist named Gary Trudeau launched *Doonesbury*, filled with unrepentant cold sarcasm, and became the voice of a new generation in the same way *Peanuts* once had spoken to the alienated and discontent of the 1950s. Charles Schulz despised *Doonesbury*. Aside from seeming unprofessional and downright disrespectful, in the aging cartoonist's estimation, Trudeau's work rested on what Schulz believed was the cheapest and least durable form of humor: political commentary. Schulz prided himself on building *Peanuts* on more solid ground, focusing on timeless human experience and eternal values of love, friendship, and hope. But *Peanuts* was never as timeless as Schulz liked to imagine, not even when it came to politics.

The book concludes with a CBS miniseries titled *This is America, Charlie Brown*, which aired over the 1988–89 television season. In this program, Schulz tried to encapsulate what he saw as the common history and culture that had brought prosperity to the United States in the twentieth century. This program was a unique blend of conservative Christian traditionalism and progressive historical revision. The result was a miniseries largely panned by critics and audiences alike. By trying to comment to a broad audience—a strategy that had been effective throughout Schulz's career—by the twentieth century, *Peanuts* was losing its prominence. It had fallen out of step with a society in the throes of what historians now refer to as the "culture wars." Because Schulz tended to play to the middle and downplay his political opinions, a strategy that had made him a cultural darling for the better part of forty years, his work now seemed quaint and antiquated in the polarized world of *The Simpsons* and Pat Buchanan's "War for the Soul of America" speech. Newspapers like the *Chicago Tribune*—one of the original seven newspapers to publish *Peanuts* in 1950—openly called for the retirement of Charlie Brown and the gang. Schulz's strong base of evangelical readers too came to question the depth and authenticity of the artist's faith as he expressed a growing discomfort with evangelicalism's preachiness and insistence on moral conformity.

In the end, Schulz found himself right where he had always been: stuck in the wishy-washy middle of the American political spectrum. And where that centrism had actually served as a virtue during the political battles of the Cold War, it left *Peanuts* without a side in the fever pitch of a new age of open partisanship.

The epilogue examines the legacy of *Peanuts* today. In 2001, ABC purchased the rights to the television specials and in the 2010s experienced the highest ratings since their premieres in the 1960s and 1970s. In 2015, 20th Century Fox premiered the first feature length *Peanuts* movie in over thirty years to great critical and commercial success. That summer Charlie Brown was once again the focus of American media attention, though in a drastically different political moment than the one he had walked into sixty-five years earlier. There were signs, however, that he was as relevant as he had ever been. The film inspired a summer trend of *Peanuts*-themed avatars on Facebook that signaled a clamoring among some Americans for a return to a more cordial, wishy-washy political middle in the midst of a historically contentious and crude presidential campaign. It was as though they were joining President Barack Obama as he wrote with longing nostalgia in his introduction to the twenty-fifth and final volume of "The Complete *Peanuts*" collection in 2016: "Like millions of Americans, I grew up with *Peanuts*. But I never outgrew it."

But in other ways, America did seem to be outgrowing *Peanuts*. This was most apparent in 2016 when MetLife ended its prominent thirty-year advertising deal with *Peanuts*. Schulz had produced an art empire that had expressed the concerns of Cold War America, but at the same time left a body of work inextricably linked to that past era.

1

You're a Good Man, Charles Schulz

The Making of an American Original

January 2, 2000 marked a sad beginning to the new millennium, announced Ann Shields of the *Los Angeles Times*. The melancholy had nothing to do with the long-feared consequences of the "Y2K bug" or the looming disaster of the dot-com bubble burst. No, it was a sad day because Charles Schulz, creator and artist of the *Peanuts* comic strip for nearly fifty years, officially retired. For fans of Charlie Brown, Lucy, Snoopy, and all the "gang," contract stipulations meant that the end of Schulz's career also signaled the end of *Peanuts*.[1]

Schulz's retirement would leave an immense void, not just in American cultural life, but in the everyday routines of millions of Americans. Schulz's "words are read in more homes than many literary giants," Shields wrote without the slightest sense of hyperbole. *Peanuts* had been such a consistent part of daily life for the last half century (even an emergency bypass surgery in 1981 had barely slowed the cartoonist's daily output). This loss felt personal. When the cartoonist passed away from complications of advanced colon cancer only six weeks later—the night before his final comic strip ran on Valentine's Day—the loss became permanent.[2]

Peanuts had made Charles Schulz a millionaire. It had also made him a rather unlikely celebrity. He had been friend to presidents, professional athletes, world-class artists, and musicians. His artwork had been exhibited to international acclaim at some of the most important cultural centers in the world. He had also mentored countless other newcomers to the world of comic strips. He had been a husband, a father of five, and a generous philanthropist to many laudable causes.

But for most Americans, he was renowned because he was "Schulz," the man who brought those quirky, delightful, sympathetic, vulnerable, and deeply authentic cartoon children to life every morning in the newspaper and every holiday on television. Postwar Americans had grown up with Charlie Brown and Snoopy and Linus and Lucy and Peppermint Patty and Franklin and all the rest. The end of *Peanuts* truly marked the end of an era. The end, perhaps, of what *Time* magazine publisher Henry Luce had famously called "the American Century."

Every story with an ending, of course, had to have a beginning. Charles Schulz's story could only be described as exceptional. The world mourning Schulz's loss could hardly have been more different from the world that had made the cartoonist. His time had not been one of high speed digital connectivity or nationally televised broadcast events. His time was a distant remnant of a past world. But it was this world that gave birth to the country's—and perhaps the world's—most loveable loser and his unlikely creator.

Charles Monroe Schulz was born into the booming 1920s, but grew up during the nation's Great Depression. Schulz had fond memories of those years in Minnesota's Twin Cities. Many of his childhood memories revolved around playing sports. He especially loved baseball and played every warm day he possibly could. "We played on vacant lots, with baseballs that had the covers knocked off and had been taped up with black electrical tape . . . and we used cracked bats," he would later recall. He also played hockey with neighborhood friends, though seldomly on actual ice rinks. Instead, Schulz's father would flood their tiny backyard in the winter months and the boys would wait for freezing weather. Only occasionally did they ever slip onto the local school rinks, and even then they had to do so after dark and on a night when the moon gave enough light to play. More than any other sport, however, he loved golf. In high school, one of his few accomplishments—his academic performance had gone from solid in middle school to downright dreadful—was landing a place on the school golf team. Sam Snead—one of the early legends of American golf—was one of his personal heroes and he dreamed of earning a spot in the US National Open tournament. But no sport compared to his love for drawing.[3]

"If there is such a thing as being born to do something I think I was born to draw comic strips," Schulz told a *Penthouse* reporter in 1971. In countless interviews throughout his career, journalists saw destiny in the fact that at only two days old Schulz's uncle had nicknamed him "Sparky," after the new horse "Sparkplug" in the comic strip *Barney Google*. Whether fate or journalistic license, this anecdote demonstrated the ubiquity of comic strips in American popular culture in the early twentieth century. The boy took to drawing at an early age, beginning as far back as he could remember. Years later, when asked if he ever dreamed of such success, Schulz would reply, "Well, frankly, I guess

I did expect it, because, after all, it was something I had planned for since I was six years old."[4]

In school, he quickly distinguished himself as a budding artist. During his first week of kindergarten, the teacher asked the students to draw a picture using crayons and paper. Schulz combined an image of a man shoveling snow with a palm tree in the background. The child had blended a very familiar Minnesota image with the much more exotic plant life his mother had described to him while reading aloud letters from her relatives in Needles, California. As the teacher made her rounds in the room, she stopped over young Schulz and announced, "Someday, Charles, you're going to be an artist." His classmates took notice as well. "I used to decorate my loose-leaf binders with drawings of Mickey Mouse, the Three Little Pigs, and Popeye," he wrote. "Whenever friends in class would see these cartoons, I would be asked to draw them on their notebooks as well." Though it was still rough, this was the type of talent that demanded sharing and Schulz's personality, always seeking the affirmation of others' happiness, was just the type to share it.[5]

There were no other artists or authors in Schulz's family, but the boy received plenty of encouragement to pursue his dream. His father, a barber who owned a shop in downtown St. Paul, possessed a practical mind and a strong work ethic. Carl Schulz was the primary reason his son did not remember those Depression years in the harsh tones of so many of his contemporaries. "I always admired him," Schulz told one interviewer, because he only had a third-grade education but "worked pitching hay in Nebraska one summer to earn enough money to go to barber school, got himself a couple of jobs and eventually bought his own barber shop." Though his father worked tirelessly to maintain his business and pay his employees—especially during the dark days of the Depression—he took special care to foster his only child's passion: comic strips. "He loved to read the comic strips," Schulz remembered of his father. "We discussed them together and worried about what was going to happen next to certain of the characters." Every weekend Schulz and his father took turns reading four different newspaper comics sections—two Minneapolis papers and two St. Paul papers. While it was not unusual for a family in these years to subscribe to a couple of papers, their dedication to the funnies section was extraordinary.[6]

His mother was no less encouraging. Though she could not entirely appreciate her husband's and son's obsession with comic strips—"How could you sit there and laugh at something out loud?" she would ask the two; "I don't understand that!"—she wanted her son to pursue his dream. In fact, she was the one who suggested he work to hone his skills as an artist through professional training. During his senior year of high school she came across an ad for Art Instruction Schools, Inc., a cartooning correspondence course located in Minneapolis. The cost was $170, a whopping sum for the family and yet he never heard his parents complain. Such a course suited Schulz perfectly for he was deathly afraid of sitting in a regular art school classroom "because I'd be right back where I was in high school—in a class with a lot of people who could draw better than I could" (or so Schulz later claimed). Fears of inferiority plagued the aspiring cartoonist. "I really was afraid of art school," he told another reporter, "because I didn't think I was good enough." Even when he was given the option to drop off his lessons in person, he opted to mail them in so as not to have to face the instructor.[7]

But as he studied the instructors' responses, practiced, and improved, he slowly gained the courage to go to lessons in person. His growing confidence paid off as he found that he was indeed good enough to stand among his peers. "The first night, [the instructor] put up different cartoon characters from the papers that we had to copy," he remembered. Studying the smooth, curving lines of Chic Young's *Blondie* characters, he swiftly completed the assignment. "I was done way ahead of everybody else," he reminisced, "and I could draw them just as well as [the instructor] could." The young man was soaring: "Now, that made me feel good. Because I knew then that I really had something special." He had possessed the passion for cartooning since childhood, and finally his diligent study and practice were paying major dividends as he raced to the head of his art school class. Not even a rejection letter from Walt Disney Animation Studios following his high school graduation could stand between the budding artist and his lofty dream of writing his own syndicated strip. Then the war came.[8]

He received his draft notice in late November 1942, just days after his twentieth birthday. Photos from that year show a pleasant yet uncertain young man with boyish looks and slicked-back hair, slouching back on his heels, so slim as nearly to disappear in his loose-fitting clothes. The government's form letter could not have come at a worse time. For the last couple years after high school graduation, the teenager had watched his mother crumble from treatment for cervical cancer. Stationed at Fort Snelling, nestled at the confluence of the Minnesota and Mississippi rivers just south of the Twin Cities, Schulz took full advantage of the generous leave time in this phase of his service and returned home every weekend to be with his parents. All the while his mother went in and out of the hospital, her health declining faster than doctors could keep apace.

On Sunday evening, February 28, as the draftee prepared to make his trip back to base, he reluctantly slipped through the doorway of his mother's room. There in the darkness, his mother looked away toward the wall. Like

Figure 1.1 Schulz was drafted in 1942 and served three years in the Army during World War II. Courtesy of the Charles M. Schulz Museum and Research Center.

her son, she did not wish to face the moment that lingered before them. Schulz finally broke the silence to tell his mother he must be going, it was time to say goodbye. "Yes, I suppose we should say goodbye," she responded rather calmly. Slowly, painfully, she looked at her son. "Well," he recalled her saying, "Goodbye, Sparky. We'll probably never see each other again." Those words hung in his mind for the rest of his life.[9]

The next day, the first day of a still wintry March, his mother's prophecy came true. Though his father raced to retrieve his son, it was not quick enough. As Schulz entered the main hall at the base to meet his father he found him across the room on the phone, first stoic, then quietly weeping. The dreaded day had come, and the two were now alone. "Our tiny family was torn apart," Schulz lamented.[10]

The funeral followed in a blur and then off he went to Fort Campbell, Kentucky to prepare for deployment. Schulz was alone in a sea of unremarkable, barely distinguishable recruits like himself, one of more than four and a half million men serving in the Army by the end of 1942. Few things were worse than being drafted, Schulz believed. Years later the experience still brought up memories of childhood summer camps, which for him, "was the equivalent to being drafted." This was such a bewildering time for the newly motherless young man. Instilled with his father's sense of faithful duty, he still "met [World War II] with the same lack of enthusiasm" with which he had once faced those boyhood summer camps. In many ways, Charlie Brown's lingering depression was born of Schulz's coerced military service at this formative moment in his life. "The three years I spent in the army," he later confided, "taught me all I needed to know about loneliness."[11]

Schulz found it "almost unbearable" to never know when he or any of his fellow soldiers would be returned home. "We used to sit around in the evenings and talk about these things," he recalled, "and we were completely convinced that we were going to be in for the rest of our lives." Trapped so far away from his father—"the only person in the world I had to worry about"—Schulz faced a conflict "that seemed to have no end in sight." Part of his uncertainty was rooted in ceaseless training and waiting. Drafted in early 1942, he would not be deployed until February 1945 when his company boarded a retooled luxury liner in the Boston Harbor for a thirteen-day voyage to the newly liberated beaches of Normandy.[12]

Schulz did manage to maintain a sketchbook while he was off at war. With its cover decorated much like the notebooks he had illustrated for his classmates a few years earlier, he titled the sketchbook "As We Were." This title established a theme for the types of drawings that filled the pages. Many of them were rather realistic sketches of the mundane daily life of soldiers: resting by their vehicles, shaving, ironing their clothes, sleeping in their bunks. These sketches resembled stylized photos, with the slender, long lines that had characterized action art in comic books and elsewhere in the 1940s. In other sequences in the book Schulz employed a more cartoonish style with the rounded shapes that would come to define his style. These pieces were done in the form of a single-panel editorial cartoon and the substance lampooned the daily life of the soldier, much like the work of Bill Mauldin's *Willie and Joe* then running in the military's publication *Stars and Stripes*. While the pages of the notebook were filled with artwork, the inside of the cover—filled with names, addresses, and personal notes from the soldiers he met along the way—told the story of a man deeply connected to people.[13]

By the time of his Atlantic passage, Schulz had proven himself to be an able soldier, working his way up to staff sergeant and leader of a light machine gun squad. In retrospect, though he would credit his time in the army as "the source of many of my problems," World War II became a major source of pride for him. Never really a tough kid, Schulz felt "exonerated by World War II by becoming a squad leader" because "you couldn't be a sissy and be that." Nonetheless, his brief experiences with combat almost pushed him beyond his limits. After taking fire on their position outside Dachau, Schulz aimed his 50-caliber machine gun and squeezed the trigger, but no shots rang out as two German soldiers rushed out of hiding to surrender. To his own relief, Schulz had forgotten in the haste of the moment that the 50-caliber had a safety that required a second pull of the trigger to engage. Another instance required the young Minnesotan to make certain a German artillery building was clear of enemy soldiers. As he approached the entrance to toss a grenade, a small dog scampered inside in search of food. Schulz could not bring himself to harm the dog and opted to investigate the building in person. It was empty.[14]

Schulz's combat experience put him on the brink of realities that deeply unnerved him: the brink of Hitler's Holocaust, the brink of killing with his own hands. But he was never forced over. In his own estimation he managed to fight "a pretty civilized war." He returned home twenty-five pounds heavier and more confident than before. In a photograph with his father in late 1945, the once retreating, slender boy had clearly become a man, muscular and tall. He had survived, but was also acutely troubled by the whole experience. He was convinced "that there is nothing glorious about war."[15]

Living in a small apartment above the barber shop with his father, the young veteran had no desire for a college education or a regular job. He was in pursuit of a dream deferred. After being turned down for jobs in several Twin City area art departments, he nearly landed a job lettering tombstones. He was quietly grateful when the employer never telephoned to offer him the position. In March 1946, he finally found work lettering panels at the Catechetical Guild Educational Society, publishers of a series of Catholic comic magazines titled *Topix Comics*. This job did not accomplish the goal of publishing his own strip, but at least it was work in the comics field. He was even given the opportunity in February and April of 1947 to draw his own cartoon in *Topix Comics*. Titled "Just Keep Laughing . . ." and pinned under his nickname, "Sparky," the artwork only vaguely resembled the first panels of *Peanuts* that would follow three years later. Terribly unfocused, the characters included adults, children, and even ants in a rather unremarkable page of panels. It did, however, include a few sports-related jokes, staples in his later work. One of the panels showed a boy and girl sitting on a sidewalk, the boy with a baseball bat in hand. "Y'know, Judy," the boy reasoned, "I think I could learn to love you if your batting average was just a little higher." This was the first time Schulz demonstrated his potential for developing a strip about children. When his friend and mentor Frank Wing saw the strip he remarked, "Sparky, I think you should draw more of these little kids. They are pretty good."[16]

Four months later, Schulz was hired as an instructor at the Art Instruction School where he had previously been a student. This opportunity was beneficial to the budding artist in a number of ways. It provided him a steady income as an artist, even if it was in an educational capacity. It allowed him

Figure 1.2 In one of Schulz's earliest published cartoons the cartoonist was already exhibiting his humorous take on childhood. Courtesy of the Charles M. Schulz Museum and Research Center.

abundant practice on the fundamentals of line and style that would come to define his expertly composed later works. It also gave him time and space to continue honing his own original ideas and a circle of other skilled young artists to provide constructive criticisms of his work.

The late 1940s were also a period of deep spiritual awakening for the young war veteran. In part to find friends and in part to explore the deeper meaning of life, Schulz began attending a Church of God congregation in St. Paul. The pastor of the church was the same man who had conducted his mother's funeral. Here he found a very active group of young people and began regularly studying the Bible with them. "The more I thought about the matter during those studying times," he wrote, "the more I realized that I really loved God." He came to attribute his surviving the years after his mother's death, the draft, and the war to the work of God. "I accepted Jesus Christ by gratitude," he articulated. There was no emotional conversion experience nor revivalist altar call. Schulz approached Christianity the same way he approached everything else: calmly, quietly, and with his full intellect.[17]

For artistic inspiration, Schulz turned to the comic strips he loved. George Herriman's *Krazy Kat* was perhaps the greatest influence on young Schulz's art. "I always thought if I could just do something as good as *Krazy Kat*, I would be happy. *Krazy Kat* was always my goal," Schulz told *Psychology Today*. *Krazy Kat* was an anomaly in the comics. The story revolved around three characters: Krazy (a cat), Ignatz (a mouse), and Officer Pupp (a dog). Herriman set his strip in an expansive fantasy world and engaged his trio in a unique reversal of roles where Krazy loved Ignatz (though the cat often lamented his confusion over his own gender), Ignatz tormented Krazy with bricks, and Officer Pupp worked tirelessly to protect Krazy from Ignatz. The strip's biggest fan was George Herriman's boss, William Randolph Hearst. While *Krazy Kat* was never a commercial success it delighted numerous intellectuals, reportedly even President Woodrow Wilson, who would often read the strip before entering war cabinet meetings during the Great War. Herriman's greatest strength was his unrelenting experimentation with his art and literary forms, weaving a tale that often read more like ancient fable than a mere cartoon on cheap paper.[18]

Schulz loved Herriman's "wonderful scratchy-pen effect" and the fact that the strip was "quite literate." Like Schulz's own work, *Krazy Kat* chronicled a never-ending tale of unrequited love. Schulz did not have access to the strip as a boy because it was not published in any of the Twin City papers—the strip only ran in thirty-five papers at the time of Herriman's death in 1944. When a collection of *Krazy Kat*—with an introduction by poet E. E. Cummings—was published in 1946 it was a revelation for the young artist. He rigorously studied Herriman's style and techniques, which drove Schulz to think more deeply about his own, "to create a feature that went beyond the mere actions of ordinary children." Years later when Schulz was establishing his own place in American culture, an original *Krazy Kat* page hung on the wall of his studio as he drew.[19]

There were other influences as well. Milton Caniff, artist of *Terry and the Pirates* (1934) and *Steve Canyon* (1947), was one of Schulz's favorite action artists. Known as the "Rembrandt of the comic strip," Caniff's work was cinematic with rich plots, well-developed characters, exotic settings, and lightning-fast pacing. He was enormously influential to artists of Schulz's generation and was a founding member of the National Cartoonists Society. Most of the action strips of the early fifties imitated the Caniff style, featuring dark shading and perfectly sculpted heroes and femme fatales. While Schulz did not draw an action strip, he did focus on character development and extended storylines, keys to Caniff's success. Al Capp's *Li'l Abner* (1934), a wildly popular comic strip that parodied rural America, was also an important influence. Capp's strip was highly political, sarcastic, and satirical—nothing like *Peanuts,* but influential on Schulz's love for comic strips nonetheless. Roy Crane was perhaps the greatest influence among the artists Schulz followed as a child. His famous *Wash Tubbs* (1924) mixed realistic characters and settings with a more cartoonish lead character. He also mixed in minimalist panels alongside his more detailed ones. These prominent cartoonists all influenced an entire generation of artists after them. Schulz was only unique in the way he blended their particular strengths and contributions with his own style and ideas.[20]

In the summer of 1947, Schulz published a few panels with the *Minneapolis Tribune* and then landed an interview with the senior editor of the St. Paul *Pioneer Press.* The editor liked what he saw and gave Schulz the opportunity he had been searching for: a weekly comic strip of his own. *Li'l Folks*, as the artist titled it, was a page of three to four single panel gags featuring a group of unnamed children and a small black and white dog. The panels had no linear progression or interrelation to one another. Each was a story unto itself. On two different occasions in 1948, Schulz introduced a character named Charlie Brown. These two Charlie Browns resembled their later namesake in title only. One was blonde and the other dark-haired, neither looking like each other nor the smiling, bald little boy in the opening day of *Peanuts* to come in 1950.[21]

The *Li'l Folks* panels were hardly remarkable. The artwork was not particularly impressive, though it improved considerably over the strip's two-year run. The stories centered around children trying to act years beyond their age in a world built much too large for them. These children were often concerned with the future, such as the little girl in a December 26, 1948 panel who could not enjoy the passing parade because she interpreted it as a sign "that life has passed me by." While *Li'l Folks* was a major personal milestone for Schulz, it does not appear to have been enormously popular. It is unclear exactly why, but the strip always appeared in the women's section of the paper. Perhaps the editor assumed that only women would be interested in a strip that focused solely on children or that only women would appreciate Schulz's insistence upon flipping traditional gender roles, often making the girls the dominant characters in these panels. Nonetheless, publishing a strip of his own enhanced his resume as he continued his weekly practice of submitting cartoons to national publications.[22]

His strategy and determination paid off when, beginning in the spring of 1948, the *Saturday Evening Post* published seventeen of his panels. These drawings evidenced his new focus on drawing children. The first panel in this group carried no caption and showed a boy reading a book seated at the very end of a chaise lounge with his feet stretched out to the ottoman. The artwork was notable for its clarity. Schulz's clean, thin lines gave form and meaning to an otherwise blank page. His later minimalist style was born of these efforts for the *Post* as he labored to deliver the broadest possible emotional response with the simplest possible image. This was an enormous step forward. Schulz had reached a national audience and finally felt confident enough to call himself an artist when introduced to new acquaintances. He was finally discovering his own style.[23]

In the long run, achieving national publication would be a great benefit to Schulz, but not in the short term. With newfound confidence, he approached his editor at the *Pioneer Press* and asked for a daily publication. The editor refused, citing limited space and his abundance of syndicated material. No, *Li'l Folks* would have to continue its weekly Sunday printing. Schulz pushed his luck and asked for a raise on his ten dollar per week fee—the standard rate for a weekly syndicated strip and an amount the cartoonist had felt fortunate to receive. "Absolutely not," the editor responded. There was no more room in the *Pioneer Press*'s comics budget. Admittedly riding high after his several publications with the *Saturday Evening Post*, Schulz went all in. "Well, perhaps I should just quit drawing it," he blurted out. The response rang in his mind long after he walked out of the downtown office. "All right," replied the editor.[24]

Just like that, *Li'l Folks* was gone. Amazingly, this barely gave the typically shy and self-conscious Schulz pause. He knew how much he had improved his artwork over the past decade and he was certain his childhood dream of a daily comic strip lay just before him. So in early 1950, he set out to sell a comic strip

Figure 1.3 The minimalism and subtlety of Schulz's style was on full display in his first comic strip *L'il Folks*. Courtesy of the Charles M. Schulz Museum and Research Center.

to a national syndicate. Working from his desk at the Art Instruction School, he began redrawing his best panels from *Li'l Folks* and started taking weekly trips to Chicago to try and sell his comic feature in person. He found some editors, like National Newspaper Syndicate's John Dille Jr., to be quite friendly, giving welcome advice for revisions. Others were not so kind. The comics editor at the *Chicago Sun* was very interested in Schulz's work. "I certainly cannot say no to this," the editor exclaimed as he looked over the drawings, "We'll have to take it in to the president." Excited by the response, Schulz followed the editor into the president's office. The artist's mood was quickly tempered. Barely giving the panels a glance, the president crushed any hope with a firm, "No." For the time, whether gently or abruptly, every editor he spoke to rejected him.[25]

By the spring, however, it seemed as though he had found his break. The director of the Newspaper Enterprise Association of Cleveland wrote to Schulz expressing interest in his work. Over the course of a few months, the syndicate worked out a deal for him to draw a Sunday feature. Finally, a regularly appearing national strip, the dream realized. It was too good to be true, though. At the last minute, the editors had second thoughts and canned the deal. Schulz was back at square one with nothing but a portfolio full of unwanted cartoon panels.[26]

Throughout this series of face-to-face rejections, he had continued his practice of mailing out his work to essentially every publisher with a US mailing address. One of the many packages he sent out that spring was addressed for the offices of United Feature Syndicate (UFS) in New York City. After more than six weeks without a reply, he decided the panels must have been lost in the mail. Finally, Schulz wrote a letter to UFS describing the drawings he had included and inquiring whether they had ever been received. By this point, he was sure that UFS would reject him like all the others and was merely interested in locating his lost artwork, he wrote. What he received was a letter from the UFS editorial director, Jim Freeman, praising his work and requesting that he travel to New York to meet and discuss his ideas.[27]

"That was an exciting trip," the young midwesterner recalled. "I loved New York immediately." He brought along with him some of his most successful *Li'l Folks* panels converted into a comic strip. "We liked the panel—its charm, its characters, its style of humor," Jim Freeman recalled, "but since the market was flooded with panels I asked him to convert it into strip form and try to retain the same attractiveness." Still donning his military haircut—a physical symbol of just how deeply the war had affected this once reluctant soldier—the neatly dressed midwesterner hurried his way through the urban maze of lower Manhattan on a gray and misty morning. He arrived at the offices so early that morning that only the receptionist was in. Helyn Rippert, the woman sitting at the front desk, remembered Schulz as "a tall, slim" out-of-towner who showed up more than an hour before the editors typically arrived. She offered to hold his artwork for him because of the rainy weather and encouraged him to go get breakfast and come back at ten.[28]

By the time Schulz returned to the receptionist's desk, his artwork was no longer there. While he had been eating, the editors had gotten a hold of his strip and were busy passing it around to anyone who would look. All agreed: the strip was even better than the panels that had originally caught their attention. The editors ushered Schulz directly into the syndicate president's office. There the stunned artist found the president, Larry Rutman, dictating the terms of a new contract—five years, offering a fifty-fifty split of the profits with the copyright belonging to UFS, a standard industry contract. Schulz barely hesitated before signing the document, symbolizing the achievement of his life-long dream.[29]

He celebrated with a steak dinner and returned to St. Paul to share the good news. He was changed. "I remember thinking, 'Now I'm a cartoonist, not just an instructor at a correspondence school,'" he would tell his biographer. But Schulz was not so confident in his new job to quit his old one. In fact, he remained on staff for another year and did all the work for his new strip at his art school work station.[30]

Schulz quickly found out the limits of his power over his own strip once it legally belonged to UFS. Shortly after signing the contract, his editor notified him that they would not be able to use the title *Li'l Folks* because of a standing copyright on the title *Little Folks* held by the *Chicago Tribune*. They also felt it was too close to UFS's most successful strip—and one of Schulz's personal favorites—Al Capp's *Li'l Abner*. The *Little Folks* title had already gone far enough that one industry publication, *Editor & Publisher*, had reported the new title in their July 8 issue. Had he been given the chance, Schulz likely would have renamed his strip *Good Ol' Charlie Brown* after the main character. But he was not given a choice. Instead, *Peanuts* was selected from a list compiled in a brief staff meeting. "It was the most descriptive of the all-kids strip," argued editor Jim Freeman. It also matched the strip's unique size. Schulz's strip would be scaled down smaller than any other strip then in syndication, and its four equal sized panels would allow newspaper editors to arrange the strip both vertically or horizontally to maximize their space. "There was a movement on among publishers to shrink the size of comic strips," Freeman explained, and thus, "because of its size, *Peanuts* was an apt title."[31]

Schulz was insulted. In his own estimation it "was the worst title ever thought up for a comic strip." He felt the title had no meaning or relation to the actual strip and that it undermined the subtle dignity of his humor. Even more, it confused early readers. "The very first year," Schulz lamented, "I [began] to get letters saying, 'I love this new strip with Peanuts and his dog.'" To the end of his life, he could not get over the fact that what became his life work was so rudely given such an insignificant name. In most cases, he avoided using the official name, choosing instead to say, "I draw that comic strip with Snoopy in it, Charlie Brown and his dog."[32]

While it is unlikely that the UFS editors were deliberately trying to insult their newest artist, it was clear that they did not envision *Peanuts* becoming anything more than another daily gag strip. This was evident in the way they marketed it to newspaper editors. A promotional brochure called *Peanuts* "the

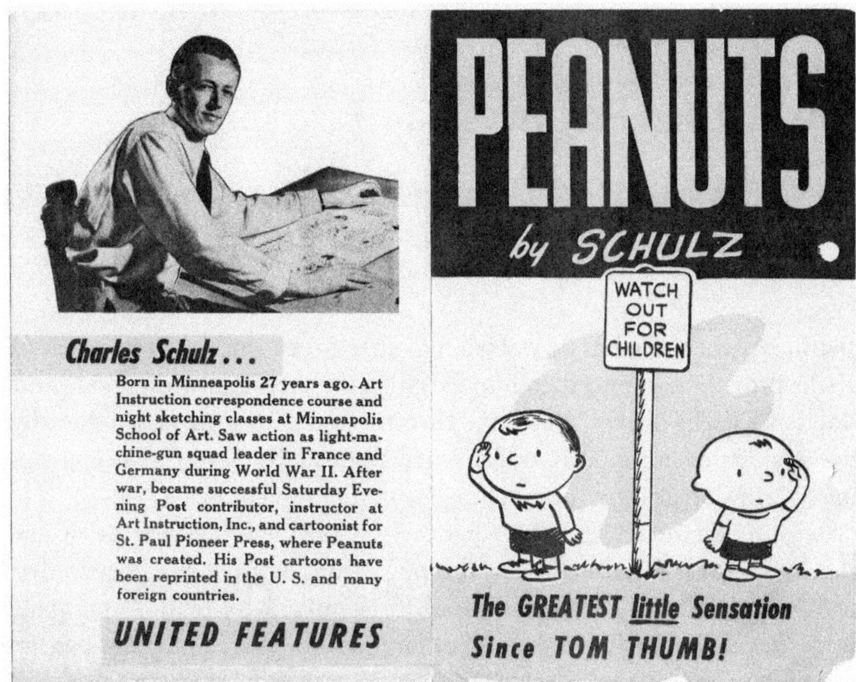

Figure 1.4 This 1950 promotional brochure for *Peanuts* tried to capture newspaper editors' interest by selling the strip as smaller and more flexible for fitting shrinking page layouts. Courtesy of the Charles M. Schulz Museum and Research Center.

greatest *little* sensation since Tom Thumb." While the promotion highlighted Schulz's service in World War II, his work for the *Saturday Evening Post*, and the strip's "clever, subtle humor with universally appealing characters," the primary selling point was that it "solves tough make-up problems" for newspaper editors. The images in the brochure were not primarily meant to show off Schulz's artwork or humor, but to display the many different ways the panels could be rearranged and resized to fit every nook and cranny of a newspaper page. The fact that Schulz's first paycheck from the syndicate was $338.88 for the artwork on this promotional was proof that this strip, like the whole medium, was meant first and foremost to please editors and sell newspapers.[33]

But that does not mean that Schulz was not attuned to his national audience, small as it might be. In fact, he was about to connect with readers in some peculiar new ways that few comic strips had managed before. And he was going to do so on a scale previously unimaginable in the industry. From just a small handful of major and mid-level newspapers, *Peanuts* was about to soar.

None of that was clear yet in 1950, though. No one knew Charles Schulz or Charlie Brown yet, but that was all about to change.

2

The Future Frightens Me

The Cold War Origins of *Peanuts*

Charlie Brown smiled as he walked into an anxious world. "Here comes ol' Charlie Brown," announced a boy to the girl in the checkered dress beside him, "Good ol' Charlie Brown." But as the cheerful Charlie Brown passed them by, the boy's expression quickly transformed from mild interest to strong animosity. "How I hate him!" he exclaimed with furrowed brow.

It was an odd introduction for Charles Schulz's brand-new comic strip and at least one reader was disturbed by the tone. "Don't we have enough hatred on the frontpage," one Lutheran minister wrote later that week to the *Minneapolis Star Tribune*, "without having it in the comic section?" As strange and unsettling as this first day's strip was, it served as a rather perceptive reflection of the growing tensions between Americans' optimism and anxiety about their world following victory in World War II. Defeating totalitarianism had not restored a world of peace, but instead had created a new world of constant and increasing concern.[1]

The newspaper headlines for October 2, 1950 certainly revealed cause for such concern. The *Denver Post*, which ran *Peanuts* on the front page to promote the strip in its first week, blared significant developments in the new Korean conflict raging on the opposite side of the globe. "U.N. Troops Hurdle 38th," the bold print announced. Just three months earlier, North Korean communists had shocked American officials with their blitzkrieg across the United Nations-imposed boundary line at the 38th parallel. For many Americans, it appeared that their worst fears of an atomic age war were being realized. "It looks like World War III is here," President Harry Truman jotted in his diary, revealing the same ominous feelings that plagued 57 percent of Americans that month. While American troops—acting under the UN flag and the command of General Douglas MacArthur—had helped turn back what weeks before had seemed to be certain defeat, this most recent thrust into North Korean territory marked a new stage in the conflict, one that threatened the terrible prospect of communist China's involvement.[2]

Figure 2.1 The initial *Peanuts* strip, which introduced Charlie Brown, was jarring for some readers. Charles Schulz, *Peanuts*, October 2, 1950. © 1950 Peanuts Worldwide LLC.

The Cold War, which emerged unintended from the aftermath of World War II, loomed large in the newspaper that Monday morning. One hundred thousand police officers swarmed to arrest 1,400 communist "agitators" in West Germany over the weekend. "Red" North Koreans were accused of a civilian massacre in South Korea's Taejon City, with estimates of the dead ranging from 1,100 to as high as 6,000. In Indochina, the French delivered a seemingly decisive blow to the Viet Minh "nerve center and military capital" fifty miles outside of Hanoi. A US destroyer hit an alleged Russian mine off the coast of North Korea, killing seven. The day's newspaper page, still printed in only black and white in 1950, was covered in "red."[3]

A distinct sense of fear and unease pervaded all of these stories. Americans, so recently victorious in history's greatest war, quickly found themselves disoriented in a destabilized world. In May 1950 public opinion polls found that 58 percent of people were worried about the possible danger the bomb posed to their families. When asked what they intended to do, a majority responded that they either did not know what to do or else did not believe there was anything they could do. As a *LIFE* magazine feature at the end of the decade put it, Americans in the 1950s "had the fatalistic idea that it was no use trying to do anything about protection against a nuclear bomb. If the blast did not kill them . . . radiation certainly would." Despite a decisive victory in World War II, this generation felt scared and vulnerable. This was, as historian J. Ronald Oakley has called it, "the age of fear and suspicion." It was the age of Joseph McCarthy and loyalty oaths. The age of the House Un-American Activities Committee. And this was the dawn of the age of Charlie Brown.[4]

Peanuts became the fastest growing US comic strip in the 1950s because cartoonist Charles Schulz was unafraid of addressing the fears and concerns of the Cold War era. Eschewing the machismo of the action comics like *Dick Tracy* or *Steve Canyon*, while avoiding the escapist simplicity of *Dennis the Menace* or *Blondie*, *Peanuts* thrived on its vulnerability about real life issues. In growing mountains of letters to the cartoonist, fans expressed how the humorous exploits of Charlie Brown reflected their own experiences in an anxious age.

Early 1950s newspaper readers from Washington, DC to Seattle found the boy Charlie Brown buried in the pages alongside all the hopes and fears of the near future. The cartoonist went by the simple name "Schulz"—or "Schultz," as the *Denver Post* misprinted it. Were it not for the strip's conspicuous placement on the front page of the Denver and Seattle papers or United Feature Syndicate's small ads in the *Washington Post* promoting *Peanuts* as "a new kind of comic strip" that would be loved by "kids eight to eighty," the four small panels would likely have drowned in a sea of black newsprint. Decades later Americans would be essentially unable to define the funny papers without some reference to *Peanuts*. Early on it was just another comic strip struggling to keep a handful of editors' subscriptions.[5]

Each of the seven papers to run *Peanuts* were crowded with numerous other strips competing for readers' eyes. Action, adventure, and drama seemed to dominate the declining space for comic strips, as evidenced by the prominence of strips like *Dick Tracy*, *Terry and the Pirates*, *Steve Canyon*, and *Brenda Starr: Reporter*. Like the news copy surrounding them, these strips seemed acutely concerned with elements of the Cold War, especially espionage and guerilla warfare. There was a reason why the medium followed this trend so closely: that was what sold subscriptions. In many ways, *Peanuts* did not fit the formula and ran the risk of slipping into obscurity.

Standing apart, however, wasn't always a bad thing. In fact, in such a competitive environment—between 1946 and 1966, a quarter of all syndicated dailies failed—it might be a new strip's only chance. Most all of the comics running had one characteristic in common: they used a lot of bold ink. The action strips were especially detailed and dark, appearing cluttered to the eye. When stacked atop one another these dark strips blended into one continuous sheet of ink haphazardly broken by fleeting wisps of white space. *Peanuts* could not have been more different. Schulz's style was decidedly minimal, providing the reader only the slightest indications of setting. On this first morning, a single thin line was all that separated heaven from earth. There were no trees, no houses, no fences, no cars. Reversing the accepted wisdom of the profession, Schulz drew only what was absolutely necessary for readers to comprehend the dialogue. On a page painted in black ink, Schulz's minimal, modern lines and open spaces stood out.[6]

Peanuts stood out in other ways, too. The strip dealt with children. This much was evident from the *Chicago Daily Tribune* ad that portrayed Charlie Brown and a friend peering off in the distance beneath a sign reading "Watch Out for Children." The most prominent strips of the day focused on adults. Even those strips like *Little Orphan Annie* or *Nancy*—or *Dennis the Menace*, which would start in the spring of 1951—that featured children did not do so to the exclusion of adult characters. Adults played a prominent role in every major strip of the period.[7]

Stories of children had played a major role in the comic strip since the medium's first great feature: Richard Outcault's *Yellow Kid*. That feature, which utilized the best color printing technology of its time and played an integral role in the Hearst–Pulitzer newspaper wars of the 1890s, had centered on the exploits of a rough gang of kids in fictional Hogan's Alley. These children were urban, working-class, and poorly educated. They reflected the state of turn-of-the-century city spaces as well as immigrant influences and prejudices in American popular culture. Schulz updated this standard motif by making his children suburban, middle-class, and deeply active in school. This variation would be essential to *Peanuts*' enormous appeal throughout its fifty-year run.

Peanuts' art design also separated it from the predominantly realistic work of other artists. Where the look of many characters in action and adventure dailies imitated styles found in the movies, Schulz's characters, with large heads and tiny bodies, were decidedly more cartoonish. Of course, not all comics copied the live-action cinema. Walt Disney's *Donald Duck*, Mort Walker's *Beetle Bailey*, and Chic Young's *Blondie*—the most read strip of the day—were all notable exceptions.

Three decades later, Schulz would admit to biographer Rheta Grimsley Johnson that this opening scene of the children's hatred for Charlie Brown was the only one he ever regretted drawing. Nonetheless, it is telling that the young artist chose to begin here. This was the American mood in 1950. "Never had the nation been more powerful," one historian wrote, "but not since the early dark days of World War II had the American people felt so puzzled and so threatened by world events." At a moment of such uncertainty in the world, as Asia—like eastern Europe—seemed to be falling under communist influence and Americans were warring amongst themselves to root out spies and political enemies, that first day's *Peanuts* engendered the mood of the times. Even more, it revealed the mood of this obscure cartoonist known to new readers only as "Schulz."[8]

For some readers, *Peanuts* emerged as a gem of existentialist angst. Charlie Brown was less about wise-cracking children and more a daily meditation on "the tiny incidents of experience." Rather than viewing Schulz as the clean-cut, dutiful veteran that UFS so often wanted to present in those early days, the student writers of the *Yale Daily News* saw him as a "lighthearted renegade," subverting adult expectations of the younger generation. In fact, early *Peanuts* strips quite often joked about a growing generational gap, an issue of considerable hand-wringing among parents of the growing baby boom generation. Schulz just seemed to understand young people, the students writers felt, in a way that other adults did not. "Does Charlie Brown represent the existential situation of the Beat Generation?" the young interviewer asked. Schulz quickly dismissed the question with a self-deprecating quip, as he often did when pressured to answer a question he was uncomfortable with, yet other young readers got the same sense, including young Garry Trudeau, who would grow up to draw the comic strip *Doonesbury*. Trudeau later claimed that he always thought of *Peanuts* as "the first Beat strip" because of how much the strip "vibrated with '50s alienation."[9]

During another interview with the *Saturday Evening Post* in fall 1956, Schulz was interrupted by an unexpected telephone call. On the line was a young female representative from the Democratic National Convention calling to inquire whether Schulz would be willing to do some artwork for Adlai Stevenson's presidential campaign. The campaign wanted Schulz's work, she insisted, because they consider him "the youngest existentialist." As the interviewer soon discovered, the cartoonist was hardly a student of existential philosophy, being barely aware of leading thinkers such as Jean Paul Sartre. Regardless of the artist's awareness of his own philosophical depth, *Peanuts* was beloved as a popular existentialist text in the 1950s and 1960s. As one journalist later put it, Schulz was able to take Charlie Brown's social isolation and translate it into "one of the great voices of 1960s existentialism."[10]

Much of this young existential intrigue with *Peanuts* stemmed from the character early readers so often confused with the strip's title: Charlie Brown. He was a habitual loser, and in the postwar era losers had a special resonance. Historian Grace Elizabeth Hale has argued that white middle-class young people participated in a cultural phenomenon she has called "the romance of the outsider." It was such a salient cultural force, in fact, that "by the end of the twentieth century, the romance of the outsider had become so pervasive that few scholars questioned how odd and uncanny it was, how historically unprecedented, to understand politically and economically enfranchised people as marginal and alienated." The United States became, in Hale's estimation, an unlikely "nation of outsiders," and Charlie Brown was nothing if not the poster child for it.[11]

Many of *Peanuts*' most recognizable devices were born out of Cold War anxiety. In the summer of 1954, for example, Schulz introduced Linus Van

Pelt's "security blanket," or "security and happiness" blanket, as Charlie Brown called it later that fall. For the cartoonist, Linus's new favorite accessory simply came from observing childhood behavior in the Schulz household. "That came, of course, from our first three children," Schulz later told *Newsday*. "Three out of five of our children dragged blankets around, and that was one of those observation things which I started." But this simple observation went far beyond anything he ever anticipated. "That is probably the single best thing that I ever thought of," he claimed in 1977. By that point, his usage of the term "security blanket" had even been added to the *Oxford English Dictionary*, thanks to *Peanuts*. Popular connections to Lucy's lovable little brother, however, obscured the true Cold War origins of the term.[12]

"Security blanket" was a term that initially emerged during World War II. The term referred to the military's secrecy surrounding troop movements in Europe. One of the first such instances came in the *Dothan Eagle* (Alabama) on September 4, 1944 when the newspaper reported its difficulty in keeping precise track of US troops' progress toward Berlin because of the "security blanket" surrounding updated information. The *Los Angeles Times* complained of the same on March 27, 1945. Over the subsequent decade, the security blanket came to refer specifically to government and military secrecy surrounding atomic weapons and atomic research. Australian officials' security blanket surrounding their first atomic bomb test in 1952 "thickened" as the event got closer. The atomic security blanket even became a central sticking point of US Cold War diplomacy with the nation's allies. British naval officials accused the Pentagon of slowing advancements on atomic propulsion systems because of the security blanket surrounding atomic secrets. In early 1955, the Eisenhower administration launched an international effort to share atomic secrets with allies in an effort to bolster the anti-communist position in the West. Clearly, the term "security blanket" had entrenched Cold War connotations in the United States and abroad.[13]

Figure 2.2 Schulz's use of a "security blanket" transformed the popular meaning of a term that had previously been used to describe military actions in the early Cold War. Charles Schulz, *Peanuts*, June 1, 1954. © 1954 Peanuts Worldwide LLC.

With Linus's security blanket, the Cold War moved from an exterior confrontation of military maneuvering and strategy to an interior, personal conflict of containing one's own mental and emotional "weaknesses" for the good of a stable and prosperous democratic society. Devices like an infant blanket became coping mechanisms for dealing with the social anxieties of a world of alienation and social policing. This is why Schulz's simple idea resonated with much of postwar intellectual culture. Bestsellers from David Riesman's *The Lonely Crowd* and C. Wright Mills's *White Collar* to Benjamin Spock's *Baby and Child Care* and J. D. Salinger's *Catcher in the Rye* were all expressions of concern over the social dislocation and isolation commonly felt in the era. Linus's security blanket was a fitting metaphor for an uneasy and perhaps repressed society.

It was such an effective shorthand that academic psychologists began turning to *Peanuts* for useful analogies in textbooks and even research monographs. D. W. Winnicott, a famed English pediatrician and pioneer in child development psychology, was one of the first to reach out to Schulz for access to the comic strips. "I would very much like to include one of the *Peanuts* brilliant cartoons as it exactly illustrates a point in one of the chapters," Winnicott wrote concerning his two upcoming volumes *The Child and the Family* and *The Child and the Outside World*. Schulz and his publishers were happy to grant permission. They also granted reprint permissions to a young researcher at the Kaiser Foundation in Oakland, California named Timothy Leary. The Berkeley doctorate and future champion of psychedelics sought the rights to reprint "a masterful and amusing illustration of a most common psychological phenomenon" that involved "the unusual tendency to say one thing about oneself and to act in a way which may be quite different" for his revised dissertation titled "The Interpersonal Diagnosis of Personality." A year later, Leary wrote again requesting "to both lighten and enlighten the reader by including Mr. Schulz's witty and wise illustration." Both requests were granted.[14]

Lucy's psychiatry booth, another classic *Peanuts* scene, emerged amid the deep days of Cold War anxiety. Lucy first opened her stand in spring 1959, as Soviet premier Nikita Krushchev and Western leaders lobbed heated threats back and forth over the future of a divided Berlin, the hotbed of Cold War tensions. Lucy's first patient, of course, was Charlie Brown. "I have deep feelings of depression," Charlie Brown confessed. "What can I do about this?" The self-confident (and self-trained) psychiatrist replied with a jolt, "Snap out of it," before demanding her five cent fee. As with much of Schulz's work, this scene and its many subsequent renditions could be read multiple ways. Many readers may have identified with Charlie Brown's openness and vulnerability

Figure 2.3 The first appearance of Lucy's psychiatry booth played upon the explosion of therapy culture in mid-century America. Charles Schulz, *Peanuts*, March 27, 1959. © 1959 Peanuts Worldwide LLC.

about feelings that could be uncomfortable and arresting in the real world. Others, however, could identify more with Lucy, who made light of the psychotherapy trend in postwar America by using it to make her spending money instead of the more conventional childhood lemonade stand.[15]

Peanuts reflected the political culture of its time in other, more subtle ways, too. For example, Charlie Brown and his friends regularly played "cowboys and Indians." Cultural critic Richard Slotkin has argued that the twenty-five-year period following the Berlin crisis in 1948 was "the Golden Age of the Western" in American popular culture. Whether on radio, television, or the big screen, Westerns were everywhere in the 1950s and early 1960s and consistently garnered high ratings and awards. Indeed, the theme of cowboys fighting Indians in a struggle to tame the Wild West permeated Cold War culture and expressed deep anxieties about the dangers of the mid-century world. As Slotkin has noted, these Westerns were both influenced by the political culture of the moment, but also provided the culture with fictive settings to imagine new policy scenarios. This dual dynamic played out in Schulz's artwork.[16]

Frontier motifs played a prominent role in *Peanuts* in the 1950s. Foremost among these was regular games of cowboys and Indians. Charlie Brown and Shermy often appeared in cowboy hats, boots, and kerchiefs, shouting "bang" with their toy guns as they chased one another around, at least until their voices went hoarse (meaning they were out of ammunition) or hiccups got in the way. The female characters took part in many instances, sometimes acting as Indian princesses, other times playing gun-toting cowgirls. Schulz relied heavily at times on the consumer aspects of 1950s childhood play for jokes, simultaneously connecting his characters to the common experiences of young families across the United States and mocking attempts at material authenticity in the children's make-believe world. The cartoonist freely utilized ethnic stereotypes prevalent in the cultural iconography of the popular Western genre, perpetuating images of "otherness" and natural, violent

Figure 2.4 The *Peanuts* gang often played cowboys and Indians, playing on a popular Cold War metaphor for the conflict between East and West. Charles Schulz, *Peanuts*, February 10, 1952. © 1952 Peanuts Worldwide LLC.

conflict between cowboys and Indians. Nostalgia-fueled conflicts of the imagined wild West played out in the same days the Cold War exacerbated the anxieties over the United States' tenuous control over a world where Soviet Russia possessed atomic capabilities and the massive Chinese populace had embraced communism.[17]

Sometimes, the *Peanuts* children quite literally played the Cold War. On June 18, 1954, Schulz used his minimalist approach to humor with chilling effect when he introduced *Peanuts* to the nuclear age. In that strip, Charlie Brown and Lucy played "H-bomb test" with Lucy's roaring voice as the explosion. There were no scenes of mass destruction, casualties, or environmental fallout, yet still the strip was haunting. Like so much of Schulz's work, the impact lay in the subtle, largely assumed truths of the cartoon. By playing at nuclear warfare, the children were normalizing it in their daily lives. Like millions of children across the United States, "the bomb" and routine "duck and cover" school drills became an accepted part of their lives. To a school child reading this strip in 1954, this might have been unremarkable. To their parents, however, it might have felt more like a modern tragedy.

Figure 2.5 The hydrogen bomb, first successfully tested in 1952, made its way into *Peanuts* in the form of childhood play and imagination. Charles Schulz, *Peanuts*, June 18, 1954. © 1954 Peanuts Worldwide LLC.

While such connections with the Cold War might have seemed inappropriate or excessive, it appears that for readers in the 1950s it seemed like a logical choice. In January 1955, the research director for the National Science Foundation (NSF) wrote to Schulz in praise of *Peanuts*. After extolling the comic, Richard Axt requested an original of one strip where Lucy explained her own misguided understanding of a scientific theory. And Axt already had the perfect place in mind to hang it in the NSF offices. The original comic strip "would be most warmly received," he assured Schulz, "and would be proudly displayed next to a large photo of the first H-bomb explosion!"[18]

Americans in the 1950s could hardly escape the looming glow of the bomb. Newspapers and magazines early in the decade were filled with features exploring the possibilities of atomic explosions in the homeland. In fact, Schulz likely saw one such article that ran in his hometown newspaper. On January 8, 1950, the St. Paul *Pioneer Press*'s Sunday magazine featured a cover article titled "When the A-Bomb Bursts on St. Paul." The opening lines of the article set the fictionalized scene: "a bright fall day sometime in the future" where the distant rumble of a new war that has been going on for "about six months now" hardly touches the picturesque life of this fantasized Midwest. The article suggested an air of denial that sheltered everyday life from the dark atomic possibilities ("If the enemy does have the A-bomb why haven't they used it by now?" neighbors discuss in passing). This sense of invulnerability is suddenly ruptured, however, when a bomb rips through the morning sky, detonating over downtown St. Paul, the district and its people instantly melted away "like a chunk of paraffin tossed into a foundry furnace." If the literary imagery was not enough to terrify readers, the *Pioneer Press* artists added frighteningly realistic maps and photos to the mix, showing a block-by-block diagram of the destruction and an aerial photo of St. Paul with an atomic mushroom cloud superimposed on top. The sense of dread and helplessness was palpable.[19]

And so, when Schulz published his comment on the debate in early 1958, he struck a delicate balance between fear and optimism. That January Linus van Pelt, Lucy's little brother, went for his first winter stroll. As he walked he noticed large white flakes floating down around him. It took only a moment for him to become panicked, racing down the sidewalk in search of shelter. In his mad dash he ran headlong into Charlie Brown who, thus far, diligently mentored young Linus about life—despite Lucy's best efforts to mislead and confuse him. "It's happening, Charlie Brown," Linus yelled hysterically, "It's happening just like they said it would!" Charlie Brown replied pleasantly, "Of course it's happening . . . it's snowing. What else did you expect at this time of year?" Calm now, Linus looked around in a mixture of wonder and relief. "Good grief," he exhaled, "I thought it was the fallout."[20]

Schulz's critique was twofold, and each of the characters carried a side of the argument—one obvious, one subtle. The first side of the critique is obvious: the fear Linus feels in this moment of misunderstanding. For Linus, and many other American children in the fifties, the bomb and its consequences were more than they could handle. One young man recounted his own childhood reaction to the bomb to sociologist Kenneth Keniston years later. While he remembered celebrating the World War II victory the atomic bomb achieved with a parade around the neighborhood with the other children, his introduction to the bomb itself came four years later. In the late 1940s his mother purchased the first volume of an encyclopedia from a traveling salesman. As the boy thumbed through the pages of the "A" section, he came across an article on the atomic bomb, which included a photo of the mushroom cloud and then a tank driving over the aftermath of the explosion. The boy's reaction was primal: "I think I became hysterical," he confided in the interviewer. Like this boy, Linus van Pelt was a child carrying the enormous burden of his own nuclear awakening. In his character, the cartoonist was pointing out the degree of real terror adult decisions over the previous decade had caused.[21]

The other side of Schulz's argument lay in Charlie Brown. Here the artist made an appeal to rationality in the face of paralyzing fear in the atomic age. In this strip, nuclear irradiated matter falling from the sky is the farthest thing from Charlie Brown's mind. He does not feed into Linus's hysteria, but calmly and reasonably refutes it. Charlie Brown's level-headed response to nuclear night-terrors served not only as a corrective for his younger friend, but as a rebuff to those in the media who seemed to feed the national hysteria by exaggerating the dangers and focusing only on the negatives. Dr. Douglas Courtney, psychologist and director of the Institute for Research in Human Relations in Philadelphia, warned that the American society's "overemphasis" on the atomic and hydrogen bombs was "endangering the emotional security of children and may lead to the development of neurotic fears" or even "atomic neurosis." These elaborate reports were so persistent that even the toddler Linus, who regularly watched television and listened to the radio with the older children, had heard of the horrors that awaited him outdoors. And yet the frightened boy's fears were not entirely unwarranted, just overblown. In this simple strip, Schulz highlighted both real American anxieties about the new nuclear reality and the nation's propensity for overreaction. While demonstrating the terror children faced in the nuclear age, he used those same children to rebuke those who would take advantage of those innocent fears and uncertainties.[22]

Even in dealing with domestic issues of youth culture, Schulz balanced humor and critique. One of the biggest and most surprising issues to arise about youth culture in the 1950s was a backlash against comic books. Without any content standards or censors, comic books of the postwar era covered a range of vulgar and gruesome topics. Following the publication of psychiatrist Frederick Wertham's *Seduction of the Innocent* in 1954, which suggested that comic books could be a leading cause of juvenile delinquency, the issue rose to the level of a Congressional hearing. Comic books were so concerning, comics scholar Lara Saguisag has argued, because they cut out parents as cultural mediators, much like the rest of youth consumer culture. Pressures on the comics industry were so serious that the leading publishers finally agreed to form their own censorship protocols—the "Comics Code"—to avoid full-fledged congressional oversight.[23]

In the 1950s, Charlie Brown and the children in the strip regularly read comic books. In fact, comic books were one of the most commonly recurring themes in the first five years of *Peanuts*. Schulz even went so far as to label comics on the drugstore shelf with such names as "Mangle Comics" or "Kill Komics," as in a June 22, 1952 strip, reflecting the questionable nature of comics as a children's medium. And yet these comics never seemed to have any deleterious effects on the children in Schulz's world. The children did not descend into juvenile delinquency. They did not murder or steal or deface property or run away from home. For all their alienation, Charlie Brown and his friends were surprisingly resilient and unchanged. As Saguisag has demonstrated, Schulz "avoided a direct and explicit attack on . . . comic books." He did so by balancing humor and social anxiety once again.[24]

By the end of his first decade as a nationally syndicated comic strip artist, Charles Schulz had won the National Cartoonist Society's "Cartoonist of the

Year." He could hardly believe the honor. "Isn't it fantastic to be recognized by your own craft!" Schulz blurted to a reporter for an industry magazine as he fumbled to call his wife and father with the news. But *Peanuts* was being recognized far beyond the banquet halls of the cartooning world. It was becoming the most popular new comic strip in the United States. By 1959, UFS counted a daily US circulation of 18 million, with fans ranging from suburban moms, elementary school children, and parish priests all the way to some of the most prominent people in the country. Both Secretary of Agriculture Ezra Taft Benson—the lone "Old Guard" conservative in Dwight Eisenhower's cabinet—and FBI Director J. Edgar Hoover had signed original *Peanuts* strips hanging in their Washington offices by the end of the decade. "It really is flattering and very thrilling to have someone like J. Edgar Hoover express approval," Schulz gushed to one of his friends at UFS. Even more, Schulz had won the attention of Madison Avenue executives, a relationship that would change the humble cartoonist's life and American pop culture forever.[25]

The first major *Peanuts* advertising deal was a set of original illustrations for an instructional book for amateur photographers released by Kodak Eastman in 1955. The booklet was intended to accompany their new mass-market Brownie camera in hopes that consumer education in an attractive package would capture a broader customer base, especially among young people. It was a simple, one-time, $2,000 contract, not a career changing deal by any means.[26]

Schulz's big break came when the J. Walter Thompson advertising firm approached UFS to secure the rights to use *Peanuts* in advertising Ford's first compact car line. By the late 1950s the appeal of the full-sized, elaborate, and expensive cars that had characterized the decade was waning as smaller, more fuel-efficient imports from Europe were entering the market. Ford's Falcon line became one of the first serious compact offerings from the American automakers. To promote this new line, J. Walter Thompson planned "one of the largest media blitzes in history" to include the likes of Frank Sinatra, Debbie Reynolds, Rosemary Clooney, and "Tennessee" Ernie Ford in the campaign. But Ford wanted a mascot for the line, too. That was where *Peanuts* came in. Pairing their diminutive size and witty banter, *Peanuts* was meant to both illustrate the concept and persuade consumers that these new compact cars were a "smart choice." The campaign would include both print and television ad spots. The campaign was a tremendous success. After the first two quarters of 1960, the Falcon had sold over 250,000 units and was the clear leader in the compact category.[27]

The television spots for the Ford Falcon campaign proved to be immensely important in *Peanuts*'s transmedia evolution to animation, becoming a

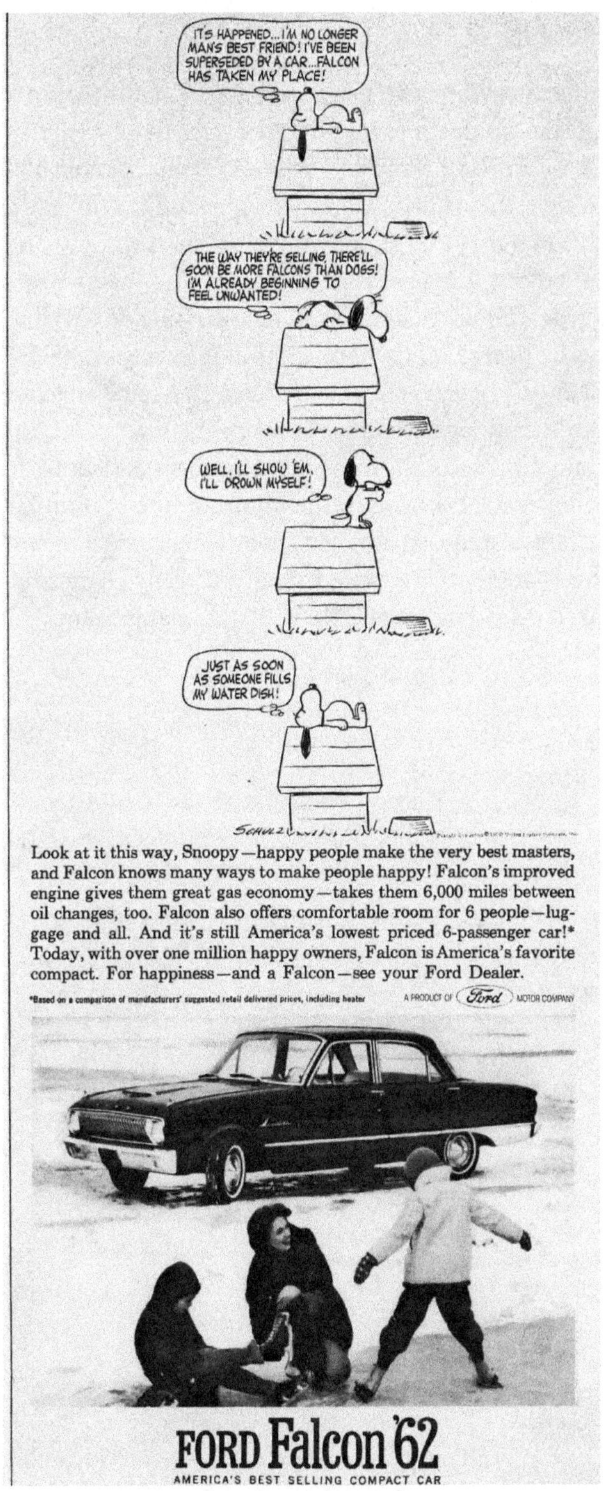

Figure 2.6 This Ford Falcon ad featured in *Life* magazine displayed the sometimes bleak existentialist humor of *Peanuts* in the 1950s. Courtesy of the Charles M. Schulz Museum and Research Center.

precursor to the later holiday television specials. But the print ads revealed just how deeply the Cold War existential ethos permeated Schulz's early work. In many cases, the Ford ad campaign capitalized on the often bleak humor of Schulz's 1950s style. In one print ad, which appeared in *LIFE* and the *Saturday Evening Post* in March 1962, Snoopy lay atop his doghouse and bemoaned the fact that the Ford Falcon was replacing him as "man's best friend." The wounded pup's despair drove him to contemplate suicide. "Well, I'll show'em," Snoopy said as he peered off the roof ledge at his water dish. "I'll drown myself!" Fortunately for *Peanuts* fans, Charlie Brown had failed to refill the water dish, so Snoopy simply lay back down to mope.

It was certainly a strange juxtaposition against the happy image of the mother and children ice skating in the photo on the bottom half of the ad. Though some fans feared that a major advertising campaign would sacrifice *Peanuts*'s offbeat "authenticity," Schulz had not really changed anything. He had simply taken his strange new Cold War style mainstream.[28]

3

Bless You for Charlie Brown

Peanuts and the Evangelical Counterculture

On December 9, 1965, sixty-nine-year-old Lorene Burns sat down to write her first Christmas card of the year. Only fifteen minutes earlier, she and her husband, a prominent judge in Sioux Falls, South Dakota, had finished watching a new cartoon Christmas special on CBS. "Why am I crying?" she rhetorically asked the cartoonist Charles Schulz in her red and green card. Her tears were so steady that she could "scarcely see to write" her handwritten note. She had been so deeply moved by Schulz's *A Charlie Brown Christmas* that she was compelled to express her gratitude immediately. "It is a classic," she wrote, that would "take its place with those other treasures we wait for each year at this time."[1]

Burns was hardly alone in her feelings. She was one of more than fifteen and a half million Americans—almost half the nation's entire television viewing audience that night—who tuned in to watch the broadcast. Hundreds of viewers like her picked up pen and paper immediately after the special ended to write their feelings about the program. Hundreds more would write in the week that followed. Just as Burns predicted in her note, Schulz's mail was "heavy" with plaudits. But he was not the only one to receive bags full of mail about the cartoon special that week. The program's sponsor, Coca-Cola, also collected countless cards, letters, and telegrams about *Peanuts*' television debut. One viewer after another wrote to express gratitude for what they perceived to be a new thing in the popular culture of the mid-1960s: a television program with Christianity explicitly at its heart.[2]

In the late 1950s and early 1960s, Schulz struggled to strike a balance between sharing his deep Christian faith and not offending secular audiences or editors. "I have a message that I want to present," *Christianity Today* reported him saying, "but I would rather bend a little to put over a point than to have the whole strip dropped because it is too obvious." It seems surprising in hindsight that in a period that saw church membership as high as 69 percent by 1960, the most popular new comic strip in the country might be in danger of cancellation if it openly addressed Christian themes. The *Charlie Brown Christmas* special very nearly failed to make it to broadcast because of its bold statement about the "true meaning of Christmas." The story of *Peanuts'* ventures into religion and theology reveal how Schulz navigated the highly contested field of civil religion in postwar America. By using ambiguity, copyright, and a religious character, Schulz was able to control his message and navigate the treacherous waters of religion in the 1960s.[3]

Religious faith had played only a nominal role in Schulz's life before World War II. He had grown up Lutheran, but the liturgy had done little more than provide him with a set of values to which he could aspire. When he returned from the war, though, religion had taken on a new importance in his life. By the mid-1950s, faith was becoming a part of his work as well.[4]

Schulz became the kind of artist "who takes his religious principles into his career," according to the *Gospel Trumpet*, a publication of Schulz's denomination, the Church of God (Anderson, Indiana). Schulz believed that his faith should influence his work. One of the central ways he saw it influencing his work was by maintaining a moral innocence and decency in the comic strip. The cartoonist told Allen Keller of the *New York World-Telegram* that according to Jesus in the Gospel of Luke, "It were better for him that a millstone were hanged about his neck, and he be cast into the sea, than that he should offend one of these little ones." He took his moral role as a popular artist seriously. "Comic-strip artists have a responsibility to be uplifting and decent," he asserted. "I am still a believer in what the church refers to as 'holy living,'" he declared in 1963, and he wanted his work to reflect that personal conviction. Cultural producers, Schulz believed, had a moral obligation to the public and his Christian faith should inform that morality without overpowering his strip. In most cases early on, this meant maintaining a wholesome product without being overtly religious.[5]

One of the most successful early examples of providing wholesome entertainment, but not necessarily a religious message, was his 1962 book *Happiness Is a Warm Puppy*. The brief picture book could hardly have been simpler. It consisted of twenty-nine full-page *Peanuts* panels opposite a statement defining happiness in terms of childhood experiences like "Happiness is a thumb and blanket" or "Happiness is being able to reach the doorknob." The project was largely the idea of Connie Boucher, who owned a small printing shop in San Francisco called Determined Productions. Boucher and her husband had originally approached Schulz about doing a *Peanuts* calendar. With the success of that calendar, Boucher suggested taking a set of his comic strips that had attempted to define happiness and making a children's book. "I was rather doubtful that there would be enough material here to carry a complete book," the artist admitted, but he went ahead with the project anyway. By the end of 1962, *Happiness Is a Warm Puppy* was the bestselling book of the year.[6]

For Schulz, the small book made a powerful statement. "We were able to prove a good point," he asserted. "One needs only to look quickly around him to see the great quantity of useless literature being published, and yet there was a market for a book which was absolutely pure in content to the extent that it immediately sold a million copies." The book, he told *Time* magazine, "is completely innocent; yet in 1963 it outsold every other book, despite the waves of smut sweeping the nation." Again, Schulz challenged his fellow cartoonists to consider the example of the Christian scriptures, this time pointing to the New Testament epistle of Philippians in a piece for the Crusade for Christ publication *Collegiate Challenge*: "Finally, brethren, whatsoever things are just, whatsoever things are pure, whatsoever things are lovely, whatsoever things are of good report; if there be any virtue, and if there be any praise, think on these things." Even when Schulz was not directly discussing religion or scripture, the Christian faith influenced his work, just as he believed it should direct anyone who wanted to speak to the American public through entertainment.[7]

The success of works like *Happiness Is a Warm Puppy* placed Schulz squarely within what historian Michelle M. Nickerson has termed the "cult of wholesomeness." In the midst of widespread concerns about the state of American youth in the mid and late 1950s, many conservatives decried a loss of parental authority, blaming the decline of traditional family structures for everything from juvenile delinquency and the urban crisis to failing public education and changing sexual norms. While these conservatives' beloved traditions clashed with the postwar generation's "youth culture of experimentation," many came to believe that their children might best be reached by positive role models in popular culture. Pat Boone, a pop singer and influential evangelical spokesperson, fit the bill perfectly. If young people loved Pat Boone's music, their parents loved his values. Boone was a clean-cut young man from Tennessee who could claim Daniel Boone as an ancestor and was raised in a devout Church of Christ home. He had studied theology at David Lipscomb College, a private Church of Christ school, and had regularly preached to local congregations. He completed his education at Columbia University while he and his wife, Shirley, raised their four daughters. In 1958, Boone authored the number one bestselling advice book *Twixt Twelve and Twenty*, which chronicled his experience being "born again," and encouraged young people to follow his example. Boone quickly cemented himself as one of the faces of a growing "cult of wholesomeness" that sought to stave off the rise of what many Americans saw as a licentious and dangerous youth culture in the late 1950s. Similarly, Charles Schulz created a wholesome world where children held an unblemished innocence in the face of modern life's challenges, despite the fact that the *Peanuts* kids lived in an essentially adult-less environment.[8]

Schulz mostly kept his overtly religious themes separate from his acclaimed comic strip in the early years. But in the summer of 1957, things changed. That August he traveled to New York City on syndicate business, as he typically did several times throughout the year. When he arrived the city was abuzz with discussions of evangelist Billy Graham's popular crusade meetings at Madison Square Garden. Originally scheduled to run for six weeks beginning on May 15, Graham ultimately extended the crusade to sixteen weeks. Over that period attendance totaled more than two million, with over 52,000 religious decisions recorded.[9]

Schulz was enthralled as he watched Graham command the stage at Madison Square Garden. "I was amazed to see all the people going forward to receive Christ," he wrote in 1963. Though some questioned Graham's methods, if not his intentions, Schulz felt he had taken part in a real spiritual revival in the heart of New York City. "I had come to the conclusion that it was the result of earnest prayer, and of the working of the Holy Spirit," he said, "rather than simply the result of the speaker's message." When he returned to Minneapolis it was clear to Schulz's friends that he had been deeply touched. Schulz "was very high on Billy Graham," said one of his artist friends, Hal Lamson. "It was just a little uncomfortable for me," Lamson admitted, "because he was not ordinarily emotional about something that was personal." Lamson watched in amazement as his friend recounted the details of Graham's sermon, including hand gestures.[10]

As Schulz was thinking more and more deeply about his own spiritual life in the late 1950s, he became more bold in discussing religion in *Peanuts*. "Everything that you know becomes part of this comic strip," he told the *Christian Herald*. "Of course, I do have an interest in spiritual things. I do like to study the Bible." Much of Schulz's early discussions of Christianity began with his character Linus Van Pelt. Linus first appeared in the strip in September 1952, but he spent the next few years as an infant. It was not until 1958 that Linus reached the age of five and began attending school with the older children. Linus was clearly intelligent, though he was prone to misinterpret situations because of his youth (and because of faulty information from his older sister, Lucy). Linus was popular with readers, as evidenced by his central role in many of Ford Motor Company's television and print advertisements that began running in 1959.[11]

Linus got his first real shot to proclaim the Christian message during Christmas. On December 21, 1958, the Sunday strip showed the *Peanuts* children reciting the tale of the first Christmas on stage at a school program. "We are here to tell you of a wondrous light," Violet told the audience. The recitation followed the biblical story of the three wise men who followed a bright star in search of a newborn king. "They found the stable in the night," Charlie Brown chimed in, referencing the nativity scene, "beneath the star so big and bright." Though Linus was so nervous that he feared he would forget the final line, when his time came he shouted out, "The star that shone at Bethlehem still shines for us today!" This scene, while never explicitly mentioning Jesus, made clear that Schulz believed that celebrations of the Christmas holidays should focus on Christ's birth because his old message of rebirth and hope was still relevant for audiences in modern times.[12]

The following Christmas, Linus was tasked with reciting scripture to tell the Christmas story. This time the production was set at the Van Pelt family's church, not the children's school. This coincided with the fact that the children's message was also becoming more explicit, communicated through scriptural quotes rather than Christmas carols. "And the angel said unto

Figure 3.1 In 1958, Linus got his first chance to participate in the scripture recitation for the Christmas program. It was still a bit much for him that year. Charles Schulz, *Peanuts*, December 21, 1958. © 1958 Peanuts Worldwide LLC.

them," Linus would have to recite, "'Fear not; for, behold, I bring you good tidings of great joy which shall be to all the people." Once again, the scene in the Christmas strip centered around Linus's nervousness about forgetting his important line. Schulz would continue developing this theme over the next few Christmases. In 1960, Lucy threatened Linus with her fist to get him to remember the scripture verse he needed to recite. All indications in the strip pointed to the Christmas program that year being held at the local church and not the public school. Schulz was slowly developing not a religious strip but a religious character.[13]

While he was still struggling to remember his verses in the Christmas program, it was clear by the early 1960s that Linus had fully become a Christian character. On January 29, 1960, Linus knelt at his bedside to pray for his school teacher. That summer, as Charlie Brown pulled the petals on a flower to try and divine whether the "little red-haired girl" loved him or not, Linus complained, "It is difficult for me to believe that a flower has the gift of prophecy." Readers found out that Linus's father was a member of their church's board of deacons. On August 1, 1960, Linus found that religion could be "a very touchy subject" when his sister berated him for asking her if she spent time praying to God. Linus's growing biblical knowledge was on full display on August 14, 1960. That Sunday, Linus, Lucy, and Charlie Brown lay on a small hilltop and looked for figures in the passing clouds. Linus pointed out a scaled map of British Honduras, famous portraits, and, most importantly for the developing character, this scene: "That group of clouds there gives me the impression of the stoning of Stephen. . . . I can see the Apostle Paul standing there to the side." Of the unlimited number of references Schulz could have made, he chose the killing of the first Christian martyr as witnessed by the religion's first evangelist. Increasingly, Schulz was using Linus to incorporate the language and forms of evangelical Christianity into what had been a largely secular, albeit morally decent, comic strip. By introducing religion as a character trait of a likeable character and not the overarching theme of the entire strip, Schulz could fulfill his desire to share elements of his faith while minimizing the potential of pushing a sizable portion of his audience away.[14]

For the 1961 Christmas program, Linus was given an especially complicated scripture to recite. This time he would have to memorize a statement from the Old Testament prophet Jeremiah: "A voice was heard in Rama, wailing and loud laments; It was Rachel weeping for her children and refusing all consolation because they were no more." In the context of the New Testament Christmas story, these lines were believed to be a tragic prophecy of King Herod's search for the newborn king of Israel and his order to kill all Hebrew male infants under the age of two. This particular story clearly nagged at

Figure 3.2 Schulz would later reveal in an interview that this was one of his most commonly requested strips in the early 1960s. Charles Schulz, *Peanuts*, August 14, 1960. © 1960 Peanuts Worldwide LLC.

Schulz long after this strip appeared on December 17, 1961. "Did you ever wonder whether Jesus knew that at his birth other children were killed because of him?" he asked one interviewer for the *Christian Herald* several years later. "If he did know, how did he carry that burden?" After considering the question himself, Linus commented that Christmas had become "too commercial," leaving little room for the more somber details of the biblical Christmas story. This text was a peculiar part of the biblical Christmas story, one much at odds with the "spirit of Christmas" so often referred to in television programs and holiday films of the period. But this scene revealed Schulz's interest in studying the most intricate details of the Christian faith and his growing discomfort with secular holiday celebrations that focused more on gifts and decorations than the spiritual lessons of the season.[15]

During Christmas week 1962, Linus walked to school with Charlie Brown and Lucy at his side. As the three bundled children trudged through the snow, Linus pulled out his item for "show and tell" to share with the others. "These are copies I've been making of some of the Dead Sea Scrolls," he said as he showed off several tattered papers covered in Hebrew writing. The document to which Linus referred had been discovered by Arab shepherds in a partially closed cave just north of the Dead Sea in 1947. By 1956, archaeologists had uncovered nearly a thousand ancient texts far older than any existing Old Testament manuscripts. This discovery was a major find for conservative Christians who argued for the inerrancy of the Bible because the Dead Sea Scrolls, dating as far back as 408 BCE, corroborated the accuracy of much later existing copies of the Old Testament. The scrolls had great popular interest even a decade after they had all been collected. In 1962, Israel announced that it would be lending seven scrolls for a pavilion at the 1964 New York World's Fair.[16]

So while Linus's scrolls might not have held much significance for his young classmates, they represented a topic of current interest to many Americans, especially evangelical Christians. "This is a duplicate of a scroll of Isaiah chapters 38 to 40," Linus said as he unfolded his sheepskin replica of the first scroll discovered. "Here I've made a copy of the earliest known fragment ever found," he continued as Lucy and Charlie Brown looked on, dumbfounded. "It's a portion of I Samuel 23:9–16." As always, Schulz did not reference any specific item without first researching it in order to add just enough detail to delight the expert, but never so much as to lose his general audience.

Figure 3.3 Linus elevated his credentials as a young Bible scholar by reproducing replicas of the famed Dead Sea Scrolls. Charles Schulz, *Peanuts*, December 23, 1962.

Linus made no mention of copying any of the non-canonical books discovered with the Old Testament scrolls, which had stirred some controversy among scholars over why such books had been left out of later manuscripts if they had been used by earlier synagogues. Linus assured his friends that he would educate his classmates not only on the original construction of these documents, but also on "how these manuscripts have influenced modern scholars." Conservative evangelical readers likely would have read this as a nod to their own debates about the divine inspiration and authority of the Bible in the twentieth century. It was also another piece in Schulz's now yearly effort to reassert the Christian roots of the Christmas holiday. "I thought it might be at least faintly appropriate to the season," Linus remarked, acknowledging that week's celebration.[17]

In 1962 and 1963, the Supreme Court decided two cases that left many evangelicals reeling. The first of the two cases, *Engel v. Vitale*, ruled that public schools could not mandate or direct prayer. The second decision, *Abington School District v. Schempp*, offered a similar ruling concerning Bible readings in school. Both cases, the Justices pointed out in vain, only prohibited school administrators and teachers from directing prayers or Bible readings but did nothing to restrict the free exercise of the children's religion. The cultural shockwaves reverberated across the country. "Not since it struck down racial segregation in public schools in 1954," wrote the editor of the *Chicago Daily Defender*, a popular African American newspaper, "has the Supreme Court caused as much confusion as it did in its recent decision on official prayers in schools." Four years after the ruling, a staggering 70 percent of Americans still believed the Supreme Court had gotten the ruling wrong. "Millions of U.S. Christians emotionally reject the Supreme Court's successive decisions against prayer in schools," reported *Time* magazine.[18]

These two court decisions and their aftermath were the immediate context for one of the most controversial strips Charles Schulz ever produced. In the October 20, 1963 *Peanuts* strip, Sally Brown came home from school to find her older brother sitting in front of the television set. "Guess what," Sally demanded of Charlie Brown. "What?" he asked. Rather than replying immediately, Sally turned to make sure that no one was eavesdropping. She then quietly led her brother around the house, checking around corners and even out the front windows to ensure that privacy. She then crawled behind the couch, Charlie Brown in tow. When the two had settled in their hideout, she finally revealed her news: "We prayed in school today!" Charlie Brown clasped his hands over his mouth in disbelief.[19]

The cartoonist's sparse eleven panels and eight words of dialogue generated numerous emotional responses from readers. The audience's interpretations of this particular strip were varied, but that was exactly what Schulz had expected. "Of course, there is lots of meaning [in *Peanuts*]," Schulz assured a *Time* reporter, "But I can't explain it. What people see in it, that's what's in it." Still, he would later admit that this strip had "stirred up far more trouble than I had anticipated." The wave of response to this strip showed how Schulz's subtlety could sometimes cause him to lose control of the point he was attempting to make.[20]

Those who reached out to Schulz about this strip tended to be those who opposed the Supreme Court's decisions in *Engel* and *Schempp*. But while these letter writers tended to agree on the harmfulness of the rulings, they could not agree on how they felt about Schulz's October 20 strip. Some felt that he should not be joking about something so serious to the United States's spiritual health. "With this nation fast becoming a godless country," wrote one anonymous reader in comments attached to a facsimile of the strip, "I thought

Figure 3.4 Schulz stirred both praise and criticism with this remarkably understated response to the *Engel v. Vitale* decision. Charles Schulz, *Peanuts*, October 20, 1963. © 1963 Peanuts Worldwide LLC.

this comic strip in very bad taste." Carol Sue Henry of Ohio found it equally distasteful. "This is funny?" she wrote. "This is a serious thing not something to be made a joke of," because "without prayer our nation is *nothing*!" Moreover, this ruling must be understood in the context of the Cold War, she claimed, asserting that "outlawing prayer in school is nothing but a form of *Communism*!"[21]

Frank Goldman of Abington, Pennsylvania, was equally disappointed, though he held a very different opinion on the school prayer issue. The October 20 strip was "a very sad performance for a cartoonist of your talent," Goldman wrote. He figured that Schulz "must have been suffering from a truly desperate shortage of ideas to select the topic of prayer in schools." "I believe," Goldman explained, "the place for prayer, bible reading and all other practice of religion is primarily in the church or synagogue and may be supplemented by the home." Consequently, he did not believe that public schools were the proper place for such practices and was "now thoroughly convinced that religion is no fit subject for a cartoon." "Especially since yours was neither funny, clever nor cute," he closed. George Ramos agreed, seeing an official prayer as a clear violation of the first amendment. He wrote that "as much as I love *Peanuts*, if I have to choose between your strip and the U.S. Constitution, I will choose the Constitution!" To him the strip read as "mawkish and disquieting, to say the least of it."[22]

The overwhelming response of the writers was, however, disdain for the court ruling and praise for Sally for taking a stand against school authorities. Helen Mulherin, an elementary school teacher, wrote that the teachers at her school had posted the strip in their teacher's lounge as a means of protesting the court's decision. "Of the many hundreds of words I have read concerning recent Supreme Court decisions about prayer in schools," Texas H. Stevens told the artist, "these eight words in the settings which your genius provided for them are the most eloquent, forceful, and to the point I have seen." He requested copies of the strip to disperse throughout his Church of Christ congregation so others could enjoy the message. Even thirteen-year-old Marlene Turner of Illinois wrote to commend Schulz for "the cleverly written column." In her estimation "it was a real slam to all those opposing praying in public schools." "I debated seriously," another woman wrote, "whether to send this strip to [President] Kennedy or [Chief Justice] Warren, with the suggestion that you might be far more effective on our Supreme Court than a few of the incumbents."[23]

Many letters associated peaceful resistance to the Court's ruling with standing up to Communism and the rise of atheism. The best example of readers making connections between the court decisions and the rise of Communism was a lengthy letter from a man named John W. Oliver of Pennsylvania. "Every American must realize," Oliver insisted, "that removing Bible reading from our schools is the first step into Communism." He was thankful that Schulz had taken a stand and thought the artist deserved public recognition. "You should be given a medal for services rendered to the slumbering American people," he praised Schulz. The *Peanuts* strip on the *Engel* decision proclaimed a "patriotic Christian message," Oliver believed. He only wished that the rest of the country would take these developments as seriously as he and Schulz did. "May God forgive us," he wrote, "for rolling over and playing dead in accepting this infamous court ruling." Oliver was just one example of a large number of readers who saw the October 20 strip as an important statement in the Cold War, a conflict that they understood in both ideological and religious terms. While there was a range of different reader interpretations of this particular strip, this interpretation was by far the most common.[24]

Ironically, Schulz did not agree with these readers. He actually believed that the Supreme Court had made the right decision in both the *Engel* and *Schempp* cases. As was typical, Schulz did not make a public statement on the meaning of this strip. He did, however, later engage in discourse within his church that revealed how he truly felt. The spark that finally got Schulz to talk about his thoughts on the court rulings was a Christian magazine article. In September 1964, the Chief Justice of the Indiana Supreme Court Harold E. Achor wrote an article in *Vital Christianity*, the main publication for the Church of God (Anderson, Indiana), opposing the US Supreme Court's rulings on officially sanctioned prayer and Bible reading in public school. These rulings were, Achor wrote, "a regression from America's noble destiny" and were part of the Court's "ultimate resolve to prohibit all the religious activity and recognition of God in the affairs of government." The decisions were in complete contradiction to the way the founding generation had originally applied the First Amendment, Achor argued, and the Court had exceeded its authority by overruling the rights of the people by removing their autonomy over local schools. In an addendum of sorts, Chief Justice Achor wrote to the editors again in October to update his article. Achor cited a recently released FBI study that showed an 11 percent increase in juvenile arrests in the first full year following the Supreme Court's decisions. "This information supports the fact," Achor told the editor, "that an educational program in which worship and an understanding of God is denied will leave tomorrow's generation devoid of the moral stature required in a free society."[25]

Schulz disagreed, so much so that he wrote to the editors that "the fear of Chief Justice Achor and others . . . show [*sic*] a profound lack of faith." The success of the Church of God and their mission "needed no government approval." Instead, they would succeed the same way the early Christian church had: "due to its holiness." No government decrees could stop the Christian mission, Schulz argued. Only disobedience to the teaching of the Bible could hinder the mission. "If our spiritual lives need the support of government laws," he reasoned, "then we are already doomed." Christians should rely on the power of the gospel message taught by Jesus. "Our faith must lie in the ability of the gospel to save the individual," he concluded, closing with a reference to Romans 8:31, "If God be with us, who can be against us?"[26]

At least one reader picked up on the humor of the October 20 strip. William J. Butler had been the attorney for the plaintiffs in *Engel v. Vitale*. He wrote to Schulz because his mailbox had been stuffed with copies of the October 20 comic strip for more than two weeks. "Permit me to say, I thought it was extremely well done," Butler wrote in admiration.[27]

Butler, like many of those who celebrated the strip, asked for the autographed original. There is no record of whether the cartoonist complied, but it is doubtful. As Schulz later revealed in an interview, his typically supportive editor at United Features Syndicate was "disturbed" by the response. "It disturbed him when both sides wanted to reprint the strip to promote their beliefs," Schulz recalled. The two men met to discuss the situation and "decided that we wouldn't let anybody reprint [it]." Schulz's copyright protection ultimately enabled him to maintain final control over his message when it had run afield.[28]

The reality, Schulz later admitted, was that he had intended to make light of the fervor over the *Engel* case. The joke was on Sally for believing the fearful claims of some that the ruling meant it was now illegal for individuals to pray in public schools. The artist made it clear in an interview years later. "I don't believe in school prayer," he declared. "I think it's total nonsense." Prayer was a personal act, a private one, he told the interviewer. Beyond this, with public school prayer there was the question of who would be leading the prayer. "Who is the teacher there that is going to have them pray?" Schulz wondered. "Is the teacher going to be Catholic or Mormon or Episcopalian or what? It just causes all sorts of problems. And what are the kids praying about anyway?" Schulz's opinion on the issue reflected Americans' controversy in implementing the civil religion that business leaders in the 1940s had championed as an antidote to the New Deal and that government leaders in the 1950s had cemented in pledges, mottos, and presidential prayer breakfasts. Where such vague references and acknowledgments of a god could function at a national level, the practical application of public prayers and Bible reading

Figure 3.5 Growing up in Cold War America, Sally Brown had trouble distinguishing the pledge from prayer, school from church. Charles Schulz, *Peanuts*, September 11, 1963. © 1963 Peanuts Worldwide LLC.

led to intense theological and legal controversy at the local level and ultimately transformed national law through the judiciary.[29]

Schulz did not agree with public school prayer and he did not want to be the champion of a "patriotic Christian message," as John W. Oliver of Pennsylvania had written. "This is a frightening trend," Schulz told the *Christian Herald* in 1967, "people who regard Christianity and Americanism as being virtually the same thing." Schulz's criticism was obvious in his September 11, 1963 strip that pictured Sally Brown completing the Pledge of Allegiance with her hand over her heart. As she sat down to begin her school day, she suddenly jumped back to her feet, embarrassed that she had forgotten to formally close her moment of secular devotion. "Amen!" she shouted. Growing up in a society that often blurred the lines between Christian faith and national pride, Schulz seemed to argue in these panels, Sally Brown struggled to distinguish the pledge from prayer. Schulz was not trying to promote a nationalist Christianity, but he was trying to deliver a Christian message to his audience in a palatable form. To do that, he would need to further develop the religious character of Linus.[30]

Despite Charlie and Sally Brown getting so much of the religious attention in fall 1963, Linus Van Pelt was still the strip's most overtly religious character and was becoming more explicit in his faith with each passing month. In September 1963, for example, Linus, carrying an antique wooden piece over his shoulders, met Charlie Brown for their walk to school. "What in the world is that?" Charlie Brown asked. "This is a yoke," Linus replied and explained that he was taking it to his class for a special report. Linus went on to elaborate on his project, describing the different ways that the Bible used the imagery of the yoke, whether in the story of Jacob and Esau, the prophecies of Ezekiel, or the tales of Israel's disobedience to God. With each example, Schulz included specific scripture references in parentheses for his readers. He then finished the Sunday strip with one of his most explicitly religious comments yet. Linus would "wind up by talking about the yoke of sin suggested in Lamentations 1:14 and the 'easy' yoke of Matthew 11:29." This final cited passage was a direct reference to the messianic claims of Jesus, Schulz's very first use of the Christian gospel in *Peanuts*. For any curious newspaper reader with access to a Bible, Schulz had used Linus's discourse in this instance as a sort of Christian evangelical tract.[31]

Even when he was confused, Linus's misconceptions served to comment on religious faith in 1960s America. This was most evident in a series of annual strips Schulz wrote beginning in 1959 concerning the Great Pumpkin. The story of the Great Pumpkin began when Linus conflated the stories of Santa Claus with Halloween. Each Halloween Linus would wait in the pumpkin patch all night rather than participating in trick-or-treating, confident that the Great Pumpkin would bring gifts to the "most sincere pumpkin patch." Year after year, the Great Pumpkin never showed. Utterly disappointed and embarrassed in 1959, Linus bemoaned that he was "a victim of false doctrine." But the very next year Linus was back to arguing with Lucy about whether the Great Pumpkin or Santa Claus was superior. Overhearing the fuss, Charlie Brown turned and left, saying, "I'm always disturbed by denominational squabbling." By October 1963, though, Charlie Brown had finally engaged in the argument with Linus. "How can you believe in something that just isn't true?" Charlie Brown shouted at his friend in the pumpkin patch. "When you stop believing in that fellow with the red suit and white beard who goes, 'Ho, Ho, Ho,'" Linus demanded, refusing to name Santa Claus, "I'll stop believing in the Great Pumpkin!" Charlie Brown sighed at that point, exhausted by the impasse. "We are obviously separated by denominational differences," Charlie Brown grumbled. These strips were filled with the language of religious faith, belief and unbelief, denominationalism, and spiritual hypocrisy.[32]

Figure 3.6 Linus refuses to acknowledge Santa Claus because of his fervent faith in the Great Pumpkin. Charles Schulz, *Peanuts*, October 28, 1963. © 1963 Peanuts Worldwide LLC.

By the mid-1960s, Schulz had developed Linus from an infant to a junior Bible scholar. The naiveté and misunderstandings of the young boy provided comic relief for many strips, but it also gave Schulz an avenue to express his feelings about his Christian faith, a topic of great personal importance to him. In 1965, the maturity of this theme in the strip would coincide with a major opportunity for *Peanuts* to make the jump from the funny pages to the small screen.

A Charlie Brown Christmas actually began as a documentary about the cartoonist. The project, titled *A Boy Named Charlie Brown*, was the idea of a young filmmaker named Lee Mendelson and centered around Schulz's everyday life, from his time at the drawing board to his daily drive in his kids' school carpool. The half-hour film included about two minutes of *Peanuts* animations directed by Bill Melendez, the same creative director responsible for the earlier Ford commercials. For a year and a half, Mendelson shopped the special to the television networks with no luck. Perhaps, Mendelson thought, the documentary was a loser just like its title character.

Two things changed for Schulz in 1965. First, in April of that year, *Peanuts* was featured as the cover story of *Time* magazine. The article highlighted the rise of "comment in the comics." "More and more," *Time*'s editors wrote, "the [comic] strips are offering political satire, psychology, and comments of varying subtlety on the rages and outrages of everyday life." They chose *Peanuts* for the cover because Schulz's work, they felt, best characterized this "new style" in American comics. "Religion, psychiatry, education—indeed all the complexities of the modern world—seem more amusing than menacing when they are seen through the clear, uncompromising eyes of the comic-strip kids from *Peanuts*," the cover story asserted. Life's greatest challenges were made more palatable in the morning funnies, but not because they made light of serious concerns. Instead, *Peanuts* offered a "simplistic yet somehow impressive understanding of the assorted problems that perplex their elders." More than anything else, the *Time* cover story gave *Peanuts* a level of national visibility that helped turn a beloved strip among avid comic strip readers into an American icon.[33]

Second, *Peanuts* became the source for a hugely popular 1965 book, Robert L. Short's *The Gospel According to Peanuts*. Short, who was pursuing a doctorate in theology at the University of Chicago Divinity School, had never met Charles Schulz. Other than the comic strips that were included within the text, the book had very little to do with *Peanuts*. The text focused more on debates over the place of art in Christianity, the doctrine of original sin, the sufferings of Job, and Christian typology. Short quoted extensively from theologians and scholars like Soren Kierkegaard, Karl Barth, and Blaise Pascal, all names with which lay readers would have been only vaguely familiar. *The Gospel According to Peanuts* became the bestselling nonfiction book of 1965. Selling more than 375,000 copies in twelve printings in just the first year, it was by far the biggest book that John Knox Press, a small Christian publisher in Atlanta, Georgia, had ever produced. With some four thousand copies selling per week in 1965, numerous Americans were exposed to Short's contention that beneath the surface of *Peanuts* lay a fundamentally Christian worldview. The reality, however, was that just like the majority of readers who wrote to congratulate Schulz on the school prayer strip, *The Gospel According to Peanuts* merely reaffirmed what the author already believed: *Peanuts* was a slyly Christian production in a period of perceived spiritual decline. For his part, Schulz took no credit for any of Short's findings or success. "Robert Short wasn't trying so much to show what I was saying in the strip," Schulz explained again and again. "What he was trying to show was that even such an insignificant thing as a comic strip could promote certain spiritual thoughts." In this sense, *The Gospel According to Peanuts* was a major event for conservative Christians, in light of the perceived dismantling of American civil religion in the early 1960s. "This could be one of the most important Christian books published in our time," declared the *Young Calvinist* magazine. "In a 'post-Christian' culture infiltrated by existentialism and brainwashed by 'the new morality,' " the reviewer went on, "Christians may well rejoice in the creative efforts of [Schulz]."[34]

The *Time* cover and *The Gospel According to Peanuts* led to a phone call. John Allen of McCann-Erickson, one of the nation's largest advertising firms, contacted Lee Mendelson, who had tried several times to sell his *Peanuts* documentary to the firm, to ask if Schulz had ever considered making a Christmas television special. "Of course," Mendelson lied. "Well, the good news is that one of my clients, Coca-Cola, is looking for a Christmas special," Allen explained. "The bad news is that today is Wednesday and they'll need an outline in Atlanta by Monday."[35]

Mendelson recalls that he immediately telephoned Schulz to announce, "I think I may have just sold a Charlie Brown Christmas show." Bewildered by this project of which he had never heard, Schulz inquired, "And what show might that be?" "The one you need to make an outline for tomorrow," Mendelson replied. Without hesitation, Schulz accepted and the two men, along with animator Bill Melendez, met at the artist's home in Sebastopol, California—where the Schulz family had moved in 1958—to write the next day. By the weekend, they had submitted a script for Coca-Cola's approval. Schulz's plans called for a number of unconventional features for a family Christmas special. The soundtrack would feature jazz music, originally composed by San Francisco pianist Vince Guaraldi. Rather than professional voice actors, the *Peanuts* characters would be voiced by actual untrained children, some as young as six. For those who could not yet read the script, Mendelson and Melendez would have to feed them lines, sometimes a syllable at a time. The animation would also be quite odd compared to anything produced by larger animation productions like Disney because Melendez's artists struggled to figure out how to put Schulz's flat characters in motion. There would be no laugh track to cue the audience and Schulz's subtle humor led to what CBS executives believed was awkward, slow pacing. But the most controversial component of the program would be the penultimate scene.[36]

Though some readers had criticized Schulz for using quotes from the Bible in "such a lowly thing as a newspaper comic strip," he always took such quotations very seriously. "These scriptural references have always been done with dignity and, of course, with much love, for I am extremely fond of studying the Old and New Testament," he told readers in one interview. Linus's recitation of the birth of Jesus from the Gospel of Luke was no different. "Isn't there anyone who knows what Christmas is all about?!" Charlie Brown shouts from the stage of his failed Christmas pageant as he stands next to his sparse, pitiful Christmas tree in the climax of *A Charlie Brown Christmas*. "Sure, Charlie Brown," replies young Linus, the only child who had not stomped off laughing at the round-headed boy, "I can tell you what Christmas is all about."[37]

Linus marched out to center stage, his blue blanket trailing behind him. "Lights, please," he called to the control booth. The house lights went black and a single spotlight focused on Linus as he began his monologue. Linus recited Luke 2:8–14, which told the story of shepherds keeping watch over their flocks outside of the small town of Bethlehem when an angel appeared to them. "Unto you is born this day in the City of David a Savior, who is Christ the Lord," the shining angel told the shepherds. Linus completed the passage by telling of a great multitude of angels appearing in the sky to sing praises to God. There was no sign of forgetfulness or hesitance from the boy as he spoke, unlike the many Christmas programs he had spoken at before in the comic strip. When he finished his piece, he confidently picked up his blanket from around his feet and walked back to his friend. "That's what Christmas is all about, Charlie Brown," he said matter-of-factly before sticking his thumb back in his mouth.[38]

If friends, producers, and executives had had their way, Linus would never have quoted scripture in *A Charlie Brown Christmas.* The decision to include the passage from Luke had come only after a long deliberation. As Schulz, Mendelson, and Melendez searched for a way to get at the point Schulz so desperately wanted to convey, the cartoonist "finally decided that every idea we had was an idea that really avoided the essential truth which was that the true meaning of Christmas could be found only in the Gospel according to Saint Luke." There was no way, in the cartoonist's mind, around using "the famous passage about the baby Jesus." But Mendelson admitted that both he and Melendez were reluctant. "Oh, gee, I don't know if you can animate the Bible," Mendelson slowly replied. Schulz, however was determined: "If we don't do it, who will?" CBS executives were equally uneasy with the religious content, saying, "The Bible thing scares us." As Mendelson remembered it, "The network thought it was awful" and did nothing to hide its disappointment with the investment. At that point, the only thing that helped the program make the airwaves was the fact that Coca-Cola had already signed off on the early script and that CBS did not have time to pull their own advertisements for the program.[39]

So on December 9, 1965, *A Charlie Brown Christmas* debuted, not to the feared blowback against animated religious content, but as the second highest rated show of the night. According to the Nielsen ratings, the special attracted 15.5 million primetime viewers, only slightly behind *Bonanza*, the most popular television show of the mid-1960s. Even more, the show received wonderful reviews. *Variety* noted that Schulz was so well known for his "religious content" that "it is no surprise . . . that this little video fable on the meaning of Christmas should come off so well." "It was a religious show," the magazine summarized, "and a good one." The reviewer celebrated the fact that it "did not deal in the usual Yuletide homilies and euphemisms for Christian faith." Instead, the special's "fundamentalist message was that man can find certitude only in the word of God as revealed in the Bible." And he felt that the trimmed down, simple style of the production—that is, the very things CBS executives had hated—actually served to communicate Schulz's religious message. Likewise, *Time* magazine deemed the program "a special that really is special" and called for it to become an annual tradition.[40]

The most telling reviews, however, came from viewers who wrote to express their feelings about *A Charlie Brown Christmas.* Many of these letters were directed to the show's sponsor, Coca-Cola, which in turn forwarded them to Schulz. There were some common themes in this correspondence. First, most letters were written on the day the special aired on television, December 9, 1965. Many viewers even commented that they were picking up their pen or sitting down at their typewriter within moments of the program's conclusion. These letters, then, represent an immediate response from the audience. A large number of those writing admitted that this was the first time they had ever written a fan letter. This demonstrates the level of response *A Charlie Brown Christmas* elicited. Finally, the letters overwhelmingly focused on Linus's monologue. Like Reverend Philip A. Jordan of the Trinity Lutheran Church in Fresno, California, many viewers believed this scene was a "spiritually significant" statement in the context of the mid-1960s.[41]

While Christmas trees and Santa Claus were common fare, the Christian Nativity or scriptural references were nowhere to be found in most Christmas television specials of the 1960s. In his own right, Schulz saw Christmas as a time of child-like innocence. His trusty study Bible, covered in countless handwritten notes and marginalia from years of reading and rereading, evidenced as much. "Christmas is primarily a children's day," he wrote next to the Gospel of Matthew's account of Jesus's birth, "for it takes the innocent faith of a child to appreciate it." In his mind, declaring the birth of Christ to be the "true meaning of Christmas" was less about making some claim of religious exclusivity and more about redirecting attention to the "innocent" origins of the season, the very thing Schulz feared was being lost in modern commercialization. And, as Schulz would tell a gathering of the National Cartoonists Society, "there is a market for innocence. . . . There's still a market for things that are clean and decent."[42]

Many viewers felt that *A Charlie Brown Christmas* addressed a topic—explicit Christian faith—that was largely missing from American television. Media studies of 1960s holiday television supported this impression. Throughout the 1960s, less than 9 percent of television Christmas episodes and specials contained any substantive religious references. "The message that Christmas is the celebration of the birth of Christ," wrote Judith Anderson of Napa, California, "is one that has been ignored or rejected for much too long by the television medium." "Thank you," another writer said, "for putting Christ into Christmas." Coca-Cola, too, received credit for televising this uncommon viewpoint. George DeAngelo wrote to the company to say, "Thanks to your company, the real meaning of Christmas has gotten through to our children and my wife and I have had our faith restored by a company who cares." Most importantly for Schulz, readers suggested the Christmas special could have an important influence on those who did not know the Christian message. "It could be that many persons who wouldn't sit still for a sermon," Art Vermillion of the Christian Church in Indiana wrote, "would gain some realization of the true meaning of Christmas by watching *Peanuts*."[43]

A number of viewers even connected Schulz's religious statement in *A Charlie Brown Christmas* to the backlash against the Supreme Court's rulings in *Engel* and *Schempp*. It was a "dark day" in which Americans were living, wrote Betty J. Knorr of Miami. People were "afraid to mention Jesus and the Church for fear of some group boycotting their product or getting a Court Order handed down." It was a time of "prayer being banned from schools and public meetings," a time when "the evil and vile things receive banner headlines" and "the mention of God in general [was] being hush-hushed." That was why she felt that Schulz's program was a "timely presentation," and she was sure that "most concerned parents" agreed. John A. Carter of Los Angeles certainly concurred when he called the program "a perfectly delightful show and in spite of our Supreme Court." The court's rulings in *Engel* and *Schempp* had had nothing to do with limiting Americans' freedom of religion—indeed, the justices believed they were protecting those freedoms by excluding school public officials from such matters—but many conservative evangelicals believed the opposite. Of these, at least some saw Charles Schulz's religious statements as a counterattack against a secular onslaught.[44]

In reality, *A Charlie Brown Christmas* would likely not have been able to command the viewership it did if it were exclusively a religious program. This is why it was so important that the larger message of the show be anti-materialist, not religious. Viewers not only found the program spiritually outstanding; they saw it as special in its tone and presentation. One viewer praised it as a much-needed escape from the numerous concerning events on television like the Vietnam War and the Watts riots, writing that it was "a welcome relief from current depressing presentations (press and TV)." Another, picking up on the same high morality that Schulz had always championed in his comic strip, wrote that "amidst the rage of vulgarity and indecency portrayed to the public and especially to our children, your production of *Peanuts* stands out as refreshing" and extolled Schulz's "wholesome philosophy." Shell Storrier, the vice president of WKTV in Utica, New York, felt confident that the kindhearted tone of *A Charlie Brown Christmas* would make it "the most remembered Christmas special that we will see in many years." While "there are people who say 'comics' and say it disdainfully," wrote another, "but with so much violence, mistrust, and trouble in this country, this short thirty minutes was an oasis." By keeping the Schulz's personally important religious message to a single scene of just a couple minutes he was able to reach a much larger audience with the other themes of the show.[45]

By all measures, *A Charlie Brown Christmas* was an enormous success for all involved. The week after the premiere, the associates at McCann-Erickson, Coca-Cola's advertising firm circulated a memo celebrating all the positive press surrounding the program that simply read: "Last Friday All Heaven Broke Loose." The show would go on to win an Emmy in 1966. CBS was so impressed with the response that it ordered four more specials within a month of the original debut. As successful as the subsequent television specials were none would ever be as highly revered as the first. That Christmas special had tapped into a part of the population that felt its influence quickly slipping after the tremendous revivalism of the 1950s. In Charlie Brown and Linus they found tiny yet powerful voices for their faith. The program's enormous critical success only reinforced their faith in the power of the Christian message amid what they believed was a rising tide of secularism. "Bless you for Charlie Brown," wrote Helen J. Shupe, articulating millions of evangelical Christians' newfound love for *Peanuts* and Charles Schulz. And Schulz had maximized the mass appeal of the special by containing the religious message within the larger message of anti-materialism, a message popular in other holiday programming like one of the era's other animated classics *How the Grinch Stole Christmas* (1966).[46]

Just before Christmas in 1966, perhaps in response to the overwhelming number of requests to rerun the Christmas special on television (which CBS happily did), Schulz reran the message of *A Charlie Brown Christmas* in a

Figure 3.7 Linus reprised his famous Christmas monologue, this time questioning the point of Santa Claus in a religious holiday. Charles Schulz, *Peanuts*, December 18, 1966. © 1966 Peanuts Worldwide LLC.

Sunday comic strip. As Linus and Charlie Brown roamed through a wintry scene, Linus read from the Revised Standard Version the same passage of Luke he had recited in the Christmas special. At the conclusion of the reading, Linus reiterated, "That's what Christmas is all about, Charlie Brown," to which Charlie Brown affirmed, "You're right." In this strip, however, Schulz added a new tag to the end of the scene. Rather than ending where *A Charlie Brown Christmas* had, Schulz pushed his criticism to the chief icon of a secularized Christmas by having Linus ask, "So who needs Santa Claus?"

Just as with the Christmas television special, fan letters poured in to celebrate the cartoonist's statement. These readers hoped that Schulz's message would resonate with his large audience and that he would be fortunate enough to continue delivering his Christian message for many years to come. A mother from Connecticut wrote, "I have three children and your December 18th comic strip had more influence on them than all the sermons our priest could ever give them." Amos Morgan of Portland appreciated the addition of Linus's criticism of Santa, commenting that, "Perhaps Linus doesn't speak for the majority of people when he throws Santa Claus out of Christmas, but he is a Number 1 hero so far as I'm concerned." Again, Christian religious leaders joined the chorus. "Keep on bringing your truly Christian philosophy to us through the lips of little ones," penned Father Joseph Adams of St. Charles Borromeo Church in St. Louis, Missouri. "When I read it," wrote another, "I prayed and asked God to bless you and thanked Him for gifted people who are Christians." And the cartoonist's membership in the "cult of wholesomeness" was still up to date. R. W. Massi of Tuscaloosa, Alabama, who read *Peanuts* to his children every Sunday morning before going to church, wrote that "in this present day of social moral standards on the decline it is difficult to continue to fight the battle for good," but he encouraged Schulz to "keep up the good wholesome work."[47]

By the mid-1960s, Charles Schulz had succeeded in delivering his Christian message to a national audience of millions without causing major offense. He had managed this feat by incorporating these beliefs into the personality of a single, likeable character. When the message and critiques verged on being engulfed in larger social debates, Schulz maintained his control by utilizing his copyright. When he attempted to expand the reach of his message through television, he worked the message into the larger and more popular critique of postwar materialism and vulgar popular culture. Whether he agreed with them or not, he had become a cultural hero to American evangelicals for his willingness to incorporate Christian messages and biblical texts into the cultural spaces whose secularization troubled them so deeply.

4

Crosshatch Is Beautiful

Franklin, Color-Blindness, and the Limits of Racial Integration

On August 21, 1949, a young Charles Schulz used his *Li'l Folks* comic strip in the St. Paul *Pioneer Press* to address a topic that was rising to the forefront of national consciousness in postwar America. The panel showed a girl and a boy—the boy bore a striking resemblance to Schulz's early drawings of Charlie Brown—staring down at two dogs: a dark dachshund and a small, white beagle with black spots. The boy appeared worried as he looked over the two canines. "It's difficult to say which you prefer," the boy said of the dogs, "without showing racial prejudice."[1]

This single panel encompassed Schulz's thoughts on the problems of race in America. He was not afraid that picking one dog over the other would reveal any real personal racism. Instead, the boy worried that making a choice would lead others to think he was racist. This was, of

course, a child's misunderstanding of what racism really meant and misappropriating the terms of America's central social conflict. But, as Schulz did in all his work, the real message was buried just below the humor of the innocent situation. This was the key to all of Schulz's social criticism: using his adorable child characters to disarm readers as he addressed sensitive topics. He was acknowledging just how difficult it was to comment upon the complex problems of race in America without offending anyone. Though he consistently demonstrated his commitment to racial equality throughout his career, he would struggle with how best to use his national platform to aid the civil rights movement without patronizing African Americans or alienating white middle-class Americans. He worried that a white midwesterner like himself might be unable to fairly voice a black character. And he knew that if he did not hit exactly the right tone, any statement he made on one of the most controversial domestic issue of the 1960s could have terrible consequences for his career (and even the culture) when tens of millions of Americans sat down to read their morning paper.[2]

In one of the boldest social statements in *Peanuts*, the cartoonist integrated his comic strip during a tremendously volatile moment in American history.

Figure 4.1 A panel of Schulz's *Li'l Folks* comic strip featured in the *St. Paul Pioneer Press*. August 21, 1949. Courtesy of the Charles M. Schulz Museum and Research Center.

Public reactions ranged from celebration to dissatisfaction to condemnation. The integration of Franklin into *Peanuts* would become a defining moment in Schulz's public legacy. But his execution of this event would also demonstrate the limitations of black characters in the mainstream popular culture of the 1960s to accurately represent African American voices. Schulz's measured, unassuming approach to racial integration was at once revolutionary and restricting. The story of the character Franklin, the first African American character to integrate a nationally syndicated newspaper comic strip, is the story of the mainstream struggle between acknowledging the fight for black rights and maintaining white control of American popular culture in the 1960s and 1970s.

In the 1950s, *Peanuts* was as white as Levittown. There was almost no hint that Americans were wrestling over the legacy of segregation in the decade. *Peanuts* only hinted at the subject once during those years. In March 1953, Schroeder blazed through a gleeful piano tune as Snoopy—a transient neighborhood dog not yet attached to Charlie Brown—danced around the living room to the other children's delight. When all the laughter and play was done, Violet walked over to Snoopy and thanked him for his performance. "We're going to serve lunch now," she told him, "You'll have to eat in the kitchen." Snoopy could hardly believe his ears. "The kitchen?!" the pup thought to himself in dismay. "I'm good enough to entertain them," he continued, brewing over the implications, "but not good enough to eat in the same room with them!" The scene harkened back to the classic 1926 Langston Hughes poem "I, Too":

> I, too, sing America
>
> I am the darker brother.
> They send me to eat in the kitchen
> When company comes . . .
>
> Tomorrow,
> I'll be at the table
> When company comes.
> Nobody'll dare
> Say to me,
> "Eat in the kitchen,"
> Then . . .
>
> They'll see how beautiful I am
> And be ashamed[3]

Mealtime was one of the most segregated moments in postwar American daily life. By the end of the 1950s public lunch counters would become a battleground at the center of the civil rights movement. Snoopy's recognition of his second-class status—fit for entertainment but not for intimacy—was

Figure 4.2 Snoopy experiences some of the insult and shame of racial discrimination against black performing artists in the 1950s. Charles Schulz, *Peanuts*, March 15, 1953. © 1953 Peanuts Worldwide LLC.

an obvious nod to the social injustices of the day. But Schulz complicated his message in the final panels of that Sunday strip. Snoopy had determined that he would rather go home than endure such treatment. Just as the dog went to leave, Violet entered the kitchen with a plate for Snoopy that included multiple sandwiches, a salad, cake, ice-cream, and a cup of hot chocolate. Upon seeing this, Snoopy wistfully abandoned his principles with the dismissive comment, "Pride is a foolish thing." Like much of Schulz's work, this punchline could be read in multiple ways. On the one hand, he could have intended to say that African Americans could enjoy the fruits of American affluence in exchange for some of their personal dignity. On the other hand, and more likely, he could have simply been trying to lighten the criticism of his predominantly white readership by taking a step back from his very pointed and hardly veiled social criticism. Either way, it exemplified how Schulz attempted to challenge older ideas about race and society without alienating too much of his audience.[4]

The 1950s in *Peanuts* largely proceeded like the previous decade in terms of racial diversity. But as the civil rights struggle intensified in the United States, race became much harder for Schulz to avoid. The decision in *Brown v. Board of Education* in 1954 gave the first federal force behind public integration and pushed the issue to the forefront of the American consciousness. In 1955, NAACP activist Rosa Parks refused to give up her public bus seat to a white rider, setting off a boycott that would force southern business owners to choose between profits and prejudice and would also introduce the nation to a local preacher and civil rights leader named Martin Luther King Jr. In 1960, four black students from North Carolina A&T University sat at the lunch counter at the Greensboro Woolworth's and demanded service. Their demonstration sparked similar anti-segregation protests across the Deep South and forced local communities to grapple with their own racial regulations. The next year, the Congress for Racial Equality (C.O.R.E.) sponsored what came to be known as the "freedom rides" to test new court prohibitions on segregated public transit. James Meredith integrated the University of Mississippi in 1962 amid violent white backlash. In the summer of 1963, Martin Luther King Jr. headlined a protest march that saw more than 250,000 people descend on Washington, DC to force Congress to act on their behalf. President Lyndon Johnson signed the Civil Rights Act into law in 1964, followed by the Voting Rights Act the next year. And in the summers of 1966, 1967, and 1968, urban riots erupted across the nation, signaling the failure of recent legislation to address entrenched poverty in inner-city black America.[5]

With this growing social and legal momentum, the stereotypical black comic characters of the past—primitive, lazy, unintelligent, animalistic, and sexualized—became increasingly distasteful to media executives and their sponsors. As readers' expectations slowly changed, white artists became more uncomfortable with producing and reproducing black characters. Underground comics innovator Robert Crumb would be one of the very few to continue using these exaggerated stereotypes in his black characters, much to the distaste of critics. Perhaps Crumb was using his grotesque black characters to provoke just such visceral responses from readers and force them to face their own true feelings about blackness. Nonetheless, such images were considered extremely offensive to progressive-minded whites by the 1960s and most artists were unsure of how best to handle black characters in this new era. For these reasons, black characters largely vanished from mainstream comics in the first half of the 1960s. Not until the mid- and late 1960s would a new brand of black comic character arise in the wake of the great legislative successes of the civil rights movement. Marvel Comics' Black Panther, introduced in 1966, would be one of the few examples of positive black characters in a field of comic arts that was otherwise exclusively white.[6]

Similarly, positive black character types were not common in television and film until later in the 1960s, though there were some exceptions. The earliest black characters on television relied on old Jim Crow-era stereotypes. The first television program with a black lead was ABC's *Beulah*, starring Ethel Walters in a mammy-type role. The show struggled over its three-year run to keep a lead actress because of the offensive nature of the role. As Walters expressed upon leaving the show, she did not feel comfortable starring in "a white folks kitchen comedy." Another early show with black leading actors was CBS's adaptation of the popular radio show *Amos 'n' Andy*. The television program suffered low ratings and only lasted two seasons, ultimately canceled following the NAACP's protest against the stereotypical characterizations. Outside of these two shows and black appearances on programs like the *Ed Sullivan Show* or sporting events, black people rarely appeared on television before the mid-1960s. As one scholar has pointed out, popular shows like *Lassie* (1954) and *Bewitched* (1964) were set in worlds in which African Americans did not seem to exist. Film actors Sidney Poitier and Sammy Davis Jr. experienced success in the 1950s and 1960s, but often played characters that were largely de-sexualized, educated, conservative, and well-mannered. Even shows like *I Spy* (1965), for which Bill Cosby received the first ever Emmy award won by a black actor, portrayed a highly educated, elite black character with little racial consciousness. Similarly, *Julia*, a sitcom led by actress Diahann Carroll, depicted an African American nurse for a prominent doctor and rarely pushed very far in challenging the racial status quo. Nichelle Nichols, who played the African American communications officer Uhura in the progressive science fiction program *Star Trek* (1966), only remained on the show after being persuaded by Dr. Martin Luther King Jr. not to give up one of the few visible black roles on television. As Dr. King realized, there were few black voices in 1960s American popular culture and almost no complex portrayals.[7]

Late in the decade, Schulz made his first subtle attempt to embrace racial diversity in *Peanuts*. In March 1967, Peppermint Patty telephoned Charlie Brown with a surprise. She had found a new slugger for their baseball team. "This guy is terrific!" she trumpeted over the phone, "José Peterson!" Peterson was a short boy with a powerful swing and instantly became the star hitter of Charlie Brown's team. Though the boy never spoke for himself (it was unclear if he knew English), Peppermint Patty explained that his family had lived all over the West, from New Mexico to North Dakota. Though José did not work out as a player on Charlie Brown's team, he became a lasting member of Peppermint Patty's rival baseball team. Schulz would later explain this strange boy as the product of a dream. José, he had imagined, was half-Mexican and half-Swedish. So it was through Schulz's off-beat sense of humor that he first introduced ethnic diversity to *Peanuts*, though most readers likely missed it. José only appeared in the strip three times over the course of one week in

March 1967. Furthermore, Schulz did not publicly explain the boy's ethnic background until 1975. José Peterson, then, was the exception that proved the rule: *Peanuts*, like the rest of comic arts at the time, was the story of children in a white middle-class suburb.[8]

This was the status quo in Schulz's work until one day in April 1968, as he sorted through his weekly mountain of fan mail. There he found a letter from a California stay-at-home mom named Harriet Glickman. Nothing on the envelope indicated how significant this letter would be for Schulz's career.

Harriet Glickman was a forty-one-year-old Southern California woman who had recently left her public teaching career to stay at home with her three young children. One of two children of Russian-Jewish immigrants, Glickman was regularly taught during childhood about the "importance of all people." Her parents expected her and her sister to have "a sense of responsibility for others," she recalled. Her mother and father had been active in organizing steelworkers in Chicago. Though she had not become a labor activist herself, she never lost a passion for the equal treatment of all people and a respect for human dignity. Thus the motivation for the letter to Schulz "really grew out of my whole life," she later reflected.[9]

Glickman's letter, however, was most immediately the product of tragedy. On April 4, 1968, Martin Luther King Jr. was assassinated in Memphis where he was supporting striking sanitation workers. The moment demanded that Americans ask themselves, as Robert Kennedy told a campaign rally in Indianapolis that night, "what kind of nation we are and what direction we want to move in." "People realized how white everything was," cartoonist Morrie Turner told the *Los Angeles Times*. "They finally realized what Dr. King was talking about." In the wake of the murder, Glickman began looking for ways to help influence change in race relations of the late 1960s. "I've been asking myself," she admitted in her letter to Charles Schulz written shortly after she heard the news, "what I can do to help change those conditions in our society which led to the assassination and which contribute to the vast sea of misunderstanding, fear, hate, and violence." In the midst of this, Glickman knew that progress would be "a very long and tortuous road." In fact, she predicted that it would be "another generation before the kind of open friendship, trust and mobility will be an accepted part of our lives." Nonetheless, she was compelled to do something and so she reached out to Schulz.[10]

Glickman described herself in three telling and deeply interrelated ways. She was "a suburban housewife," a mother, and "a deeply concerned and active citizen." Through activities like individual and collective letter writing, local book clubs, and engagement with Parent-Teacher Associations, suburban housewives helped shape the grassroots politics that would transform the political culture of the nation by the 1980s. While there were numerous personal reasons Glickman might have given for her engagement in public life, she declared her primary reason to be the protection of her young children. As she thought through how best to fulfill her roles as housewife, mother, and concerned citizen, she arrived at "the areas of the mass media which are of tremendous importance in shaping the unconscious attitudes of our kids," namely "our comic strips and . . . that violent jungle of horrors known as children's television."[11]

Glickman had a simple request for her favorite cartoonist. "It occurred to me today," she wrote, "that the introduction of Negro children into the group of Schulz characters could happen with a minimum of impact." She was confident it would work because of "the gentleness of the kids." Glickman well understood that, while this all seemed so simple "sitting alone in a California suburbia," the reality was that "one doesn't make radical changes in so important an institution without a lot of shock waves from syndicates." But she had confidence in Schulz. "You have . . . a stature and reputation which can withstand a great deal." In her mind, *Peanuts* was perfectly situated in popular culture to break the color barrier in newspaper comic strips.[12]

Schulz responded to Glickman eleven days later. He thanked her for the letter and wrote that he appreciated her "suggestion about introducing a Negro child into the comic strip." Schulz felt constrained, however, by "the same problem that other cartoonists are who wish to comply" with such a request. While "we would all like very much to be able to do this," Schulz explained, cartoonists were "afraid that it would look like we were patronizing our Negro friends." Though he had discussed the idea with colleagues before, he was left without a clear vision for how to address what he believed was an inadequacy in his field while remaining sensitive to the complex racial politics of the day. "I don't know what the solution is," he confessed. The *Peanuts* scene printed at the bottom of Schulz's letterhead seemed an apt illustration of the artist's feelings: Charlie Brown's kite string was tangled hopelessly around Snoopy's doghouse as the kite itself lay crumpled in the dog's water dish. The boy stood next to the doghouse with his shoulders slumped and a dejected look of confusion on his face.[13]

As he noted, Schulz was not the only artist struggling with how to handle race in his work. In fact, he was not the first artist Glickman had contacted. She had also written to *Mary Worth* cartoonist Allen Saunders, who replied that while he believed in promoting integration in the comic strips, he feared that the syndicate would drop him. In later interviews, Saunders would express his sense that newspaper comic strips were "the most conservative of the popular media" and that any comic strip artist was drastically censored by "the Puritanical nature of the readers and of the editors, who insist that a strip not lose too many readers." Schulz found a similarly critical audience and editorship. "The artist is also forced to serve many masters," he wrote a few years later. "He must please the syndicate editor, as well as the countless editors who purchase his comic strip." Even the fearless social critic Al Capp shied away from the topic. In his popular *Li'l Abner* strip, Capp lampooned everyone from Richard Nixon and Joseph McCarthy to radical student protesters and even Schulz himself. "I'm willing to take on any group," he bragged to *Newsweek*, "I've taken on all the liberals already." But when it came to the issue of race, he was reluctant. "Right now," he supposed, "I don't think the Negro can be caricatured." In his mind, African Americans could only become a part of mainstream humor "when he is so much a part of the U.S. he can be laughed at." Thus, when Schulz worried over how to handle race, he was far from alone among his colleagues.[14]

Popular opinion was just as conflicted over the issue of integration. The month that Glickman wrote to Schulz one poll found that 40 percent of Americans felt more favorable toward racial integration than they had been in the past. Yet the same poll found that 34 percent felt less favorable toward integration. Another poll that month found that 39 percent believed the Johnson administration was pushing integration too quickly, while only a quarter felt comfortable with the pace. In May, the number of those who felt rushed into integration rose to 45 percent. By September 1968, more than half (54 percent) of all respondents to a Gallup poll expressed discomfort with the pace of racial integration. In short, the American public was unsure over the trajectory of the civil rights movement following King's assassination and a majority were reluctant to rush ahead into this unknown. Despite Glickman's heartfelt plea, this was hardly an optimal time to integrate *Peanuts*.[15]

Schulz's letter declining Glickman's request presented "an interesting dilemma," she replied at the end of April. But she would not give up so easily. She devised a plan to convince the cartoonist that a black *Peanuts* character was not only desirable, but culturally necessary to change the racial thinking of the next generation. "I would like your permission," she requested, "to use your letter to show to Negro friends." Glickman was confident that "their response as parents may prove useful to you in your thinking on the subject." Schulz responded that he would be "very anxious what your friends think of my reasons for not including a Negro character in the strip." He was not, however, backing off of his earlier position, he made clear. "The more I think of the problem," he confided, "the more I am convinced that it would be wrong for me to do so." "I would be very happy to try," he assured her, but he was not confident in his ability to create and write a black character. "I am sure," he worried, "that I would receive the sort of criticism that would make it appear as if I were doing this in a condescending manner." Well aware of the nation's long history of appropriating black identities and bodies for the sake of reinforcing the color line and subjugating African Americans, Schulz was reluctant to draw a black child for fear that he might inadvertently do more harm than good. If he was going to include a black character in *Peanuts*, he wanted him to be authentic, not contrived.[16]

Before Glickman had the chance to collect all of her African American friends' letters for Schulz, Robert F. Kennedy traveled to California in the hopes of riding a primary victory there to a presidential nomination from the Democratic Party. By night's end, Kennedy had won California but fell victim to an assassin's bullet at Los Angeles's Ambassador Hotel. Just nine weeks after losing King, the civil rights movement lost another prominent advocate.

On June 11, five days after Kennedy died in a Los Angeles hospital, Glickman wrote to Schulz once again. She had decided to forward the two letters she had already received rather than waiting for the rest to come in. Clearly, the action for which she lobbied could not wait any longer. "A number of my friends had indicated they were formulating letters," she told Schulz, "but last week's newest tragedy has nearly immobilized everyone I know." For Glickman, however, the experience had only bolstered her resolve to take on violence in American culture. "I have drafted some letters to the networks," she informed the cartoonist, "dealing with [the violence] of television which reaches the very young." As a concerned mother, she decided to attack the places her children were most likely to see television violence: in the "ugliness of Saturday morning offerings." She would continue her crusade and Schulz, she was still convinced, could be her most powerful ally. She encouraged him to consider the two attached letters and assured him that he could expect more letters from black readers within the next two weeks.[17]

The first letter Glickman included was from a friend named Kenneth C. Kelly, an African American father of two boys. He tried to address Schulz's concerns that including a black character would patronize African American readers. "I doubt that any Negro would view your efforts that way," Kelly wrote, projecting his own opinion onto others. Nonetheless, "I'd like to suggest," he continued, "that an accusation of being patronizing would be a small price to pay for the positive results that would accrue." In Kelly's opinion, American media in the late 1960s largely misrepresented race relations as constant "racial enmity." Schulz had an obligation to introduce a black character, even if the character was only a "Negro supernumerary in some of the group scenes in *Peanuts*." Kelly argued that such a character would have two benefits. First, it would give fathers like him a popular and positive African American figure to share with their sons. Second, "it would suggest racial amity in a casual day-to-day sense." Kelly purposefully suggested a "supernumerary character," endorsing *Peanuts*' gradual integration. "The inclusion of a Negro in your occasional group scenes," he explained, "would quietly and unobtrusively set the stage for a principal character at a later date." Kelly concluded, "We have too long used Negro supernumeraries in such unhappy situations as a movie prison scene while excluding [them] in quiet and normal scenes of people just living, loving, worrying, entering a hotel, the lobby of an office building, a downtown New York City street scene." This practice had "insidious negative effects" on American society and took place in movies, television, magazines, and syndicated comic strips.[18]

Monica Gunning, another African American friend of Harriet Glickman, fully agreed. The mother of two endorsed Glickman's request to integrate *Peanuts* because she saw it as "an enhancement to Negro youth" in the United States. Race relations were at a crossroads, she believed, and it was very important that black children develop a clear "feeling of identity." Schulz could have a pivotal effect on that identity through introducing a positive black character. "The inclusion of a Negro character even occasionally in your comics," Gunning wrote, "would help these young people to feel it is a natural thing for Caucasian and Negro children to engage in dialogue." It was only logical in her mind that *Peanuts* be racially diverse. "The message in your comic applies to all people," she assured Schulz, "so why not include a member of a minority group in the strip?"[19]

After reading the two letters, Schulz had no need to see anything else. On the first day of July, Schulz wrote back to Glickman. "You will be pleased to know that I have taken the first step in doing something about presenting a Negro child in the comic strip," he announced in the short note. She could expect to see the results during the week of July 29. Schulz was certain that his plan would satisfy readers looking for major examples of racial integration in the nation's daily funny pages. "I have drawn an episode which I think will please you," he closed.[20]

Glickman was overjoyed when she read the cartoonist's letter. "To say that I am heartened and pleased by your letter would be a vast understatement," she replied a few days later. Their extended conversation reinforced her "faith in communication and the exchange of ideas." Schulz's decision inspired her to keep fighting for a popular culture that reflected her own personal values. She was amazed that he was "taking a chance with the publication and showing his courage." She also informed him that both the Kellys and the Gunnings were delighted as well and all of their children "feel just a little better about the world."[21]

"Charlie Brown has a new friend," announced *Newsweek* in an exclusive story on July 29, 1968, "and his name is Franklin." The magazine described the basic details of the new character's upcoming three-day feature. Nothing about this storyline seemed unusual for *Peanuts*, except, of course, on one count. "Franklin is like most of the other moppets that populate Charles Schulz's *Peanuts*," the article explained, "with one important difference. Franklin is black." What struck the *Newsweek* writer about this new character, however, was the manner in which Schulz handled race. The article noted that Schulz had "been trying to introduce Franklin with as little fanfare as possible" (though a same day preview article in the national press was hardly avoiding fanfare outside the world of the comic). And, in the estimate of the journalist, "he succeeds admirably: Charlie Brown acts completely color-blind."[22]

Color-blindness had become a popular approach to race relations by the late 1960s, especially for Republican leaders like Richard Nixon and Governor Ronald Reagan. White leaders were not the only ones using this language. If law enforcement officers were to dispense their duties properly, argued the chapter president of the Hartford, Connecticut NAACP, they must believe that "real justice is colorblind," that is to say, that justice could only be served when race was ignored, even if the conditions of American racial inequality had spawned the circumstances of inequality and crime. Color-blindness was central to the rightward turn in American politics after the 1960s. As historian Matthew D. Lassiter has demonstrated, the social stresses caused by school integration—especially the anxieties that busing stirred—"produced a populist revolt of the center across the metropolitan South, as white-collar families became the architects of a color-blind discourse that gained national traction as an unapologetic defense of the class privileges and consumer rights of the middle-class suburbs." This is what Dr. Robert M. Diggs—a public school parent from Charlotte, North Carolina, who was outraged over the Supreme Court's recent compulsory busing ruling in his county—was articulating when he wrote to President Nixon asking how it could be possible for a federal judge to punish wealthy communities for using their earned income to buy homes in nice, clean, and safe neighborhoods. Though Diggs lived in an exclusively white suburban subdivision, he was certain that his opposition to busing had "nothing to do with race or integration."[23]

Charlie Brown's color-blindness was entirely intentional. "Charlie, Lucy, and the rest are color-blind, which obviously is the way their creator would like big folks to be," *Newsweek* asserted. "I've been thinking about this for a long time," Schulz explained to the reporter, "but up until recently I had always come to the conclusion that I wasn't capable of doing this thing properly." This was because, as he had told Glickman earlier that year, "I had always thought that Negro people might feel I was doing it in a patronizing or condescending way." Perhaps the cartoonist's reluctance came from the backlash he had faced from conservative readers who regularly derided him for using Scripture quotations in "something as lowly as a comic strip." While he was confident enough in his biblical learning to ignore such critics, he was clearly insecure about his ability to speak to the nation's racial issues. Ultimately, though, Schulz decided that the best approach to race was to ignore color and cultural difference and focus on the merits of the individual.[24]

It was true that Schulz had had very little personal experience with African Americans over the course of his life. He grew up in Minneapolis-St. Paul, where black people had comprised only 1 percent of the 879,000 people in the metropolitan area. After spending three years serving in the Army—a racially segregated force until 1948—Schulz returned home to the Twin Cities to find a metropolis that had grown in population but hardly looked more diverse than before, despite the fact that roughly a million African Americans emigrated from the South in the 1940s. Even when Schulz moved his young family to the more temperate climate of northern California, they did not settle in a particularly diverse town. While 7 percent of the 20 million people living in California by 1970 were black, the quiet town of Sebastopol in Sonoma County was home to only about one hundred African Americans out of nearly four thousand inhabitants. This is why the two letters from Harriet Glickman's friends had been so significant to the artist. "I received two letters from Negro fathers [it was actually one father and one mother] asking that *Peanuts* be integrated," he told *Newsweek*. "That was the turning point."[25]

Schulz did have one close black friend who had a tremendous influence on his decision to integrate the strip. He had known Morrie Turner, a black comic strip artist from Oakland, California, famous for his *Wee Pals* strip, for several years, and the two had discussed the possibility of introducing a black character into *Peanuts*. "Your timing was perfect," Turner praised Schulz, "and your handling and treatment of the character excellent." He was hopeful that a black character in the nation's leading comic strip would lead to more black characters in other strips. "The day Little Orphan Annie has a black boyfriend," he wrote, only half-kidding, "we'll really have it made." Always more vocal about his politics than Schulz, Turner was a significant force in the struggle for black equality in American popular culture.[26]

In the mid-1960s, Turner approached Schulz with an idea and asked for his senior colleague's advice. "What I wanted to do," Turner remembered, "was a black *Peanuts*, and sell it to black publications." Schulz found the idea intriguing and encouraged Turner to pursue it. The result was a comic strip titled *Dinky Fellas*, which appeared in the nation's most important black newspaper, the *Chicago Defender*, as well as the *Berkeley Post*. He quickly began to have second thoughts, however, about this all-black *Peanuts* he was drawing: "I was into a totally black scene which was what [white cartoonists] were doing in reverse," Turner recalled in 1972. After running just a few *Dinky Fellas* strips, he decided to develop a fully integrated strip for a national audience.[27]

When Turner signed a syndication contract in 1965 for *Wee Pals*—a strip that included black, Asian, Jewish, and handicapped children— he became the first black cartoonist to sell his work to a major syndicate. Turner would later contend that his nationally famous work was based on his childhood neighborhood. "*Wee Pals* was West Oakland when I grew up," he told an *Atlanta Constitution* reporter, "It was totally integrated. But everyone was poor." Turner argued that he could not "be angry at all white people" because he had grown up with so many as his friends, not to mention the numerous Asian children he had gone to school with in the poorer parts of the Bay Area.[28] Turner firmly believed in what he called "Rainbow Power." This was a decidedly integrationist principle that meant "all people, of every color, working together for a better world." The strip, however, was slow to find success. Not until Martin Luther King's assassination in 1968 did *Wee Pals* really take off nationally. Turner suspected that newspaper editors were simply using him to capitalize on the gravity of the moment. "The nation began to grieve," he remembered. "All the newspapers wanted to prove that we're 'OK, Jack.'" This troubled the cartoonist. "I wasn't pleased with the fact that Martin Luther King had died and because of that they were taking me, because of the grieving." Nonetheless, the rise in popularity gave him a national platform for his integrationist message.[29]

The new notoriety did not come without challenges. Some newspaper readers wrote to Turner to protest the integrated comic strip. The cartoonist most vividly recalled one reader from Detroit who repeatedly harassed him for several years by sending newspaper clippings of crimes committed in Detroit by black men. "This is for your information," the reader would comment, typically closing with "when you're through with it, send it to your friend, Martin Luther King." Instead of focusing on the potentially violent threat implied in the invocation of the murdered civil rights leader, Turner, ever an optimist, reassured himself that "he puts me on a level with Martin Luther King. That's nice, anyway." Schulz further encouraged him not to worry about reader criticisms, advising that when you write a comic strip, "You do it for yourself." Following that advice, Turner began to use the closing panel of his Sunday strips for a black history feature he called "Soul Corner." In all of his work, his goal was "to portray a world without prejudice, a world in which people's differences—race, religion, gender, and physical and mental ability—are cherished, not scorned."[30]

While Turner had sympathized with the voting rights movement going on in the Deep South in the mid-1960s, his need to provide for his young family prevented him from leaving Oakland to participate. Still, he believed he could make an important impact. "I decided that just by exposing readers to the sight of Negroes and whites playing together in harmony," he told reporters in 1970, "rather than pointing up aggravations, a useful, if subliminal purpose would be served, and ultimately would have as great effect for good as all the freedom marchers in Mississippi." In 1970, Turner was asked to be vice-chair under Fred Rogers for the White House Conference on Children. While he served his obligations on the committee, he refused to attend a White House dinner because "Nixon was in the White House." Well aware of some of Nixon's regressive policies toward integration and of the backlash Sammy Davis Jr. had received from black Americans because of his cordial relationship with the president, Turner wanted no part.[31]

Schulz's friendship was very important to Turner and throughout his career said that Schulz was "the guy I admired the most." Turner especially liked the way that he could slyly incorporate black humor into his white comic strip. Turner recalled one *Peanuts* strip where Lucy informed Schroeder that new research suggested that Beethoven, the boy's favorite composer, might have actually been black. The boy suddenly stopped playing his piano and replied in amazement, "You mean all this time I've been playing soul music?" The two men would have many laughs over jokes like these. Turner also remembered how Schulz always made him feel like a valued guest during his visits. On one occasion Schulz invited him to come to San Francisco for the opening performance of *You're a Good Man, Charlie Brown*, the critically acclaimed musical based on *Peanuts*. Before the performance began, the director brought up the house lights and recognized Schulz and his party of well-known cartoonists. The director, however, mistakenly left out Turner in his introductions. As the director went to leave the stage and begin the musical, Schulz called out to stop him and personally introduced Turner to the audience as an equally important figure in American comics. When the National Cartoonist Society held its annual awards banquet in San Francisco, Schulz invited Turner to sit with him as the guest of honor at the main banquet table. This close friendship had a tremendous influence on Schulz's feeling of obligation to integrate *Peanuts*.[32]

During the week of July 31, 1968, Charlie Brown and his family took their first ever beach vacation in the comic strip. The family had hardly arrived before Sally had taken her brother's beach ball and cast it to the tide. "Your beach ball just left for Hawaii," she announced to Charlie Brown, who had been happily building a sandcastle. As the boy stood staring hopelessly into the ocean, his ball apparently too far gone to be spotted, a new character walked up behind him. "Is this your beach ball?" the new boy asked. As the two boys stood side by side, there was no mistaking their immediate difference. They wore nothing but swim trunks, exposing the majority of their skin for the reader's view. There stood Charlie Brown as lily-white as he had ever been and opposite to him stood a smiling boy colored with a pen shading technique known as hatching. If readers had not already heard the news that *Peanuts* would be integrating, there was no doubt once they saw Charlie Brown's new friend.[33]

The scene might have surprised many African American readers. Just as a number of white school parents had tried to thwart integration efforts by founding private schools, numerous wealthy shorefront communities moved to consolidate control over their beaches through privatization or strict regulations for public beaches. In response, some local civil rights leaders challenged these new regulations, highlighting the absurdity of some of the social and even literal lines drawn to segregate space. Both black and white demonstrators were forcibly removed by authorities in 1963 when they staged a sit-in at the public entrance to Long Island state park's Jones Beach to protest racial discrimination. Malibu residents protested a plan to rezone a stretch of formerly private shoreline for resorts and recreation in 1971 in

Figure 4.3 Franklin's first appearance in *Peanuts*. By depicting the two boys in bathing suits, Schulz made clear the stark contrast between their skin colors and its irrelevance to their friendship. Charles Schulz, *Peanuts*, July 31, 1968. © 1968 Peanuts Worldwide LLC.

part because it would "cater to transients." Beach discrimination crossed class, race, and ethnic divides as well. In Larchmont, New York in 1969, a group of 200 upper-middle-class protesters—"the most well-behaved, well-dressed demonstrators I have ever seen," commented one local police officer—picketed the Larchmont Yacht Club demanding beach access for Jewish people in the community. Many times the battle over the beaches was a fight over narrowly demarcated spaces in public ordinances. In one of the more visible instances, a group in Connecticut protested the Madison Beach Club in 1974. There, club members had constructed two long stone piers on each end of the beach that extended well out into the water in an effort to protect their private space. In this protest, African American participants paddled boats up to the private beach, making sure to stay below the high tide line in accordance with the law. The new black boy in *Peanuts*, by contrast, had managed to swim up out of the water and openly stand on the beach with Charlie Brown without any protest from surrounding adults.[34]

Furthermore, Schulz introduced Franklin at a time when concerns about civil rights dominated headlines. The new boy appeared the same month that the Poor People's Campaign—the group King had been working to help organize at the time of his death—marched 50,000 people on the National Mall for Solidarity Day, an event raising awareness of black unemployment, undereducation, and wage inequalities that contributed to the stubborn problem of urban poverty that plagued late 1960s America. Sprinter Tommie Smith appeared racing across the cover of *Newsweek*, labeled "the angry black athlete" who was threatening to boycott the Olympic games. Smith and his comrade John Carlos would be immortalized that fall for silently raising black-gloved hands over their heads at the Olympic medal ceremony in Mexico City. Two weeks before Franklin arrived in *Peanuts*, the Urban League's executive director Whitney Young Jr. had told the national convention of CORE that a majority of white Americans were racist and urged young black Americans to develop "the power that America respects." This was not a rejection of the organization's history of nonviolence, he asserted, but rather an embrace of "the interpretation of black power which emphasizes self-determination, pride, self-respect, participation and control of one's destiny and community affairs." Nonetheless, it was concerning for many middle-class white Americans to hear a conservative, pro-business African American organization adopt even the mildest version of black power rhetoric. Rioting plagued both national party conventions that month, Yippies crashing the Democratic convention in Chicago and black protesters setting fire to parts of Miami where the Republican party nominated Richard Nixon and Spiro Agnew.[35]

None of this controversy reached the beach in *Peanuts*. The black boy—still unnamed in the strip—held out Charlie Brown's beach ball in his hands. "I was swimming out there," he explained, "and it came floating by." The two boys went back up the beach and set out to improve Charlie Brown's crooked sandcastle. They talked about family—Franklin's father was away serving in the Vietnam War—and baseball and periodically walked down to the ocean's edge for a bucket of water. It would take two days before Charlie Brown would mention the new boy's name as he celebrated their sandcastle-making handiwork: "It looks great, Franklin!" After three days of playing and talking, it was time for Franklin to leave. "I hate to go," he sighed to his new friend. "This has been a good day." As Franklin hurried off to answer his mother's call, Charlie Brown shouted after him, "Ask your mother if you can come over sometime and spend the night!"[36]

Schulz may have taken a risky step in introducing Franklin at such a contested location as a beach and at such a contested time as the summer of 1968, but he was still quite measured in his execution. Though Franklin had appeared over three straight days, he and Sally Brown did not appear in a single panel together. Perhaps the cartoonist felt this would push the issue too far for many readers who might support public integration, but still drew a line at interracial coupling. In a Harris poll from this period, 81 percent of people believed that most of their peers disapproved of interracial couples. Schulz avoided even the suggestion of contact between Franklin and Sally. While Sally had been the focal point of the first two strips of the week, she would not appear again until two panels after Franklin had left. The reader could reasonably assume, nonetheless, that both Sally and Mrs. Brown had been elsewhere on the beach the entire time.[37]

In writing about Franklin's first appearance, Schulz would later downplay its significance. "When Franklin first appeared in the '60s," he wrote, "his noticeably darker skin set some readers in search of a political meaning." Like so many other political and philosophical meanings readers found in *Peanuts*, these readers' search was in vain, he assured fans in the late 1990s. "The remarkable becomes unremarkable," he asserted, "when readers learn that I simply introduced Franklin as another character, not a political statement." But the political and social context of Franklin's arrival made it impossible to interpret it as apolitical or meaningless, as evidenced by the numerous letters Schulz received in the days after introducing his new character.[38]

"The reaction thus far is excellent," wrote Schulz's good friend and business manager at United Feature Syndicate Jim Hennessy in October 1968. Judging by the response, he was "sure there will be no appreciable future opposition." He could not imagine that anyone could find fault with such an inoffensive character as Franklin. He did warn his artist friend, however, that there could be a "few cranks" who might complain. The reality was, however, that there would be some who would legitimately question the efficacy and execution of Schulz's creation. Never entirely comfortable with the situation, the artist would struggle to answer such criticisms.[39]

As Hennessy had asserted, though, much of the early response from readers was tremendously positive. Glickman was certainly pleased. "You've hit on the perfect way to introduce [Franklin]," she praised him, "and have done it beautifully." She was so impressed with Franklin that she wrote to Los Angeles City Councilman Tom Bradley—later the first African American mayor of Los Angeles—to suggest that Franklin become the mascot for the city's Green Power Foundation, Los Angeles's black elite reaction to the emerging Black Power movement. "I thought it a good idea," she suggested, "if someone [from Green Power] contacted Mr. Schulz about the possibility of producing dolls, pillows, pennants, stationery, using the new little Negro character, Franklin." It is significant that she drew the connection between Franklin and a moderate civil rights organization since the character would never catch on with more progressive groups. What was clear, nonetheless, was that Glickman was ecstatic about the change she had effected through her persistence.[40]

Likewise, readers from across the country wrote in to voice their support. Ina Smith was so pleased to see that the creator of *Peanuts* "is brave enough to recognize that children come in colors." Adrienne KinKaid, a second-grade teacher from Minneapolis, "vigorously applauded" Franklin's arrival and already thought of him as "a friend." She hoped that "eventually we may even see him on television or with a book of his own." He had to succeed, she insisted, "for all the other Franklins." Bob Selly, a college student, felt that Schulz and his new character demonstrated "the conviction and forward-thinking which seems to be so lacking in our troubled time." Patricia G. Cammarata of Detroit was "sure that Franklin will gain acceptance among the various strata of our society." As delighted as she was, though, about the new black boy in *Peanuts*, that joy was shaded by the broader context of American race relations. "It is truly a shame," she lamented, "that a black man cannot be welcomed into our homes, offices, and places of entertainment as easily as he is in your most fascinating strip."

Another reader wished that "more beautiful people had your power not only to bring much needed humor to an overstressed world but influence the daily lives and thoughts of millions of readers." He saw the day's strip as a metaphor for the civil rights battles taking place across the nation in 1968. He believed that if everyone could "introduce a new character" in their lives—apparently meaning that everyone should make friends outside of their own race—then the "fight against fear, intolerance, bigotry, and hatred would soon be over." And while Franklin was carrying the ball back to Charlie Brown, "countless others have also been 'carrying the ball' too long, without help, in our 200-plus year struggle for racial equality."[41]

Detroit attorney Jordan Rossen was so impressed with the introduction of Franklin that he forwarded a copy of a recent letter he had mailed to "comic strip writers and syndicates." He made clear in a handwritten note that the "letter was prepared before *Peanuts* integrated" and that he had "great respect for the effect which these strips have on our society—especially the young." Much like Glickman's correspondence, the letter aired Rossen's concerns about the "almost total absence of Negro characters in comic strips." He did not count African characters, who regularly appeared in adventure strips like *The Phantom*, because they did not represent the black experience in America. This "omission," Rossen felt, was "an unfortunate distortion of American life." Even more, he believed the lack of equal representation was a "lost opportunity" for educating future generations. "White children should see Negroes as comic strip children (e.g. *Peanuts*, *Nancy*); as sports stars (*Gil Thorpe*); as lawyers (*Judge Parker*); as actors (*On Stage*); as policemen (*Dick Tracy*)," he wrote, apparently assuming that white children would be the only ones to read these strips to begin with. Rossen understood that it might be difficult for white artists to "think black." But, he argued, that "if we first think as human beings and then, only incidentally, of a character's race or religion, this possible obstacle can be overcome." Here Rosen shared Schulz's faith in a color-blind ethos. While he was pleased that Schulz had integrated *Peanuts*, there was still much work to be done in the funny pages.[42]

The new character even reached American servicemen at war. A young, black Army sergeant serving in Vietnam named Franklin R. Freeman wrote to share how deeply the new addition to *Peanuts* had impacted him. Schulz's work had "been very instrumental in keeping us in a good mood and high spirits while being away from home." In fact, Freeman said that reading *Peanuts* was one of the highlights of his day. So when he read the strip on October 29—nearly two months delayed from its original publication in the

States—he felt his daily "reward was doubled because I found a new character in the strip who shares my name." Even more, that character shared his race. "You'll never know," he reported, "how much commotion was stirred among my friends when they read the . . . cartoon." To a young man fighting overseas, Franklin was a welcome delight.[43]

Professional cartoonists also wrote to Schulz to show their support. Ric Hugo, a Berkeley native and political cartoonist, sent a simple note that displayed a drawing of Franklin in perfect Schulzian style. The boy stood there bare-chested and in his swim trunks, just as he had at his first meeting with Charlie Brown. Above the boy's head, a speech bubble captured Hugo's comment: "Crosshatch is Beautiful!" His quip not only referenced the style of shading Schulz used but also the slogan African Americans used to celebrate their cultural heritage and reclaim blackness from its appropriated past.[44]

Not all the correspondence Schulz received, however, was positive. Some criticisms were purely aesthetic. "Do you think that [Franklin] could be drawn with a felt pen for the coloring?" one reader asked, because "all those lines across his face . . . did not look good." Apparently, crosshatch was not beautiful to everyone. Other criticisms were more substantive. Some thoughtful readers wondered if Schulz wasn't missing an opportunity to do more for the civil rights movement. "I'm not sure that *Peanuts* is reaching people as it used to, because the message hasn't changed with the times," Rev. Cecil Williams, a black minister at San Francisco's Glide Memorial Church, told *Newsweek*. Williams had been a long-time fan of *Peanuts*, but felt reservations. "Schulz has stayed away from civil rights and social issues that relate to Third World and especially black people."[45]

A number of criticisms stemmed from the fact that after Franklin's three-day appearance he had seemed to vanish. Charlie Brown had invited him to spend the night, but week after week Franklin never showed. Mary Emily Peck sent Schulz a letter via the *New York Post* to inquire about Franklin's absence. That "appealing small boy named Franklin" had been present for a historic week in the funny pages, but then had "not been seen since." Recalling that Charlie Brown had invited Franklin to come over and play at his house, Peck wondered if Mr. Brown had objected when his son told him about the new friend. "Just when I thought you were really getting with the world as it is," she wrote, "you disappointed me by delaying Franklin." Peck struggled to figure out what had changed. "Does *Peanuts* appear in the South?" she wondered in a parenthetical aside, suggesting that perhaps Schulz had caved to some white supremacist backlash. Regardless of the reason for the absence, she was not happy and demanded that Schulz "bring him back."[46]

Similarly, H. H. Houston, principal of East End Elementary School in North Plainfield, New Jersey, was deeply disappointed with Franklin's brief run in the strip. "What has happened to Franklin?" he demanded. Houston had been a big fan of the 1965 bestselling book *The Gospel According to Peanuts* by Robert L. Short and felt that the author "spoke very well of [Schulz]." "I am afraid," he wrote, "that 'our house is not founded upon a rock.'" In other words, the cartoonist was not the man he had appeared to be and seemed to be reneging on his initially integrationist stance. Schulz needed to "make a greater effort to ensure that it is so founded," Houston commanded. In a rather gruff closing, the principal admitted that it was not solely Schulz's responsibility to change the country's race relations, but "your hands can draw black people." This letter reveals that while demands on artists to integrate their comic strips were high, these pressures and criticisms hardly ended once black characters were introduced.[47]

Some readers worried that Franklin's absence meant he had been dropped from the strip. Spurgeon Cameron described himself as a graduate student, an NAACP member, and a local Democratic Party executive. While proud of his ethnic identity, Cameron was discontent with his place in the nation, saying that, "I am a Black man, a Negro, or essentially a non-white tremendously proud of my existence in the United States even though I feel it is a lousy country" or, as he termed it, "the best of the rest." He felt that "the introduction of Franklin is great" and "long overdue." But he also understood that there could be practical consequences to Schulz for pursuing this new path. "I readily recognize," he wrote, "the dictates of economics that will govern your continued use of this Black child in the strip." Cameron went on to lobby for Franklin's return in the strip by contending that "Charlie Brown would very easily play with a child of color in any section of this country." This was because, he argued, "children are color blind, whether we adults like it or not." Cameron challenged Schulz to take some time off from his work to visit a public school and witness children of various races at play together. Such scenes were "America and the United Nations in reality," he asserted. He petitioned Schulz to "keep Franklin" and "make him a sharp kid projecting a success image all the way." In a parenthetical statement, he provided the artist with some possible positions to give Franklin: manager of his own baseball team, baseball commissioner, president, vice president, "the works." Most of all, he asked that *Peanuts* "tell it like it is"—that is, use Franklin to show the great abilities and potential of African American children.[48]

It would take ten and a half weeks for Franklin to appear again. Whereas he had first come along to help Charlie Brown, this time he showed up in

Charlie Brown's neighborhood to take advantage of the invitation to visit. As he searched for his new friend's house, Franklin met Lucy at her psychiatry booth, Snoopy pretending to fly his dog house as the flying ace, Linus preaching the gospel of the Great Pumpkin, and Schroeder announcing the approaching birthday celebration for Beethoven. At this point, Franklin had seen enough. As Charlie Brown rushed to stop him, Franklin called back in a rush, "I'm going home, Charlie Brown . . . this neighborhood has me shook." This was an intriguing twist on common narratives of white flight and avoiding the "wrong side of the tracks." Franklin was fleeing the oddities of these young white suburbanites, questioning the presumption of white communities. Still, this was hardly an integrationist message. Franklin was clearly an outsider to the world of *Peanuts* as readers knew it. Thus far, the children had only met one another during special trips. But this soon would change.[49]

Schulz's first true step toward integrating the children's lives came on October 20, 1968. That Sunday the *Peanuts* children stood in a long line at the local movie box office. Quietly standing within the queue of white children was Franklin, ready to purchase a ticket and enter another public space that had long been hotly contested in the civil rights era: the movie theater. Franklin made no production of his attendance. He casually followed Charlie Brown, handing his cash up to the box office window and requesting, "One, please." This was no thundering declaration of rights. This was a peaceful, restrained assertion of equality by virtue of Franklin simply being another kid. It contrasted starkly with the countless pictures of urban riots that had erupted once again that year. This was exactly the step Harriet Glickman's friend Kenneth Kelly had hoped for when he wrote to Schulz that "the inclusion of a Negro in your occasional group scenes would quietly and unobtrusively set the stage for a principal character at a later date." But whether Kelly would ever get the "principal character" he hoped for was yet to be seen.[50]

In 1969, Franklin would make three fewer appearances than the previous year. While this did not look promising for the establishment of an integral black character, Schulz made a few more important steps in Franklin's development that year. He played in baseball games against Charlie Brown and became a regular member of Peppermint Patty's football team. Once again, Franklin went to the movies, this time walking together with another young white boy. But the most important development for Franklin in 1969 came in November. On Wednesday, November 12, Peppermint Patty sat in class struggling to come up with the correct answers for a test for which she

Figure 4.4 Franklin integrated the classroom without any of the heated confrontations that accompanied many integration attempts across the nation after *Brown v. Board of Education*. Charles Schulz, *Peanuts*, November 12, 1969. © 1969 Peanuts Worldwide LLC.

was—as always—unprepared. Desperate for help, she leaned to the student in front of her and whispered, "Psst . . . Hey, Franklin, is the third question 'true' or 'false'?"[51]

With that simple scene, Schulz introduced Franklin as an integrated member of Peppermint Patty's class. As always when addressing controversial issues, Schulz had given no warning and wrote the scene as though it were any other day. It was completely natural, business as usual. This did not go over well with all readers. "In today's *Peanuts* comic strip Negro and white children are portrayed together in school," wrote one newspaper editor from the *Meridian Star* in Mississippi. "School integration is a sensitive subject here," he continued, "particularly at this time when our city and county schools are under court order for massive compulsory race mixing." The editor's plea to Schulz was simple and surprisingly more restrained than the typical diatribe against integration: "We would appreciate it if future *Peanuts* strips did not have this type of content." The Supreme Court had ordered in late September that all remaining segregated school districts—thirty-three in total—should desegregate "at once." In a quick appeal, the Nixon administration's attorney general had requested that the districts be given the opportunity to develop their own individual plans for implementing the ruling and asked that timing be decided in the lower courts. The next day, the US 5th Circuit Court of Appeals gave the school districts until December 31 to comply. This was one of the early signs of Nixon's "Southern strategy"—which would ultimately fail in the 1970 midterm elections—and a continuation of the Southern obstructionist tactics utilized to stall progress since *Brown v. Board* first struck down public school segregation in 1954. The immediacy of this active integration order was what the editor meant when he wrote that the comic touched a "sensitive subject." Though the letter was most directly a rejection of integrationist policies, it was also determinedly critical of the use of federal power in local school systems, most evident in his characterization that the "schools are under court order for massive compulsory race mixing." Like the Little

Rock Nine or James Meredith before him, Franklin did not really have to say a word. His very presence was enough to set off a backlash from some.[52]

Such responses from local editors worried Schulz's bosses at United Feature Syndicate. Newspaper editors were ultimately the ones making the call on whether *Peanuts* would continue to appear in individual papers. The cartoonist later recalled in an interview that his New York editor Larry Rutman telephoned to say that Schulz should take into account the complaints of such Southern editors and change the strip to keep Franklin out of the classroom. Schulz, according to his retelling, was at his most blunt in dealing with this challenge to his writing. "Well, Larry, let's put it this way," he began, "Either you print it just the way I draw it or I quit. How's that?" This was the second time in his career that he had given his editor an ultimatum. The first time it had cost him his first feature in the *St. Paul Pioneer*. This time the editor caved to the celebrated artist.[53]

After just thirteen appearances and two years in *Peanuts*, some trends began to develop with Franklin. Over the course of 1970 and 1971, he became increasingly confined to the classroom. With Franklin stuck in the classroom or as a teammate on the baseball team, he repeatedly appeared in these two highly symbolic locales of racial integration. Schulz presented him as a remarkably well-rounded and intelligent child. He studied music, joined the school swim team, and was an active member of the 4-H club. He read psychology books in his spare time. He regularly scored As and Bs on his tests and was always kind and positive with his classmates. Peppermint Patty often turned to him for advice and information. Black comic characters had been plagued by negative stereotypes in the past. Schulz was actively creating a positive one. In the process, he often left Franklin with a dry personality and none of the endearing quirks of the other characters. Just as older stereotypes had done with negative black images, this new stereotype never diverged from white readers' expectations of the "ideal" black child.

By 1973, Franklin was coming to serve a more visual role, occasionally seen but less frequently heard. This trend culminated in a jarring strip in late 1974. On November 6, Peppermint Patty was preparing to rehearse her routine for an upcoming figure skating competition. As she skated across the frozen pond, she suddenly came across Franklin intensely practicing his hockey skills. Peppermint Patty demanded to know what he was doing crowding the ice. "I'm practicing to become a great hockey player," he replied. Her anger receding, she went back to skating and calmly asked, "How many black players in the NHL, Franklin?" The effect on Franklin was clearly devastating, signaled by his reserved stance, blank stare, and the fact that Schulz left most of the boy's face colorless as though he were flushed. Over the previous

Figure 4.5 This was one of the most blatant social criticisms Schulz ever drew. It was also the only time *Peanuts* explicitly acknowledged that Franklin was black. Charles Schulz, *Peanuts*, November 6, 1974. © 1974 Peanuts Worldwide LLC.

twenty-five years of *Peanuts*, Schulz had never ended a strip with a more blunt social criticism.[54]

The chilling commentary to end Schulz's November 6, 1974 strip makes more sense when considered along with one important fact: Charles Schulz loved hockey. He was a fan of many sports—he followed baseball, regularly played golf and tennis, and was part of a championship-winning bowling team in the late 1950s—but he held a special fondness for hockey. His childhood love for hockey would span his lifetime. "Playing hockey is one of the few things that takes my mind completely off everything else in my life," he told one reporter. In the spring of 1969, he opened a $2 million public ice arena of his own just a block from his studio in Santa Rosa. There Schulz refereed weekly juniors games, hosted international tournaments, and played a weekly pickup game of his own well into his seventies. Schulz was also a season ticket holder for the National Hockey League's Oakland Seals and regularly made the two hour round trip to watch them play, despite the fact that the team never had a winning record in its nine years in the Bay Area.[55]

So when Peppermint Patty brought up the question of black players in the NHL, this was clearly a question that had nagged at Schulz. The answer to her question, for any *Peanuts* readers who took the time to look it up, was shocking. Canadian Willie O'Ree had officially integrated the NHL with a two-game stint for the Boston Bruins in 1958. In November 1974, when Peppermint Patty brazenly asked her question, there was exactly one black player in the NHL: a rookie from Canada named Mike Marson who had signed with the Washington Capitals in July (it would not be until 1981 that a black American, Val James, would play in the NHL, joining the Buffalo Sabres). The nation's other major professional sports leagues had long been thoroughly integrated.[56]

It was not just Schulz's affinity for hockey that made this particular strip so personal for him. The artist included a minor touch that most readers likely never noticed but spoke volumes about his intent in the strip. On the back of

Franklin's Oakland Seals jersey, he wore the number nine, the same number Schulz wore every time he took the ice. The cartoonist, through Franklin's dejected expression, seemed to be truly appalled that the sport he loved could so totally crush the dream of an African American boy practicing to play in a league that showed no serious signs of wanting someone like him. Furthermore, Schulz's direct insertion of himself in the form of the jersey number demonstrated that he felt some sense of personal complicity as a fan of such a racially exclusive sport. This sad strip offered no solutions, no hope, and no humor. It was a social tragedy on the funny pages.

Some newspapers found the "punchline" too jarring for a daily comic strip. For example, the London *Daily Mail* opted to alter the final panel of the strip. Rather than Peppermint Patty's blunt question, "How many black players in the NFL, Franklin?", these newspapers changed the line to read, "How many great players on your team, Franklin?" Readers would likely have never noticed the change, which removed the entire racial critique of the piece and made the joke instead a slight of Franklin's athletic skill. The change, wrote one editorial page, "left the strip with no point at all." But it certainly avoided the more abrasive point of Schulz's original work.[57]

Years later, Schulz would get particularly defensive over this strip. When one young reader wrote to question the author's meaning, Schulz replied with an uncharacteristically harsh letter. The reader felt the strip made Peppermint Patty come across as racist and wondered if the artist could defend his intent. "I can't believe that you are so ready to leap in with your criticism," the cartoonist penned in frustration. He explained that when the strip had originally appeared "there was only one black in the National Hockey League," revealing that he had indeed intended to point out the lack of diversity in the league. "Does pointing out this fact make the strip racist?" Schulz demanded. Schulz was more touchy about the issue of race than he was about any other issue he addressed. Though he did have some critical words in interviews for those who challenged his usage of biblical passages in his comic strip, this was a rare case where Schulz lashed out at a reader's criticism in such a direct manner. The reason the reader perceived a hint of racism likely had to do with the fact that this was the only time Schulz ever acknowledged Franklin's race in the strip. Until this strip, it had been left up to the reader to decide that the shaded lines on Franklin's skin connected him to a certain race in the real world. *Peanuts*, thus, had been color-blind in a way until November 1974. With Peppermint Patty's question, if there had been any doubt, there was now no denying that race was a dividing line even in the fantasy world of Charlie Brown.[58]

Where Franklin had entered the 1970s as one of the most promising characters in *Peanuts*, by mid-decade he was quickly vanishing from view. He did not appear in a single strip in 1975. In 1976, he made a brief appearance as a clumsy centerfielder on Peppermint Patty's baseball team. In 1977, he appeared in one panel of one strip as a means of setting up a punchline for Peppermint Patty. And in 1978, the tenth anniversary of Franklin's historic beach holiday with Charlie Brown, he was once again nowhere to be found. Schulz would try to explain away this abandonment when he wrote in a later *Peanuts* anthology that though some readers had looked for greater meaning in Franklin, "the remarkable becomes unremarkable when readers learn that I simply introduced Franklin as another character, not a political statement." But there was no denying the impact Franklin had made in the summer of 1968 and the hope he had inspired among some readers.[59]

What had initially been celebrated as a great step forward for racial progress in American culture seemed to have been just the sign of one particular historical moment that had come and gone. Franklin would remain a secondary character for the remainder of *Peanuts*' fifty-year run. He would never become the principal character Kenneth Kelly had once pleaded for in the wake of King's assassination. Instead, Franklin would become for many a symbol of tokenism and more unfulfilled promises.

Franklin may have made a big splash in American popular culture in the summer of 1968, but it was clear from the outset that Schulz was either reluctant or unsure of how to incorporate him as a major character in *Peanuts*. Schulz would acknowledge as much in a late 1980s interview. "I've never done much with Franklin," he explained to *Nation's Business* senior editor Michael Barrier, "because I don't do race things. I'm not an expert on race, I don't know what it's like to grow up as a little black boy, and I don't think you should draw things unless you really understand them." There was no doubting that the cartoonist's intentions were genuine. "I believe our greatest strength lies in the protection of our smallest minorities," he wrote to a school child. But the execution of these principles was a far more difficult task. Schulz slowly backed away from Franklin for the same reasons that he had so long avoided writing a character like him: he was afraid he could not relate to the African American experience.[60]

Franklin was an important part of the racial integration of American popular culture in the 1960s. But roughly like the civil rights legislation of the decade, he also became an unwitting stumbling block for white middle-class readers who saw his arrival as sufficient progress while African Americans pleaded for more. In hindsight, it is easy to see that Schulz put his new character in an untenable position. No single personality could carry the burden of representing a people. This is why Glickman had advised Schulz in her first letter that if he were to integrate *Peanuts* there should "be more than one black child." They needed to "be as adorable as the others," she insisted, but most of all, they needed to be as diverse as the people they represented. Schulz did not listen, and Franklin stood alone.[61]

5

Snoopy Is the Hero in Vietnam

Ambivalence, Empathy, and *Peanuts*' Vietnam War

By the time *Los Angeles Times* columnist Christy Fox made her way through the humid jungles of South Vietnam in the summer of 1968, American military personnel had been there for well over a decade. Her visit came during the deadliest year of fighting yet. For her part, Fox sought to avoid the controversy over the war itself, following instead an Australian magic act touring military bases to entertain American troops in their off-time. Fox could not help but chuckle when she arrived at a base near Phan Rang that boasted a makeshift, open-air stage made of bamboo that soldiers referred to—with no shortage of sarcasm—as "Happy Valley Theater." The thing that most grabbed her attention, however, was not the primitive structure or the hip, young magician and his beautiful female assistant. As she took in the scene, her eyes were irresistibly drawn to a large banner draped across the stage that read, "Snoopy is the Hero in Vietnam."[1]

This might seem like an odd connection, drawing together one of the United States' most popular cartoon characters and a long, taxing military conflict that had recently reached a new low in public opinion with the Tet Offensive of January 1968. But Fox would not have had to look very far to find a myriad of other references connecting Charles Schulz's vivacious black and white dog to the Vietnam War. Snoopy appeared on soldiers' helmets, cigarette lighters, platoon patches, and even in sketches on their canvas bunk beds. As American ground forces bogged down in Vietnam between 1965 and 1973, Snoopy, most often in his imaginary role as the World War I flying ace, also besieged American popular culture. Snoopy's war with the Red Baron spawned a hit radio single in 1966, a featured float in the Macy's Thanksgiving Parade in 1968, a prominent scene in the Emmy-nominated *It's the Great Pumpkin, Charlie Brown*, and millions of dollars' worth of licensed merchandise. *Life* magazine clearly drew the *Peanuts* connection between the home front and war front in 1967 when it pointed out the way that "at scores of colleges, *Peanuts* characters are the biggest people on campus" and "in Vietnam, pilots fly into combat with Snoopy painted on their planes." As Fox remarked, "Snoopy goes everywhere." During this period, the nation's most popular cartoon dog became intimately tied to the conflict in Southeast Asia, both in Schulz's comic strip and in the popular imagination. The question then is: What made this portrayal of Snoopy so enormously popular and significant in Vietnam era popular culture?[2]

Peanuts and Snoopy as the flying ace captured Americans' complicated, visceral feelings about the war. *Peanuts* addressed not the strategy or politics of the war, but the emotional and psychological weight of the war on American society. Schulz's support for American soldiers, hatred of the draft, and uneasy acceptance of the war connected with a conflicted public. Confusing contradictions in national polling data in the late 1960s fueled a fevered search for the "uncertain" Middle Americans, those "silent" and "forgotten people" in political discourse, the "troubled Americans" who came to

Figure 5.1 Snoopy as the World War I flying ace was the subject for millions of dollars worth of licensed *Peanuts* merchandise, like this coin bank from Determined Productions. Courtesy of the Charles M. Schulz Museum and Research Center.

feel serious doubts about the war, but utter contempt for antiwar protesters. Commentators were unsuccessful in clearly defining this group that *Time* magazine suggested might encompass as much as 55 percent of the American population. President Richard Nixon did not wait for clarity. Through numerous speeches, he appropriated this conflicted "middle" as part of his "Silent Majority," stolidly in support of the war. In so doing, he papered over the ambivalence many of these Americans felt toward the war. Schulz, on the other hand, embraced this uncertainty and it endeared him to his audience.[3]

Such ambivalence and open questioning of the war, as evidenced in Schulz's nationally syndicated strip, had a much wider circulation in American popular culture than has previously been appreciated. Comic arts in this period typically did little to challenge the politics of the Vietnam War. Often they avoided mention of the war at all costs for fear of alienating consumers. In this way, they followed other major media productions. With the notable exception of John Wayne's popular film *The Green Berets* (1968), explicit on-screen portrayals of the conflict did not appear until after the United States had withdrawn from South Vietnam. When comic arts did address the war they tended to reinforce United States policy, working "to preserve what remained of the vital center" by war's end. Comic book heroes from Batman to Spider-Man to Iron Man, addressing a largely teenage male audience, walked a fine line of sympathizing with some of student war protesters' complaints while rejecting radical techniques for resisting authority. They also maintained the righteousness of American Cold War purposes in Vietnam despite the increasing ugliness of the war. Similarly, newspaper comic strips found it largely unprofitable to deal with Vietnam during the conflict. *Dan Flagg* (1963) and *Tales of the Green Beret* (1965) were two well-written comic strips that were quickly canceled as syndicates found the American public not in the mood for war-themed adventures in the midst of escalation in Vietnam. In the wake of the Kennedy brothers' and Martin Luther King Jr.'s assassinations, comic strips came under harsh public scrutiny over their portrayals of violence, prompting the Newspaper Comics Council to host a major symposium on "Violence in the Comics" in late 1968. This public outcry further stifled the medium's ability to deal directly with a grisly war. For Vietnam era comic arts, addressing the war was a risky business.[4]

Peanuts took the troubling events of the Cold War world very seriously, and Schulz clearly wrestled with his feelings about the Vietnam War. *Peanuts*' commentary on the war unfolded in two stages. Though Snoopy's battles with the Red Baron were always far from cheery encounters for the poor pup, *Peanuts* in the pre-1968 period, like the "establishment media," did little to challenge the United States' presence in Vietnam. That is, American media's general allegiance to the dominant anticommunist narrative that a democratic South Vietnam was vital to containing communist expansion prevented it from questioning the US military presence in Vietnam, even if it might question the administration's strategy. As the war lost public support in the post–1968 period, however, Snoopy—and the media—increasingly empathized with the plight of soldiers while questioning the purpose of the war. This narrative of declining popular support would become one of the defining elements in histories and depictions of the Vietnam War in the years after the fall of Saigon in 1975. As historian Andrew Huebner has pointed out, such attitudes followed a cultural revision of the American soldier's image that had begun in earlier print media coverage of the Korean War, transforming "the heroic, selfless soldier of World War II mythology into a different sort of cultural hero, one inviting sympathy, even pity, along with respect." Schulz endorsed this revised "warrior image" through his depictions of Snoopy as the flying ace.[5]

Schulz biographer David Michaelis has argued that Snoopy's war with the Red Baron "led the culture" by providing "an explanatory as well as a descriptive character for thousands who burned draft cards and protested an unjustifiable war." For Michaelis, Schulz's comic strips and his public statements during the war "clearly set him on the same side" as other prominent Americans who explicitly denounced the war. Yet Schulz's views on Vietnam—and those of many Americans—challenged the rigid prowar/antiwar framework often imposed by politicians and traditional opinion polls. A more comprehensive view of Schulz's attitudes toward the war must take into account the reality that he, like so many Americans of his time, reacted to the conflict in a much more visceral way. Rather than a cold political experience, feelings about Vietnam could often be quite personal, especially for those who had served in the military or had family members serve, a process historian Michael Stewart Foley has called the "politics of empathy." Schulz related to soldiers through his own experience of being drafted and fighting in World War II. Schulz evaluated the war on the basis of what was best for US troops and not always what was best for the country's international image or for millions of suffering Vietnamese people. Whether Schulz's characters condemned the war or dreaded the draft, they did so because of Schulz's empathy for the soldiers' plight.[6]

In the late 1960s, Charles Schulz used his skills in metaphor and purposeful ambiguity to broach the most controversial issue of the day. His strips addressing the war, the draft, and even war protests had little to no blowback. For *Peanuts* readers in the late 1960s and early 1970s, the Vietnam War was their context for understanding the militaristic images of Snoopy's war. A deeper look at *Peanuts* during the Vietnam War reveals more clearly the potential for doubt about the Vietnam War in the mainstream culture of the 1960s. It also suggests that the culture of ambivalence, reflected in the nation's most widely read comic strip of the day, played a role in limiting the US government's ability to execute the war. Finally, it sheds light on how average Americans, both at home and at war, internalized and coped with the experience of the war. *Peanuts* readers—100 million strong by the end of the war—connected with these storylines because they communicated their own feelings about the world around them more clearly than almost anything else in their lives. Snoopy's war was many Americans' Vietnam War.[7]

Though *Peanuts* had been nationally syndicated for fifteen years by the time the United States entered official combat in Vietnam, it had only addressed warfare one time before. This single reference to the nation's past conflicts—and the strip's only reference to the Korean War, which had erupted barely four months before *Peanuts* debuted—revealed much about Schulz's opinion on warfare. On May 3, 1954, Charlie Brown's friend stood amazed at the boy's extensive war comic collection, each issue named after a different American conflict. As the friend drooled over the comic books, Charlie Brown looked distressed. Finally, he voiced his concern: "The next issue has really got me worried." Two things were clear in this strip. First, the reader had to assume that on some level Charlie Brown, like Schulz himself, had an interest in warfare. Otherwise, he would not own the comics. Second, despite his interest in the concept of war, Charlie Brown was sincerely worried about the personal experience of a new war in his lifetime. Thus, the first hints for readers of Schulz's thoughts on war were deeply conflicted.[8]

A decade later, Charles Schulz was a two-time winner of the National Cartoonists Society's prestigious "Cartoonist of the Year" award and seems to have felt much more confident addressing the emerging conflict in Vietnam than he had been addressing war as a new artist. While much of Schulz's commentary would later center on Snoopy, *Peanuts*' involvement with Vietnam did not start there. It actually began as a symptom of Charlie Brown's chronic anxiety. In March 1965, the first American infantrymen, 3,500 Marines, landed at Da Nang, South Vietnam. Thousands more quickly followed. That summer Charlie Brown's parents decided to ship him off to summer camp against his will. Boarding the bus, the boy nervously made his way to the back and sat down. Isolated from the reader by a windowpane, loneliness struck Charlie Brown. "I feel like I'm being drafted," he grumbled through the glass at the reader.[9]

Charlie Brown's anxiety about summer camp drew from Schulz's own boyhood experience being drafted for World War II and having to deploy just before his mother's death. After the war, he often reflected back on his days in the infantry as a machine gunner: "I was a foot soldier." His tombstone would make no mention of his fifty years of *Peanuts*, Emmy and Peabody awards, or multimillion-dollar fortune. It listed only his proudest achievement: "Charles M. Schulz, Sgt. U.S. Army." His experiences in World War II would deeply influence his depictions of the Vietnam War.[10]

Charlie Brown's talk of conscription also likely resonated with young men and their families facing the draft during the escalation of the Vietnam conflict. By the time Charlie Brown was lamenting his ride to camp in 1965, nearly 60,000 American troops were already stationed in Vietnam. That number would triple by the end of the year. In August 1965, the *Chicago Daily Defender* reported numerous black families agonizing over whether or not their sons would be swept up in the draft, as Defense Secretary Robert McNamara raised quotas sharply to facilitate a new level of US involvement. Concerns escalated that month amid serious talks about lifting the exemptions of married men without children. Clearly, Charlie Brown was not the only one worried about being drafted. It was no coincidence that the round-headed boy made his first trip to summer camp that year. And it was no coincidence that just as American involvement was ramping up exponentially, Schulz chose to elevate the role of *Peanuts*' fastest rising star, a small beagle with a larger-than-life imagination and a battle of his own to fight.[11]

On Sunday morning, October 10, 1965, Snoopy walked into the title panel with a leather pilot's cap and goggles on his head, a scarf around his neck, and determination in his stride. "Here's the World War I flying ace posing beside his 'Sopwith Camel,'" Snoopy narrated as he stood stoically for a photo next to his doghouse. "It's the dawn patrol! We're out to hunt down the Red Baron!" As the dog daydreamed, he narrated the scenes he imagined: "I cross over the enemy lines . . . I can see the network of trenches below . . . Anti-aircraft fire

Figure 5.2 From his very first trip to summer camp, Charlie Brown associated the experience with the draft. Charles Schulz, *Peanuts*, June 5, 1965. © 1965 Peanuts Worldwide LLC.

exploding all around me." Snoopy painted violent images of warfare with his words.[12]

This marked a major turning point in the strip. Though this first appearance of the World War I flying ace had no direct correlation to the escalating war in Vietnam, Schulz introduced the new storyline at a moment when Americans were becoming acutely aware of the conflict. At least one of Schulz's cartooning friends worried that *Peanuts* was headed down a dangerous path. "When Charlie Schulz first did Snoopy in a helmet sitting on top of the dog house pretending he was fighting the Red Baron," wrote *Beetle Bailey* cartoonist Mort Walker, "I thought Schulz was going to ruin the strip." Walker worried that the growing war would prove too unpopular a theme for even the beloved *Peanuts*. With the Gulf of Tonkin incident in August 1964, American attention had immediately swung to Vietnam, 63 percent of Americans said they were following events there. By January 1965, 45 percent favored sending more troops to Vietnam if the situation required it (though a full third of Americans preferred pulling all troops out of South Vietnam rather than escalating the conflict). As the flying ace soared across the Sunday comics page, 45 percent of Americans were sure that the war in Vietnam was only bound to get worse. Readers could hardly have missed the significance of Snoopy going to war.[13]

Snoopy's enemy must have seemed eerily familiar to readers. The Red Baron always seemed to have the upper hand. Despite his best efforts, the dog never caught the Red Baron. Nor did the readers ever see the hero's hated enemy, only the destruction he left behind. This was eerily similar to media portrayals of the Vietcong throughout the early years of coverage. "The American GI's whose mission is to kill him, call the enemy simply, 'Old Charley,'" *Newsweek* reported in August 1965, "an elusive, slippery fellow out there somewhere, beyond the next paddy field, or lurking in the next clump of bush." Similarly, television news coverage of Vietnam typically showed generic clips of "artillery firing at unseen targets far away." *New York Times* reporter David Halberstam witnessed how many of the soldiers fought a private, internal war with fear because they sensed "ambushes all around them." Snoopy's enemy seemed to mirror America's.[14]

It is also telling that Schulz chose to set so many of his reflections on combat in World War I. In the Vietnam era, the Korean conflict was still far too volatile and politicized to suit his subtle style. World War II would have seemed the obvious choice if he had wanted to celebrate the American war effort or wave the banner of patriotism. Instead, he set Snoopy's fantasies in World War I, a conflict with a more unclear purpose and ambiguous conclusion, in much the same way that the writers of the popular film and later television adaptation *M*A*S*H* used the unpopular Korean War as an analogy for Vietnam.

Snoopy's mock battle was not the first time his musings had carried him away, but it was by far the most vivid. What was unique about this new storyline was the fact that Snoopy's imaginings were becoming increasingly visible to the readers. The dog's journey deeper and deeper into his fantasy gave Schulz space to reflect on the war and its effects on the home front. It was also significant that all of the early flying ace stories ran on Sundays, which allowed the artist larger panels and three rows—as opposed to the usual single row of panels during the week—to develop both his drawings and ideas. Not only would Snoopy come to dominate the *Peanuts* strip in this period, but the flying ace—and his obsession with catching the elusive Red Baron—would come to dominate Snoopy's storyline.

The violent imagery of the flying ace storyline soon grew to the point that Snoopy's imagination could hardly contain it. Whereas the dog's next engagement with the Red Baron ended in smoke and flames in the frantic puppy's mind, by January 9, 1966, things had changed. As Snoopy fought in another aerial battle with the Red Baron, he was once again outflanked and shot. This time, however, Schulz drew the damage not in words but in ink. There Snoopy sat atop his bullet-riddled dog house with a look of shock on his face as black smoke billowed to fill much of the whitespace in the frame. This was one of Schulz's most violent images in *Peanuts* to date and much too far for a comic strip, in cartoonist Mort Walker's opinion. When Schulz "showed bullet holes in the doghouse," Walker confided to fellow artist Shel Dorf, "I said, good golly—this has gone beyond the pale."[15]

In the months that followed, a theme developed. Whereas the flying ace had once experienced the war from overhead, subsequently he often crashed behind enemy lines. On February 13, 1966, Snoopy patiently maneuvered his way across the enemy countryside in search of safety. At one point, he snuck through abandoned trenches, the uneven, muddy ground, broken wood, and barbed wire clearly visible despite being depicted in silhouette. For the first time in the strip, Schulz was showing readers the terrain as Snoopy imagined it. The final panel showed a haggard Snoopy asleep beside Charlie Brown. "I think these missions are getting to be too much for him," the boy whispered, his face wrinkled with concern. Schulz was transforming his little pilot into a de facto infantryman and increasingly showing him as a victim of warfare, brave and dedicated as he might be. The poignant image made clear the gulf between the soldier's experience, pictured in Snoopy, and the civilian, pictured in Charlie Brown. This was a gulf that only empathy could bridge. And this empathy would be sharply tested. As Snoopy collapsed on the funny page

Figure 5.3 Snoopy's war began as a figment of his imagination but soon his fantasy was manifesting itself in the visual world of *Peanuts*. Charles Schulz, *Peanuts*, January 9, 1966. © 1966 Peanuts Worldwide LLC.

that morning, the *New York Times* gave little hope for reprieve, announcing that the outlook for Vietnam was "more of the same for a long time to come."[16]

With each passing day, Snoopy seemed to fall deeper into his fantasy war, to the point that the dog and the pilot became almost indistinguishable. Charlie Brown found his dog playing war so often that he worried that Snoopy had "finally flipped." When the spring baseball season arrived in 1966, Snoopy, typically the best player on the team, was totally useless because of his military daydreams. When Lucy and Linus moved to a new neighborhood because their dad had gotten a job transfer, Snoopy was even too embroiled in battle to acknowledge Linus's farewell. As the war in Vietnam demanded more attention and tens of thousands of more troops from Americans in 1966 and 1967, Snoopy was becoming trapped in a quagmire of his own.[17]

Snoopy was not the only *Peanuts* character tormented by the prospect of war. In one strip, Charlie Brown crashed his kite and became hopelessly tangled in the string. He made his way home, undressed, took a bath, and climbed into bed, all while entangled in his broken kite and twine. The only text in the whole Sunday strip came in the last panel as Charlie Brown grumpily stated, "Years from now when I get drafted, the army examiner will ask me why I have this kite with me." Charlie Brown's fatalism about his future and the draft likely resonated with a growing number of Americans who found their country fighting an endless war they believed to be a mistake. One mother from Delaware writing to Dr. Benjamin Spock in 1966 confided that her nine-year-old son had come home from school distraught that the Vietnam War would still be raging when he turned eighteen and that he would be drafted and killed. Though she was finally able to get his mind off the depressing subject, she did "think it is a terrible cloud for any child to have hanging over him." The whole episode had changed her mind about the war, she admitted to the famed pediatrician. She was not alone. Barely a year into combat deployment in Vietnam, more than a third believed the war had been a bad idea.[18]

Central to Schulz's position on the war was his unwavering support for the troops, which he viewed separately from support for the war. In one strip in August 1966, Schulz used the only parenthetical interjection of any of his 1960s strips to note that the drafted servicemen were "good lads." The artist also made his characters' likenesses available to the servicemen in Vietnam. With Schulz's permission, Snoopy became an emblem of war-making to soldiers and airmen in Vietnam. The World War I flying ace appeared on the nose of numerous American fighter planes and short range missiles. He appeared on the helmets of assault-helicopter pilots. Soldiers even drew Snoopy as the flying ace on the bottoms of their canvas bunks on the transport ships. One Ranger pilot from the Seventh Fleet even took to dressing like the flying beagle, "sporting an ancient helmet, goggles, and a long flowing scarf," according to the *Los Angeles Times*. Schulz biographer David Michaelis argues that Snoopy outpaced every other famous canine of the day to symbolically become "the American fighting man's most trusted friend when going into combat."[19]

In many instances, *Peanuts* focused on the plight of soldiers at war. In July 1966, the flying ace was given a leave of absence to relax in Paris. Enjoying the scenery, the cafes, and the young women, Snoopy mused to himself, "The war seems so far away." But he quickly came to his senses. "This is outrageous!" he suddenly exclaimed. "I can't sit here with this beautiful French girl while my buddies are fighting the Red Baron!" Back in flight, the flying ace felt at home amongst his fellow pilots. "This is where I belong! High above the clouds searching for the Red Baron!" he sighed with some sense of relief. Schulz seemed to push his readers to remember the troops in the present conflict. Regardless of where one stood on the politics of the war, Americans must be on the side of the soldiers even if it meant stomaching an unpleasant or confusing conflict.[20]

This sentiment echoed across the country as many felt that the well-being of the individual soldier was being lost in the midst of grand strategy, politics, and protest. "Nobody wants to go to war," *Playboy* playmate Jo Collins told historian Christian Appy, "but if our men are directly involved, how can we not be behind them, right, wrong, or indifferent? . . . Here were these boys that had to go and they were like myself—they didn't know where Vietnam was. They were going because they were fighting for their country." One Clevelander wrote to Dr. Spock, "Right or wrong they are there and need our support." Another *Los Angeles Times* reader told the editors in May 1966 that for some time he and his wife had been sending magazines for any G.I.s who might not have received mail from home. They did this, the reader said, because "we wanted to do our share to help cheer [the soldiers] up by doing something, rather than merely giving lip support." He complained that recently those magazines had been returned to his house with a notice that the Defense Department would no longer forward such items. The reader confessed that he was becoming increasingly concerned that when government officials talked about public support for the war "they mean support for the Johnson Policy and not necessarily for our boys over there."[21]

Over the next year, "Support Our Boys in Vietnam" parades sprung up in New York, Los Angeles, and many other cities, drawing thousands committed to showing their allegiance to the servicemen while making no clear commitment to the larger US policy in the war. In October 1967, thousands of antiwar protesters marched on Washington, DC declaring with large banners that supporting American troops meant bringing them home and ending the war. Whether they supported or opposed the conflict, many Americans agreed with Schulz that the soldiers and airmen should be at the heart of the nation's concerns.[22]

In late 1966, the artist's estimations of the war were becoming quite bleak. In October, he featured the flying ace in *Peanuts*' third television special, *It's the Great Pumpkin, Charlie Brown*. Taking on the Red Baron in a long dogfight, the flying ace plummeted to the ground behind enemy lines. On the way down, the Red Baron's bullets ripped into the side of the flying doghouse. This Emmy-nominated children's program, which shared the week's highest Nielsen ratings with the perennial favorite *Bonanza*, turned a third of this family holiday special into a reminder of war and its consequences. On Sunday, December 11, the title panel of the comic strip featured the flying ace in flight, teeth clenched, determined in combat. But in this image Snoopy did not sit atop his dog house, but rather a bull's eye. Such absurdist humor depicted soldiers as moving targets in a conflict far out of their control.[23]

In 1967, things got even darker. Early that year, the flying ace became a prisoner of war. The opening panel on January 16, 1967, showed Snoopy sitting in pitch darkness with only a sliver of light to illuminate his sad face. He feared that he would spend the rest of the war, or even longer, locked away in this enemy prison. In reality, he escaped after three days, but even then he was almost shot down by friendly fire. This storyline could have come straight from the daily headlines. The month before, North Vietnam had publicly rebuffed President Lyndon Johnson's call for a conference to discuss the release of prisoners of war. Reports also claimed that as many as 20 percent of US casualties were the result of friendly fire. Where *Peanuts* had entered the 1960s in relative innocence, Schulz had long since abandoned escapism and blurred the lines between fiction and reality.[24]

By this point, Snoopy's nightmare war consumed him. On May 11, 1967, the flying ace made his way across no-man's land and through the trenches. The scenery offered no glimpse of Charlie Brown's familiar neighborhood or the red doghouse. Instead, artillery exploded in the sky, barbed wire and debris littered the ground, and once again the shadows in the trenches were so dark that Snoopy could only be pictured in silhouette. That Sunday, Schulz drew a Mother's Day strip where Charlie Brown took Snoopy—weeping because he missed his mother—to the store to buy her a card. The peculiar thing about this strip was that Snoopy wore his flying ace gear the whole time. These strips represented how fully the war had come to dominate arguably the era's most ubiquitous cartoon character. At the same time, Charlie Brown's comment to his crying dog that "these holidays are hard on us all" reminded readers of the numerous families separated by the war, just as Schulz's once had been.[25]

In summer 1967, the flying ace went to the dreaded summer camp with Charlie Brown. It was at this summer camp that the dog pilot uttered what would become a common refrain for the rest of the conflict: "Curse this

Figure 5.4 Like a number of American soldiers and pilots in Vietnam, Snoopy became a prisoner of war. Charles Schulz, *Peanuts*, January 16, 1967. © 1967 Peanuts Worldwide LLC.

stupid war!" This declaration came weeks after civil rights leader Martin Luther King Jr.'s public denunciation of Vietnam, a move that nearly three-quarters of Americans condemned as wrongheaded and hurtful to the cause of black rights. Clearly, Snoopy was not happy with this war, but the dog's disarming charm, unflagging devotion to the fight, and the artist's ambiguity about precisely which war Snoopy was cursing seemed to allow his subversive message to pass without considerable backlash from readers or editors. On college campuses across the country, students could voice their own conflicted feelings about the war by keeping flying ace posters or stuffed dolls in their dorm rooms or by wearing an enormously popular flying ace sweatshirt branded in bold script, "Curse you, Red Baron!" By the fall of 1967, a majority of Americans would agree with King and Snoopy that Vietnam was a mistake, though many would continue to despise the antiwar movement they saw portrayed in the media.[26]

At the same time that Snoopy was separating himself from the war's more aggressive supporters, one *Peanuts* fan took Schulz's rather subtle message and made it so explicit for readers. On October 27, 1967, Herbert Block, the famous *Washington Post* editorial cartoonist, drew the flying ace baring his fangs atop his doghouse. The label on the dog's uniform read "bomb-happy generals." The thought bubble overhead said it all: "Here goes the fearless World War III pilot all over North Vietnam, and possibly China and Russia—if only those stupid civilians would unleash me." Graffiti across the side of the doghouse took Snoopy's well-known exclamation and twisted it to suit the editorial message: "Curse you, red civilians!" Block was obviously criticizing conservatives' calls for unrestricted warfare in North Vietnam and, indeed, Southeast Asia, if necessary. He was also playing on the image of the bomber pilot and expansive bombing campaigns, like *Rolling Thunder*, that had long horrified and infuriated the war's opponents. Under his signature, Block, who often used variations on *Peanuts*' characters and scenes in his editorial cartoons, made sure to identify himself as an "Old Charles Schulz Fan," making clear that this was no criticism of Schulz, but a deeply satirical reading of the flying ace's meaning. In an exchange of letters the next year Schulz assured Block that "the two cartoons in which [he] used [Schulz's] characters were all right."[27]

To many of Schulz's readers, however, Block spoke blasphemy. Block's cartoon was "a distortion and perversion" of Schulz's work, one Toledo, Ohio reader complained to the local newspaper. The reader believed the flying ace portrayed little more than everyone's "dream of being a hero" (even though the flying ace never ultimately got to be the hero nor did he always act heroically in a traditional sense). "I don't think the . . . cartoon by HERBLOCK is either funny," wrote a *Washington Post* reader to Schulz, "or even fair to Snoopy." The reader interpreted Block's editorial cartoon as a distortion of *Peanuts*' meaning. "I protest," she exclaimed. "Does *everything* have to be tied in with the world's strife? Cannot we leave *something* unsinister and sanely wholesome?" Both readers' protests revealed that they interpreted Snoopy and the flying ace to be apolitical, in opposition to Block's reading. As was often the case, Schulz's subtle, even ambiguous, presentation left readers seeing contrary meanings in the same images. Block connected the flying ace to conservative opinions of the war while conservative Americans recoiled in defense.[28]

For three years *Peanuts* had talked about the war without referring to it by name. That changed in July 1968. When Schulz introduced Charlie Brown to Franklin, he asked if Franklin had come on vacation with his whole family. "No," Franklin replied, "my dad is over in Vietnam." In the most deadly year of the war yet, Schulz finally explicitly acknowledged its existence in a way he had not done with Korea, the Cuban Missile Crisis, or even John Kennedy's assassination. The scene even suggested that the war inequitably affected black families. Casualty statistics backed up such suggestions. Studies showed that at the height of the war, while black soldiers made up only 11 percent of the combat forces, they accounted for 16 percent of casualties. This was part of what Black Power activist Stokely Carmichael meant when he characterized the Vietnam War as "white people sending black people to make war on yellow people in order to defend the land they stole from red people." Not only did Franklin's dad fight in Vietnam while Charlie Brown's continued working in his barbershop, but Franklin's dad was also statistically more likely to die than men who looked like Charlie Brown.[29]

Schulz's empathy for the Vietnam soldiers likely only grew as he began visiting wounded veterans in the fall of 1968 at the Army's Letterman General Hospital in San Francisco. Schulz would spend hours there with recovering soldiers, drawing original sketches of his *Peanuts* characters and personalizing them for each serviceman. Major General Charles H. Gingles reported that his patients "were truly delighted with the drawings." He was impressed by Schulz's 'warm and generous manner" with each soldier and thanked the artist for staying late into the evening so he could be sure to meet every veteran and draw for them. Seeing these wounded veterans firsthand and witnessing the bloody televised images portraying troops victimized by the American war machine surely had significant consequences on Schulz's view of the war itself.[30]

The war even came to dominate the most sacred of *Peanuts* holidays in 1968. There was not one sign of festivity on Christmas Eve that year. The panels instead were filled with artillery explosions, barbed wire, debris, and mud. The same deep shading that had come to characterize the flying ace strips darkened the day before Christmas. Things came to a head on Christmas Day. In a strip that Schulz typically decorated with tinsel and lights, children caroling, or a calligraphic "Merry Christmas," he instead featured the flying ace wailing, "Will this stupid war never end? . . . I'm tired of this war!" Schulz was securely within popular opinion by this point. Fifty-two percent believed sending troops to Vietnam had been a mistake and 57 percent believed the time had come for a steady withdrawal from South Vietnam. For a comic strip that had gained universal acclaim from a television special about the meaning of Christmas, though, these holiday war panels seemed an odd choice. No reader would have placed *Peanuts* in the same category as the underground comix that were contesting the war, such as expelled Georgia House member Julian Bond's *Vietnam: An Anti-War Tale*, but clearly Schulz was losing patience with the war. As he had told an interviewer with NBC's *Today* show the month before, "We're gradually, finally, coming down to the point where we're really beginning to realize how unspeakable war is, and that we simply have got to stop this." When Schulz imagined "how unspeakable war is," it is possible that his mind flashed back to Dachau and the atrocities he had witnessed in his own war experience. It is even more likely that he envisioned the growing number of graphic reports and photographs reaching the public after Tet. Like a majority of Americans by the end of 1968, Schulz was calling for an end to the war.[31]

Snoopy's military service hit its nadir on June 1, 1969. That Sunday the title panel showed an exhausted flying ace standing in thick mud, dragging his cap and goggles behind him, muttering "Curse this stupid war!" Finally, the pilot bolstered himself and climbed aboard the Sopwith Camel for another dangerous mission. As he prepared for take-off, he began to contemplate his fate. "Is it possible that this could be my final mission?" he wondered. "That I shall never return? That this is the end?" In the next-to-last panel Snoopy sat there for a moment in a dazed silence and then quickly leapt from his plane and abandoned his mission, shouting "Forget it!" as he bolted away. After this scene in June 1969, though he still regularly appeared as the flying ace, Snoopy would not pursue the Red Baron again until the end of US involvement in Vietnam. Years later, Schulz would tell an interviewer that he stopped drawing the flying ace in combat because "we were suddenly realizing . . . this was such a monstrous war and everything. It just didn't seem funny. So I just stopped doing it." Snoopy's war had driven the dog to the breaking point. No longer the fearless warrior, Schulz made clear that Snoopy was a victim of this war as much as the thousands of American men who fell in Vietnam. And Schulz's collected papers show no record of a single letter written in protest of Snoopy's refusal to continue his chase.[32]

While Snoopy was fleeing the war, Charlie Brown and Linus were afraid of being pulled in. "What happens when you get drafted?" Linus asked Charlie Brown as the two walked along on September 15, 1969. "They send you someplace," Charlie Brown replied. Linus did not like that answer. "I have no desire to be sent wherever they'll be sending people when I'm old enough to be sent," he grumbled. Some American parents certainly understood Linus's line of thinking. "I have never seen the logic," one New Jersey mother wrote to notable peace advocate Dr. Benjamin Spock, "of raising a child thru all those hours of sickness, emotional upsets and happiness, then have someone snuff them out with one bullet." Linus's fear and reluctance reflected that of many Americans. Though they had little patience for "draft dodgers," they did not believe the draft was fair, either. White, middle-class men were the most successful in avoiding the draft by attaining higher education and family deferments or by joining reserve units. Though it was evident these young men were taking advantage of the draft system, their white-collar "dodging" was no more offensive to everyday Americans than Linus's candid admission.[33]

On Veteran's Day 1969, Schulz began what would become a yearly tradition of paying tribute to one of his personal heroes, cartoonist Bill Mauldin, who was best known for his World War II comic *Willie and Joe*, which portrayed the plight of infantrymen in bitterly sarcastic realism. While Mauldin's soldiers grumbled about their duties or criticized commanders, they remained "sturdy cogs in the democratic war machine." Mauldin initially supported the war in Vietnam out of a sense of responsibility to the troops already there. He also hoped that a resolution in Vietnam would avoid a far worse conflict with China. He empathized with those he called "peaceniks," not the "unwashed doves with stringy hair in their guitars," he clarified, but "the serious ones who are genuinely troubled"—like Charles Schulz. Mauldin even went so far as to remind his fellow World War II veterans, a group often critical of draft dodgers and resisters, that in their war "the draft board had to drag most of us, whimpering, out of the bushes." President Lyndon Johnson had embraced Mauldin as a friend for his support of the war and the two spent time together at Johnson's ranch in Texas. But after 1967, and especially after the treatment of Chicago war protesters at the 1968 Democratic National Convention, Mauldin broke with Johnson and his successor Richard Nixon and turned vehemently against the war. Mauldin's harsh criticisms were nationally known and published regularly in the *Chicago Sun-Times*.[34]

So when Schulz dressed Snoopy up as a World War II veteran and sent him to celebrate Veteran's Day by quaffing root beers with Bill Mauldin, it was a much more complex message than it appeared on the surface. Of course, Schulz was paying tribute to a man who had been a beloved voice for him and an entire generation of American infantrymen. Schulz owned Mauldin's books and read them. But this was also a serious step for Schulz, aligning with a vocal opponent of the war at this contentious moment in the conflict. And yet just as they had so many times before, Schulz's lovable characters were able to disarm many who might decry the doubt he suggested.

By 1970, Schulz's thoughts on the war had become downright cynical. Snoopy again appeared as the flying ace, but always in the midst of a heavy rain. On one mission, Linus tried to stop Snoopy from taking off in a storm, but the pilot simply called him "hysterical." "Tell him we'll all be home by Christmas," he stated determinedly. The strip sarcastically juxtaposed Linus's "hysterical" concern for Snoopy's safety against the pilot's own naive belief that this conflict would end by Christmas, just as the ill-fated young men of 1914 had once believed. The next day's strip depicted the flying ace racing home in an even heavier downpour. With each panel the rain came down harder. By the third panel the rain was so heavy and black that Snoopy was barely visible as he raced through the torrent. The dreary shading of this strip must have seemed an apt metaphor for Americans' sinking hopes for the Vietnam conflict by 1970. Still Snoopy, in his dogged determination to do his duty, represented for some the last of what was "heroic" in American society. "Of the few idols I have worshipped at one time or another, most have crumbled or dissolved into dust," wrote Chaplain Kevin Devine. "At times it seems I have no one left on a pedestal except Snoopy, of course," he quipped. Snoopy was second only to "the American fighting man."[35]

Schulz continued his criticisms of the draft in 1970. In one strip that spring, Lucy walked up to the pitcher's mound and asked Charlie Brown if he had his own room. "Oh yes," he replied, "I have a very nice room." "I hope you

Figure 5.5 Lucy helps acclimate Charlie Brown to the realities of becoming a draft-age male in Cold War America. Charles Schulz, *Peanuts*, May 13, 1970. © 1970 Peanuts Worldwide LLC.

realize that you won't always have your own room," Lucy stated matter-of-factly, "Someday you'll get drafted or something, and you'll have to leave your room forever!" This was all part of a list of "Things You Might as Well Know" that Lucy had compiled for her friend. This was the only strip on the draft to involve a female character. Still, the message was the same. The draft was a bleak reality for many of the nation's young men.[36]

For Independence Day that year, *Peanuts* addressed a number of Vietnam-era issues. It began on July 2, 1970, when Snoopy was invited to speak at a Fourth of July celebration at the puppy farm where he was born. "As long as this is going to be a Fourth of July speech," he thought to himself, "I think I should slip in a few digs about dogs not being able to vote. . . . We can be drafted into the Army, but we can't vote." Here Schulz highlighted a major political debate over the voting age that would be addressed the following spring when the United States ratified the Twenty-Sixth Amendment. As Snoopy took the stage for his speech, a violent riot erupted. The room quickly filled with a thick mix of smoke and tear gas as police rushed in to secure the scene. Back home, Charlie Brown and Linus sat riveted as the whole thing unfolded on television. Charlie Brown's local newspaper would later reveal that the riot had broken out over "some trouble about dogs being sent to Vietnam, and then not getting back." This was the second and final explicit reference to Vietnam in this period. California Governor Ronald Reagan, a "morning devotee" to *Peanuts* and acquaintance of the artist, was relieved to find "that my hero Snoopy has also experienced the joys of a campus disturbance." Of course, Snoopy did not take Reagan's hard stance against young protestors, but became the victim of aggressive police tactics along with the protesters. While Snoopy seemed willing to accept the draft in exchange for the vote, the younger dogs at the puppy farm refused to see more dogs die. Schulz was acting out the turmoil of the Vietnam era home front on the funny pages.[37]

By 1971, the flying ace could barely muster the strength to be angry about the war. After landing his Sopwith Camel without the battle damage or visual violence of the late 1960s, Snoopy stripped off his goggles and sighed, "I'm exhausted . . . This stupid war is too much." By mid-year, however, Schulz was able to put together one more comprehensive statement on the war and the draft. Once again, Charlie Brown and the flying ace were off to summer camp. "I hate going to camp," Charlie Brown complained from his bus seat. "Going to camp prepares you for getting drafted, which I don't want to do either." To cap off this statement, Snoopy added, "Curse this stupid war!" Here Charlie Brown's fatalistic fear that he was being prepped for war like a sheep for slaughter collided with Snoopy's long and bitter fight in "this stupid war." This was perhaps the clearest statement of Schulz's position on the war.[38]

Two fans' responses to this strip demonstrated contemporary polarization of opinion. One Vietnam veteran and long-time reader wrote on July 19, 1971, that he "was disappointed for the first time" because Schulz's strip "portrayed Charlie not wanting to be drafted." "I was proud to serve my country," he continued, and hoped "Charlie Brown would be just as proud." Herb Tompkins—a self-proclaimed "Peanuts follower" from Michigan—responded quite differently. "Right on, man," he wrote, "I don't blame you. Hope Congress will eventually get the message."[39]

While this strip of Charlie Brown grumbling about the draft and Snoopy cursing the war might have been Schulz's most salient comment on the war to date, it was also his last. By 1971, 58 percent of Americans believed that the Vietnam War was not only a mistake, but immoral. Schulz had ceased drawing battle scenes the year before, but thereafter abandoned the entire war theme, including Snoopy's most popular alter-ego. The flying ace would not return until after the US withdrawal from Vietnam, as an unemployed veteran seeking a paycheck.[40]

Schulz's abandonment of the war did not, however, stop another artist from using his famous imagery for one more critique of the war. In a 1971 editorial cartoon from Raleigh, North Carolina's *News & Observer*, the flying ace sat atop a doghouse labeled "Cooper-Church Amendment" wearing a scarf embroidered with the word "Congress." The proposed amendment, which sought to prohibit all US military operations outside Vietnam, was a congressional reaction to President Richard Nixon's 1969 secret Cambodian bombing. The amendment finally passed in December 1970, months after ground troops had left Cambodia. The final bill also lacked any restrictions on US air raids, which continued in Cambodia for two more years. To depict the amendment's failure, the cartoonist drew bullet holes across the doghouse. Although Schulz never showed the Red Baron in *Peanuts*, this artist made clear who he believed the villain to be. Overhead, Nixon smiled as he soared off on a fighter jet, leaving Snoopy crashed below, screaming, "Curse you, Red Baiter!" Once again, readers were offended by the overt political use of Snoopy. "Can just anyone use one of your characters?" Marie Jackson of North Carolina demanded in a letter to Schulz about this editorial cartoon. "I resent Snoopy being used in this manner." Whether Jackson opposed the Cambodian invasion or not, clearly she was most offended by Snoopy's direct opposition to the president, her voice joining those of the millions who were now against the war. The editorial cartoonists' drawing might have gone beyond Schulz's own public position, but this was only a logical conclusion to the flying ace saga.[41]

Despite dealing with the controversial war and some of its social implications, by the mid-1970s and the end of US involvement in Vietnam, Schulz had become one of the most read and best known cartoonists in American history, with his strip read by more than 100 million people each day. Comics critic Robert C. Harvey went so far as to suggest that a large part of *Peanuts*' success in this era was a direct result of the flying ace storylines, which drew in millions of Americans experiencing the social dislocation of the late 1960s. Whatever the direct impact of Snoopy's war, it is clear that critics who charged *Peanuts* with being too detached from social problems missed the ways that the comic strip connected with the concerns of American newspaper readers. While few readers took the time to write and either endorse or protest Schulz's message on Vietnam, the fact that the flying ace was so enormously popular and prevalent in late 1960s culture reveals, nonetheless, that many Americans subconsciously accepted Schulz's comment on the war. Even more so, while Schulz biographer David Michaelis asserted that Snoopy's war provided "an explanatory as well as a descriptive character for thousands who burned draft cards and protested an unjustifiable war," *Peanuts*' more conservative readers drew deeper meaning from the flying ace. For them, Snoopy's battle mirrored their own fight to support American soldiers in Vietnam and uphold their allegiance to their country. His perseverance through disillusionment, disappointment, and challenge mirrored their determination to find "peace with honor." These feelings were seen most clearly in American soldiers' own embrace of the flying ace.[42]

When Army Captain Charles R. Bailey returned home to Charlotte, North Carolina in 1971, a twelve-foot-tall flying ace greeted him with the words, "Happiness is Chuck Bailey home from Vietnam." The banner had taken Bailey's wife and friends five hours to complete. The homemade sign perfectly wed the intimate nature of Schulz's bestselling 1962 book *Happiness Is a Warm Puppy* with the militaristic nature of the flying ace. Here Snoopy symbolized both the soldier's longing for the comfort of home memorialized in every epic story since the *Iliad* and the soldier's otherness created by enduring the trauma of combat, an experience entirely alien to civilians in a society of abundance and affluence.[43]

Snoopy welcomed soldiers like Bailey home because Snoopy, in the character of the flying ace, had gone through the war with them. "When I was in Vietnam," Glen Goodson of New Mexico would recall, "mom would send me the strip." Often times his mother sent the strips collected in a small photo album. "I'd pass them around and they kept me and my buddies going." When Goodson ended up injured in a field hospital, his mother would send him Snoopy mugs and cards. It all "meant more to me than anyone can know," he confided to Schulz. *Peanuts* "brought home to us," said Vietnam veteran Pleas Davis. "Those [strips] were [some of] the things, believe it or not, we cared most about" because "you could lock yourself into what was [going on in Vietnam] and it could be pretty black." Snoopy was a connection to home and security. In David Larsen's battalion, soldiers who were nearing the final weeks of their deployment received Snoopy buttons that read "short timer" as a marker for special care. Other soldiers expressed these connections to home in more crude and sexualized images, such as those that carried cigarette lighters that transformed the title of Schulz's bestselling *Happiness Is a Warm Puppy* into the slogan "Happiness is a Warm Pussy," articulating their longing for physical intimacy with a woman. For many soldiers, Snoopy represented a safer life in a familiar surrounding.[44]

Snoopy, the exhausted yet determined soldier, served to boost morale for American troops during the war. Captain Joe Holden, a pilot for the Army, ran counter to command when he had the flying ace and the Red Baron painted across the side of his aircraft in order to raise the "*esprit 'd corps* to keep the guys motivated." Though he was later commanded to remove the artwork, "it got a lot of attention" from the troops while it lasted. For Holden, the artwork had been successful "morale-wise." Al Rampone read *Peanuts* regularly in the Army newspaper *Stars and Stripes*. As a member of the 2nd Platoon of the 281st Assault Helicopter Company, Rampone had the flying ace painted on his helmet as a call sign. For him Snoopy signified "unit pride," a solidarity with his brothers in arms and a reason to keep fighting.[45]

Snoopy even provided a safe symbol for soldiers to express their own disillusionment with the war and the antiwar protest movement. When 25,000 American soldiers who had expected to be home for Christmas 1972 were forced to stay because of President Nixon's renewed bombing campaign, an Associated Press reporter found that one handmade card best captured the soldiers' mood. It depicted the flying ace staring up at the stars in Vietnam as artillery fire rumbled in the distance. Snoopy's mind quickly turned toward home as he wondered if his loved ones were watching the same sky. "Slowly he walks back across the darkened air base," the card's creator narrated, "and then

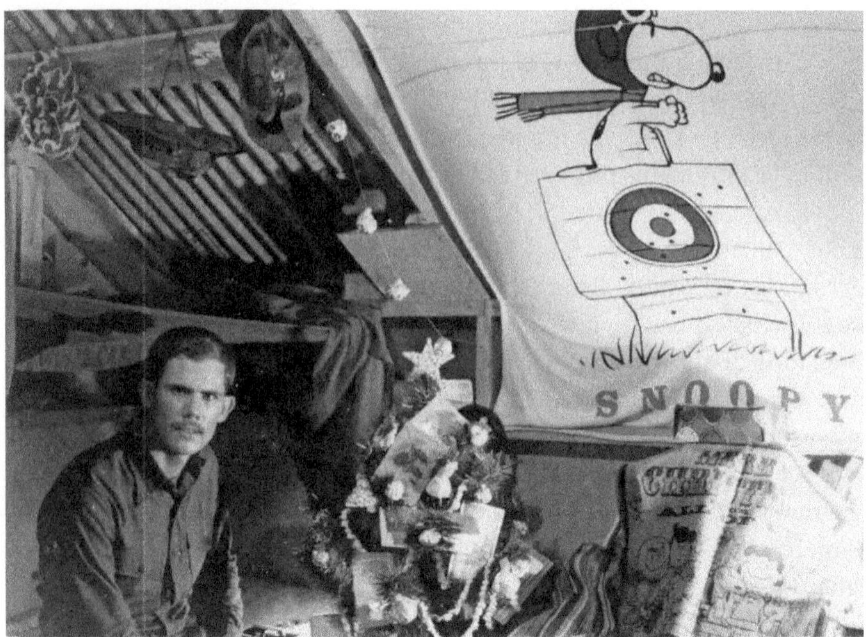

Figure 5.6 A US soldier in Vietnam poses for a picture with his Christmas presents, including a large flying ace banner. Courtesy of Richard Swan.

the thought that throbs so constantly in his mind cries out: 'I'm frustrated.'" *Washington Post* field reporter John Burgess found more signs of frustration among American airmen stationed outside of Vietnam. One embroidered patch showing "an outraged Snoopy shouting an obscenity about Jane Fonda" best articulated the feeling, he felt.[46]

For American soldiers, like so many back home, feelings about the Vietnam War did not always fit neatly into the prowar/antiwar framework. "We may find out some day that what we're doing in Vietnam is wrong," a Brooklyn man who had lost a son in the war told *Time*, "but until then, it's my country right or wrong." Like the flying ace who cursed the war but refused to stop fighting or Charlie Brown who minced no words about his dread for the draft, yet embraced his fate, many Americans faced a war they did not understand because defeat was not an option in their worldview. Although countless Americans, especially veterans, struggled to articulate their feelings about the war, Snoopy had a way of speaking for them. Snoopy was the hero in Vietnam because, even if he could not offer clear answers or victory, he could offer Americans a compatriot to commiserate with about their troubles.[47]

"I'll second that," Vietnam veteran Al Rampone chuckled knowingly in a recent interview. "He was a hero."[48]

6

I Believe in Conserving Energy

Peanuts, Nature, and an Environmental Ethos

It was just the sort of situation that suited Charles Schulz's offbeat humor. His lead character, Charlie Brown, had just bought a new wastebasket and it was still in the wrapping paper when he showed it to his friend. "Well, unwrap it, and let's see what it looks like," Patty instructed, intrigued by Charlie Brown's new purchase. The small wastebasket, decorated with flowers, appeared to please the children's eyes, but Charlie Brown had a problem. "What shall I do with all this wrapping paper?" he wondered aloud with his hands full of trash. "Throw it in the wastebasket!" Patty replied matter-of-factly. Here in this March 1951 *Peanuts* comic strip, Charles Schulz used his subtle humor to air his discontentment with capitalist materialism and to point out the consequences of affluence. Unwrapping the new wastebasket had instantly turned the wrapping paper from consumer advertising to trash. Fortunately for Charlie Brown, his purchase was made to contain this waste.[1]

Schulz's humor in this strip highlighted the disposable nature of American postwar consumer products and questioned the logic behind it all. Schulz readily acknowledged that even his own life's work fell victim to this culture. "Comic strips are not made to last," he told *Newsday*. "They are made to be funny today in the paper [and then] thrown away." This strip exposed a truth that leaders in the antilitter movement, like the corporate-backed organization Keep America Beautiful, did not want to acknowledge. The proliferation of disposable materials used in consumer packaging was a major contributor to the growing litter problem. Instead, Keep America Beautiful and the Advertising Council chose to highlight "individual thoughtlessness" as "the outstanding factor in the litter nuisance." Thus, as the environmental movement was fighting for influence in the American political economy, a pro-business movement was working to co-opt this new environmental consciousness in service to rehabilitating its public image. And Charles Schulz's *Peanuts* ended up at the intersection of the two, a national face for two opposing movements.[2]

In the 1970s, a number of America's major corporations used extensive advertising campaigns to steer the growing environmental movement away from sweeping legislation to regulate corporate production and access to natural resources and toward a "personal responsibility" that put the onus on individual consumers and communities to deal with environmental dangers like litter and air pollution. In the process, business not only avoided some increased regulation, but managed to redeem its image to become the champion of the "American way" once again by the early 1980s. In the 1970s, Charles Schulz was commissioned to participate in advertising campaigns both to promote corporate capitalism and inform the public about environmental dangers. Adopting the "personal responsibility" narrative first pioneered in corporate advertising campaigns, Schulz ultimately helped the Nixon and Carter administrations to divert attention away from large scale polluters toward individual violators. *Peanuts* thus played a public role in a key national battle over how willing Americans might be to reform their capitalist structures. Ultimately, Charles Schulz and his seemingly innocuous *Peanuts* characters helped set the stage in the decentralizing and deregulatory culture of the late 1970s and 1980s.

Though *Peanuts* began in the fall of 1950 as an urban story, it quickly and seamlessly migrated to the suburbs. This move came complete with countless suburban environmental concerns. The first tree depicted in *Peanuts* was a stump, likely cleared off to make way for new housing construction. Increasingly, advocates of an open-space protection movement bemoaned the vanishing countryside and the clear-cutting of forests. "If this 'progress' were true progress, no one would have cause for complaint," wrote one commentator in 1964. "But in fact, 'progress' has come to stand for stupidity, greed, graft, malice, and moral debasement. We have imperiled the charms of our cities; now the countryside is being laid waste." Some critics even went as far as to refer to "the rape of the land" or "the rape of the countryside." This herbicidal culture deeply affected Charlie Brown when, in March 1951, he greeted Patty's new seedling with an ax, as though trees were another weed to be exterminated like crabgrass.[3]

On January 5, 1958, a young Linus van Pelt ventured outside into winter and feared he had stumbled into a nuclear holocaust. The assumption of the strip was that during Linus's early years indoors he had heard—through his parents' conversation, radio broadcasts, and television programs— more about fallout than he had heard about the annual phenomenon of snow. In many ways, nuclear disaster was the first environmental crisis in American public consciousness. This is clear in the ways Americans processed the disaster: in numerous landscape photos of Hiroshima and Nagasaki, in the unlivable environments in postapocalyptic films like 1959's *On the Beach*, and in countless newspaper articles that diagrammed the effects of a nuclear bomb with the blast radius superimposed on various major cities. From the most mundane to the most catastrophic, *Peanuts* anticipated the rising environmental concerns of the 1950s.[4]

As silly as Linus's fears might have seemed to Charlie Brown, his terror would have been recognizable to American readers in the 1950s. By 1958, three out of four respondents to a Gallup poll said they had heard or read about the fallout associated with the hydrogen bomb. An equal proportion also feared that in the event of another world war, the hydrogen bomb would be used against the United States. This popular awareness and anxiety had developed over the course of several years, beginning with the 1949 Soviet atomic test and reaching fever pitch following the 1954 Bikini Atoll hydrogen bomb tests. In 1955, a report from the Atomic Energy Commission estimated that the radioactive fallout from a large hydrogen bomb could "kill everyone in a 7,000-square-mile downwind area." Though the commission warned that

Figure 6.1 Voyaging out of the house for his first winter experience, Linus mistook snowfall for the dreaded nuclear fallout he had heard of in the media. Charles Schulz, *Peanuts*, January 5, 1958. © 1958 Peanuts Worldwide LLC.

this was a worst-case scenario and that "the fallout radiation actually absorbed by residents of the United States from all nuclear explosions to date . . . adds up to about the same exposure of one chest X ray," this did little to slow the tide of sensational headlines that followed the Bikini Atoll bomb tests: "Expert Views on Peril of Fallout," "Fallout Radiation Is Concentrated in Food," "Fallout Now Dooms 26,000–150,000, Expert Says," and "Test Fallout Deadlier Than the Bomb."[5]

The growing concerns were echoed in the films of the era. The 1959 film *On the Beach*, starring Gregory Peck, Ava Gardner, and Fred Astaire, was the most blunt and perhaps bleak example of such anxieties manifested on the silver screen. Based on Nevil Shute's 1957 novel, *On the Beach* was a film about the end of human life. While other important science fiction films of the era used space aliens (1953's *War of the Worlds*), gigantic ants (1954's *Them!*), or prehistoric sea monsters (1956's *Godzilla*) as metaphors for their atomic critiques, *On the Beach* did nothing to mask its criticism of those societies that had developed and employed nuclear weapons. The overriding message of the movie was clear: even for those few who might survive the nuclear apocalypse of a third World War, the radioactive wasteland that would remain would make life pointless. In this story, nuclear fallout guaranteed total human extinction. It was as T. S. Eliot wrote in his poem "The Hollow Men," the verse Shute used as an epigraph for his bestseller: "This is the way the world ends / Not with a bang but a whimper." Nuclear fallout was in many ways more frightening than the bomb because it was a slow, silent, and invisible killer. Even the most potentially lethal environmental concern in postwar America found expression in the world of *Peanuts*.[6]

Schulz directly acknowledged the fledgling environmental movement by celebrating its leading voice. Marine biologist Rachel Carson cemented her place as the leader of the modern environmental movement with her 1962 bestselling *Silent Spring*. In the opening of her book, she recounted "a fable for tomorrow" that depicted a lush country town, brimming with plant and animal life. "Then a strange blight crept over the area and everything began to change," she wrote in an ominous turn. "There was a strange stillness," she imagined, "The birds . . . where had they gone?" In her fictional town, Carson deposited all of the most serious documented ecological fallout produced by American industrial action. "A grim specter has crept upon us almost unnoticed," she warned, "and this imagined tragedy may easily become a stark reality we all shall know." Carson was revolutionary in her approach, presenting the latest scientific research on the terrible effects of biochemicals like DDT in relatable examples and appealing for individual and public action.[7]

Lucy was certainly a fan of Carson. For her birthday in 1962, Lucy received an autographed baseball bat. "Whose name is on it," Charlie Brown inquired, "Mickey Mantle? Willie Mays?" Lucy stared down at the bat in her hands, a bit confused. "It must be a girl's bat," she replied, "It says, 'Rachel Carson.'" Making a mild joke by placing Carson's name on a wooden bat, Schulz poked fun at her the same way he would many other friends and acquaintances throughout his work.[8]

Lucy's affinity became more evident in another reference to Carson in 1963. Assuming her regular station reclined against Schroeder's piano, Lucy mused about what she had learned from reading Carson's earlier work on the formation and development of Earth's oceans. "Rachel Carson says that when our moon was born, there were no oceans on Earth," she reported. Suddenly, Schroeder sat up from his piano keyboard and erupted. "You're always talking about Rachel Carson!" Lucy, a bit jostled by Schroeder's exclamation, relaxed back against the piano and replied, "We girls need our heroines." This strip, first, revealed the way that Schulz would research various topics to be knowledgeable enough that experts in fields like marine biology might find a treat in the comic strip. Here Schulz refers to a trilogy of books on the oceans that Carson had written in the 1940s and 1950s. Second, this strip shows Schulz's great respect for Carson and her work, by making her the heroine of the typically anti-intellectual Lucy. Literary scholar Philip D. Beidler would later write that "the bravery and genius of Carson's achievement in *Silent Spring* are still perhaps best imaged in [this] Charles Schulz cartoon" because it revealed just how pervasive she and her work had become in American culture.[9]

While fears of nuclear fallout or other chemical degradation could paint a bleak picture of the human environment in *Peanuts* nature actually played an emotionally complex role in the strip. Nature was often depicted as a place of reflection, where the children could ponder the meaning of life in a night sky full of stars or the first fall leaves hitting the ground. This theme was perhaps presented most fully in a series of scenes in 1971 and 1972 when Charlie Brown and Peppermint Patty sat beneath a tree to ponder the meaning of love. "Explain love to me," Peppermint Patty asked of Charlie Brown in the August 10, 1975 strip. Charlie Brown proceeded to explain what was the basic theme of this series, which is that love is an abstraction that can never truly be grasped, only recognized and often only after it is gone. Schulz explored other emotions in nature, too. Loneliness, another common theme in *Peanuts*, came to be deeply connected to Snoopy's long lost brother, Spike, who lived alone in the desert and first appeared in the strip in August 1975. Spike was a generally melancholy character who sent sad letters and often conversed with the cacti

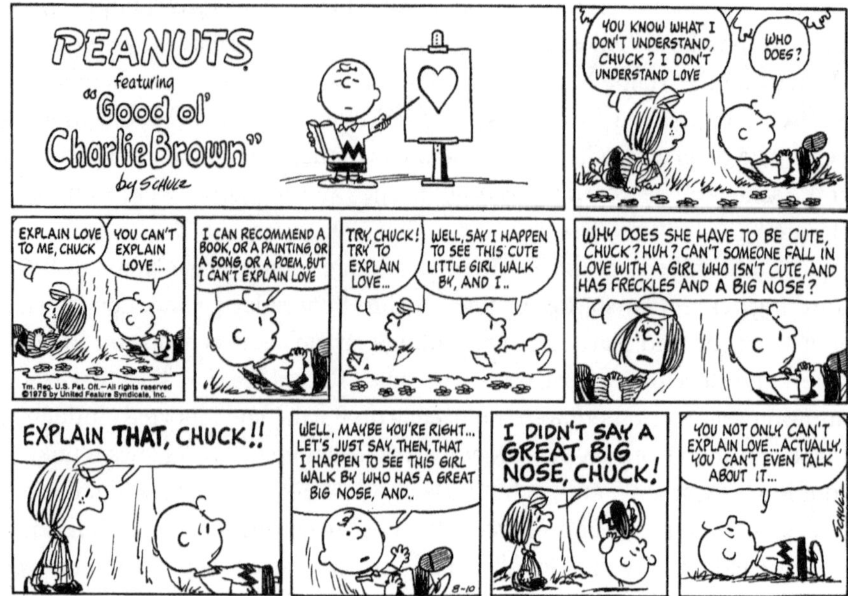

Figure 6.2 In the 1970s, nature in *Peanuts* sometimes became a site of the pastoral ideal, perfect for reflections on life and love. Charles Schulz, *Peanuts*, August 10, 1975. © 1975 Peanuts Worldwide LLC.

for friends. The barrenness of the land allegoried the emotion of the character. So nature played a complex role in *Peanuts*.

One of the primary issues of concern in postwar suburbia was raising children. As many would soon become aware, this process, too, had environmental as well as political repercussions. In the spring of 1959, Charlie Brown welcomed a new baby sister named Sally. He was a very proud big brother, as he made clear to all the other children. "I'm so happy," he told Violet when she asked about the new baby. Lucy, however, was having none of this. "Happy?" she demanded. "I suppose it's never occurred to you that over-population is a serious problem?!" While this sort of naysaying was fully in keeping with her personality, Lucy was right: overpopulation was becoming a serious issue of discussion in postwar America. This was a classic debate that had been set off by British economist Thomas Malthus with his 1798 treatise *Essay on the Principles of Population*, but it had taken on new urgency in an era of decolonization and globalization after World War II. Between 1945 and 1960 the

US population grew from 140 million to 180 million. On average, mothers in the 1950s were the youngest of the twentieth century and the average yearly birth rate of nearly 4 million in the decade was the highest since 1898. Overpopulation was more deadly than the atomic bomb, Dr. William Vogt of the Planned Parenthood Federation of America told a public forum in downtown Atlanta in 1952. "This is not a theory, a fear, or a horrible dream," Vogt said, "It is a fact." Dr. John Rock of Harvard Medical School agreed with the prognosis. According to his calculations, he told a meeting of more than 400 gynecologists and obstetricians in 1956, the world would experience a global food shortage by 1980 if population growth continued at the current pace. Ultimately, Rock argued, this would lead to a desperate nuclear war over the planet's dwindling resources.[10]

Overpopulation and its effect on global resources worried many Americans. In 1965, the *New Republic* declared that world hunger would be the "single most important factor in the final third of the 20th century." This assertion was supported by the fact that the global population grew from 2.5 billion in 1950 to 3.35 billion by 1965. This issue worried government officials, too. "Overpopulation and resource scarcity," argued one foreign aid report in 1959, created the potential for "communist political and economic domination." "No peace and no power," President Lyndon Johnson told a gathering in Omaha, Nebraska in the summer of 1966, "is strong enough to stand for long against the restless discontent of millions of human beings who are without any hope." Johnson was explaining the reasoning behind shipping five million tons of grain to relieve food shortages in drought-stricken India.[11]

Congress, too, was interested in this problem. In the summer of 1965, the Senate Subcommittee on Foreign Aid Expenditures took up the issue of the "population crisis." Chaired by Alaska Senator Ernest Gruening, a graduate of Harvard Medical School and a former governor of the "last frontier," this subcommittee was motivated by the charges from current and past presidents. The US government needed to "seek new ways to use our knowledge," President Johnson proclaimed earlier that year in his State of the Union address, "to help deal with the explosion in world population and the growing scarcity in world resources." Similarly, former President Eisenhower, serving alongside former President Truman as an honorary chairman for Planned Parenthood, wrote to the committee of his great concern over this problem. The population crisis was, in his opinion, "one of the most . . . critical problems facing mankind today." He continued in his letter: "If we now ignore the plight of those unborn generations which, because of our unreadiness to take creative action in controlling population growth, will be denied any expectations beyond abject poverty and suffering, then history will rightly condemn us."

According to the committee's report, the population explosion was partly to blame for the growing disorder, disrepair, and danger in the nation's urban areas. The committee's ultimate verdict would be that the United States must either "coordinate or become submerged."[12]

Over the course of four months in 1965, Senator Gruening's subcommittee would hear testimony from political, research, academic, and religious leaders from across the country. The committee saw the population boom as the product of longer life expectancy as well as lower infant mortality rates in the twentieth century. It also noted a wave of legal and societal changes in the mid-1960s that were making family planning more effective as a means of population control. In 1965, the Supreme Court ruled in *Griswold v. Connecticut* that an 1879 statute outlawing contraceptives was unconstitutional because it violated the "right of marital privacy." Similar laws were under challenge in Massachusetts and New York. And in 1965, eighty-one Nobel laureates petitioned Pope Paul VI to revisit the Catholic church's opposition to contraceptives.[13]

In many ways, the subcommittee debate reflected the conservationist spirit that had motivated environmental reformers in the first half of the twentieth century. Senator Gruening reminded the committee that the danger of the population explosion to Americans was the fact that, while the United States' own population was growing, it did not match the rapid growth of other nations around the globe. In 1965, the American population growth rate was 1.5 percent. That was lower than the global growth rate of 2 percent and far lower than the 5 percent or more growth rate of the developing world. It was half the growth rate, in fact, of Latin America. But Americans' disproportionate use of global resources especially troubled Gruening. With only 6 percent of the world's population, Americans were consuming half the world's resources. "The average American," Gruening pointed out, "consumes in natural resources as much as do 30 residents of India."[14]

The subcommittee reconvened in early 1966 for a second round of hearings with an even more impressive slate of witnesses, including four Nobel prize winners in both medicine and physics. Gruening also entered into the congressional record a series of *Peanuts* comic strips that he felt were "pertinent" to the topic at hand and articulated the feelings of popular concern over the population issue. "I don't think it's right," Lucy moralistically announced to her brother in one of the strips from June 1959, "to bring new babies into the uncertain world." She was upset by the addition of a new baby in the Brown household because in her opinion, "this is the wrong time." Linus had his own perspective on the population issue, though. "What are you gonna do with all those babies who are lined up waiting to be born?" he demanded. "You just

Figure 6.3 This *Peanuts* strip appeared in the record of the US Senate Subcommittee hearings on the population crisis. Charles Schulz, *Peanuts*, June 5, 1959. © 1959 Peanuts Worldwide LLC.

can't tell them to go away and wait for another thousand years, can you?" he shouted at his sister.[15]

This strip demonstrated the heated moral debate that surrounded the issue of the population explosion. "The [Planned] Parenthood movement is looked on with great suspicion among Negroes," Dr. Alan F. Guttmacher told the *Pittsburgh Courier* in late 1965. "Some think," he continued, "it is an attempt to curtail their population." There were also religious leaders who opposed efforts to manage population growth through birth control or other medical methods. One church leader in Baltimore felt that organizations like Planned Parenthood—which was discussed often in the subcommittee hearings—"encourages immoral behavior and contradicts everything we teach our children in schools, churches, and social institutions." Another religious leader, Archbishop Patrick O'Doyle of Washington, likened the rise of the population control movement to the biblical end times, writing that "surely in the glorious history of this great nation we have found better guides to the 'Great Society' than the four horsemen of artificial birth control, abortion, sterilization, and euthanasia."[16]

Gruening entered two more *Peanuts* strips into the record. The first was a July 8, 1959 strip depicting Charlie Brown and Lucy musing about the housing challenge that the baby boom posed. Charlie Brown drew a comparison between the explosion of new babies in suburbia to the growing piles of consumer disposable goods. "They seem to have a way of accumulating like old magazines," he sighed. Senator Gruening and the others certainly believed that the accumulation of unchecked numbers of new people could have serious consequences in the coming decades. Ultimately, the subcommittee recommended the passage of S. 1676, which would create an Office of Population Problems and authorize the president to call a White House conference on population in 1967.[17]

The other strip that Senator Gruening included was one that ran in newspapers on June 18, 1959. In this scene, Linus confided to Snoopy his dismay "to find out that your own sister wishes you had never been born." The more he pondered the idea, the more it troubled him and his companion. "Why, the theological implications alone are staggering," he gasped as he stood in a stupor. In his naiveté, Linus was shocked that older sisters did not always appreciate their younger siblings. But for Senator Gruening's purposes, this strip once again articulated the deep uncertainty Americans faced when they considered how their personal family planning fit into a larger global ecosystem. Given the controversial nature of population control, Gruening did not have any clear solutions, but he urged the United States to devote the resources to find them.[18]

Numerous popular books published in the late 1960s focused on the issue of overpopulation and its effects on the global environment. One such book was William and Paul Paddock's 1967 bestseller *Famine—1975!* The Paddocks referred to the population crisis as a runaway locomotive. "The collision is inevitable," they proclaimed. "The famines are inevitable." The Paddock brothers—especially Paul, who was an agronomist—made regular television and radio appearances to warn of the coming catastrophe. But their work would not have near the tremendous impact on popular culture that would come with a 1968 book on the issue of global population growth.[19]

This debate surrounding the dangers of overpopulation reached an entirely new level of intensity and public exposure when a Stanford University biology professor named Paul Ehrlich published his runaway bestseller *The Population Bomb.* As an undergraduate at the University of Pennsylvania, Ehrlich had been profoundly influenced by William Vogt's 1948 book *Road to Survival.* Ehrlich carried Vogt's urgency and spartan solutions into his own book. "The battle to feed humanity is over," he asserted. He reasoned that at the present birth rate, hundreds of millions of people around the world were "going to starve to death." To hope for technological innovations in agriculture that would help food production keep pace was reckless, only delaying the inevitable, he believed. "Sometime between 1970 and 1985," he wrote in a *Washington Post* editorial promoting his book, "the world will undergo vast famines." The only chance to avoid this was to focus resources on global regions that still could be saved through centralized population control measures. The global population had to decrease if humanity was to survive into the twenty-first century, he contended, and that could only happen through a lower birth rate or a higher death rate. "Mankind will breed itself into oblivion," he warned, if drastic means were not adopted immediately. Ehrlich even went so far, the *Los Angeles Times* reported, as to suggest that "birth control may have to be accomplished by making it involuntary and by putting sterilizing agents into staple foods and drinking water." *The Population Bomb* would go through twenty-two printings in its first three years and turned Ehrlich into a leading voice in the emerging environmentalist movement, provoking conversations on human action and resource dependency while also deeply influencing the movement's activist agenda. He would also help found a new organization to take the lead in the population problem: Zero Population Growth, an organization that soon had eighty chapters across the country. "Ehrlich is telling it like it is," wrote the *Washington Post* reviewer of *The Population Bomb*. Environmentalists came to look at the outspoken and quick-witted biologist as the "best champion we ['ve] got."[20]

Like so many pressing public issues before, Schulz made comment on the population crisis. In July 1970, Linus walked into the living room at the Van Pelt home and posed a question to Lucy. "What would happen if there were a beautiful and highly intelligent child up in heaven waiting to be born," Linus asked, "and his or her parents decided that the two children they already had were enough?" Without looking away from the television, Lucy derided her little brother for his "ignorance of theology and medicine." A bit dejected, Linus refused to concede the significance of his inquiry. "I still think it's a good question," he mumbled as he slumped away. As usual, Schulz did not take a definitive stance on the issue, though Linus's line of questioning did suggest that the artist believed the debate over the population crisis was at its heart a moral dilemma. But if a reader were to take Lucy's comment as the authentic expression of Schulz's viewpoint, then the strip became a criticism of Linus's conservative worldview. Readers replied with a wave of letters that interpreted the strip both ways.

There were many critics among those readers who interpreted Linus's question as an expression of Schulz's thought. Linus should instead ponder whether these "beautiful and highly intelligent" children should be born into a world where they are "unable to get food or water or an education because the world was overpopulated," asked one reader. "Overpopulation is a problem," he continued, "and if we don't solve it within the next several decades, it will become a crisis." He made clear that he supported Zero Population Growth and the reader hoped that Schulz would "reconsider your position."[21]

Another reader, Catherine Bodwell Malan, was deeply upset by this strip. "I would have thought such soap opera dramatics were beneath you," she charged. Malan felt that "the world is polluted with people" and wondered whether "some of the lawlessness now prevalent is not partly the result of too many people and a resultant lack of respect for life." She could not understand why Schulz would suggest bringing more children into a world already "filled with hungry, lonely, unwanted children." Malan was "sure that many of these children have the potential to be both beautiful and bright" and felt that "we are shamefully neglecting many of the children already with us." Finally, she believed that "any family which already has two children, has had their 'fair share.'" While she wished that every family could enjoy as many children as they wanted, the reality, in her opinion, was that "they cannot, and intelligent people should recognize and accept this."[22]

Likewise, Dr. Robert D. Meyers, a physician from Maryland, challenged the cartoonist to rethink Linus's position. "I don't question your theology," Meyers began carefully, but "any deep consideration of our nation's air, water, noise, crime, [and] pollution problems can only lead to the conclusion that excess population is the basis of it all." In Meyer's mind, the choice was simple. "If parents of two children *really* love their children," he reasoned, "and want them to have the chance for a life with the qualities I think you espouse—that is the love of God, love of man, love of nature, and love of beauty—then those parents *will not* have that third and fourth child." Meyer encouraged Schulz to find a way to retract Linus's position and inform his millions of readers that "our nation and our civilization have so little time left."[23]

When asked what they had done recently to help the environment in a 1971 survey, one in five Americans responded that they had "decided to limit the size of my family." The cultural shockwave of the *Roe v. Wade* Supreme Court decision would later obscure the fact that family planning and questions of population control had once been understood as environmental issues rather than religious ones.[24]

As it would turn out, Paul Ehrlich had an intellectual counterpart who saw the population crisis in an entirely different light. Julian Simon was a business administration professor in Urbana, Illinois, who had been born the same year as Ehrlich. After an undergraduate degree from Harvard and a stint in the Navy, Simon enrolled in a doctoral program in business economics at the University of Chicago, where economists Milton Friedman and Friedrich A. Hayek were challenging New Deal economics with their free-market thinking. Friedman famously asserted that economic freedom was not just the means to prosperity, but to individual freedom as well. Hayek, on the other hand, warned in his landmark *Road to Serfdom* that because the knowledge of value and demand was fragmented across all the individuals of a society, government control of economic decision-making would always lead to tyranny. These free-market ideas had deeply influenced Simon's thinking about economics. Although Simon had initially agreed with Ehrlich about the population crisis, he came to see population growth in a positive light. More people meant more ideas, better technologies, and more solutions. Humanity would not outstrip its resources because of their own ingenuity. This is why Simon referred to people as the "ultimate resource" in his 1981 book of the same title.[25]

By the close of the 1970s, Simon would put his economic faith to the test by posing a thousand dollar wager to Ehrlich that the price of five industrial metals (chromium, copper, nickel, tin, and tungsten) would decrease over the next decade. Simon was convinced that market competition and new technologies would drive prices down and demonstrate that humanity was not speeding headlong toward global shortages and warfare. As many noted during the era, this wager captured the sharpening divide between conservatism and liberalism in the last quarter of the twentieth century. But it also highlighted a less noticed reality that proponents of environmentalism and the pro-business, free-market economics of the 1970s were engaged in a high-stakes battle over the future of American capitalism.[26]

There were few signs in the early 1970s that businessmen and free-market economists would dominate so much of the policymaking and political culture of the coming decade. Business had struggled since the onset of the Great Depression and New Deal to restore its influence in American politics and convince the voting public, as President Calvin Coolidge had once contended, that "what's good for business is good for America." They waged this fight in a number of different ways, from funding public education programs to funding university business schools to lobbying Congress. Many times in the 1970s, this seemed like a losing battle.[27]

Perhaps the most jarring example of anti-business sentiment in this period came with a series of attacks against the Bank of America in the winter of 1970. The first of these incidents took place in Isla Vista near the University of California at Santa Barbara. There student protesters burned down the local Bank of America branch. To these young people, it was "the representative here of the establishment," according to one protester. The company reached out to the demonstrators and attempted to expand lending to minorities in an attempt to address protesters' concerns. Shortly after the branch reopened, however, it was attacked again. Over the next few years, Bank of America branches across the country were hit by firebombs and pipe bombs numerous times.[28]

American business responded with a tidal wave of programs to educate the American public on the benefits of free-market capitalism. "There is no doubt," said Walt Petravage of the US Chamber of Commerce's Center for Interpreting

Business, "corporate America is concerned with what it perceives as a lack of understanding towards it and the system in which it survives." This national campaign manifested itself in numerous different ways. In 1971, Arizona's Republican Governor Jack Williams signed a bill adding an economics course to the state's high school curriculum. Texas was another state that introduced an economics requirement, but rather than using state appropriations to fund the course it relied on private sponsors such as the Houston Natural Gas Corporation to provide materials and educate instructors in the program.[29]

Charles Schulz would find himself squarely in the middle of corporate America's movement against "economic illiteracy" when he signed on to illustrate a project titled "The American Economic System and Your Part in It." The initiative, sponsored by a $239,000 grant from the Commerce Department and directed by the Ad Council, had begun with an extensive national survey testing the American public's understanding of the economy. The "National Survey on the American Economic System" was conducted by the research department of the Compton Advertising company, which had long handled the advertising for Proctor and Gambles' biggest packaged-goods brands. This survey had been the direct result of a few catalysts. First, entrepreneurial organizations and business leaders across the country as well as federal officials had contacted the Ad Council's Board of Directors requesting a "public service communications campaign to create a better understanding of the 'American economic system.'" Second, a series of conferences on inflation hosted by the Ford administration in the fall of 1974 had made the economy a top public issue. This was certainly proven by public opinion polls, which showed that by August 1974 a plurality of Americans believed the economy was headed for another depression. While 53 percent of Americans had "some" confidence in American business to help deal with the sagging economy and inflation, 38 percent had no confidence at all. Third, the Ad Council believed that public understanding of the economy would be a "critical factor in the development of effective responses to the challenges posed by persistent inflation and recessionary prospects, both aggravated by rising energy costs." Finally, Secretary of Commerce Elliot L. Richardson specifically requested the Ad Council's involvement in a public campaign in October 1974. The survey, conducted in late 1974, collected some 3,000 field interviews and was published in the spring of 1975. The interview sample included Americans of various sexes, races, ages, incomes, education levels, religious affiliations, political ideologies, partisan affiliations, and levels of political activism. It also included "sufficient numbers of businessmen, 'thought leaders,' clergymen, educators and students" in the data set.[30]

The survey found that many Americans understood the US economic system in personal terms "rather than the language of economics." In describing what was unique about their economy, four out of ten expressed it in individual terms: "Anyone is free to choose or change his job, free to start a business, free to improve his condition by his own initiative." Quite troubling for the businessmen leading this campaign, only 9 percent of those surveyed cited "free enterprise, free economy, or private enterprise" when asked "what is good about the system." Conversely, when asked what was wrong with the economy, a quarter of respondents replied that big business enjoyed political and tax advantages or acted in its own self-interest to falsely restrict supply and drive up prices. One-fifth of those surveyed felt that the economy was "bad, not working, unstable or chaotic." About half of respondents agreed that the American economic system required "more than minimal changes." When asked how the problems of the American economic system should be addressed, 56 percent replied that it would require greater government regulation of things like big business, prices, wages, inflation, and foreign trade. When asked to describe the roles of various actors in the American economy, the general public best understood the role of advertising (two-thirds of respondents could accurately describe it) and least understood the role of the consumer (only 12 percent could give an accurate description of how consumers functioned to stimulate the economy). Yet while they struggled to identify the role of the consumer, two-thirds described themselves exclusively as consumers or "spenders of money." Thus, the survey found that the average American by the mid-1970s was feeling increasingly detached from the larger economy. "Although Americans value the fundamental system for the personal freedoms and potential for personal growth they see in it," the pollsters reported, "their description of their role in the system has a passive character."[31]

In response to the report's findings that "economic understanding of the American public is incomplete and fragmentary," the Ad Council embarked on its "biggest effort in [their] 34-year-history." The Council estimated it would need to spend up to $3.3 million over the first three years of the project, not including the additional funds donated by supporting business firms. The campaign was intended to run into the 1980s and would feature 35 million dollars' worth of free commercial advertising time on all the major networks, which would then direct viewers to write in for the centerpiece of the project: a 24-page booklet titled "The American Economic System and Your Part in It." This is where Charles Schulz came in. At the request of the Ad Council, Schulz provided both original artwork and previously published *Peanuts* strips to illustrate the booklet. He did this without any compensation—"as a public service," the pamphlet said.[32]

Beneath the pamphlet foreword, the artist drew an elaborate scene of Charlie Brown, Linus, and Snoopy (as the flying ace) marching beneath a set of Revolutionary-era flags. Linus wore a bandage around his head, as though he had been wounded in a battle. The three carried musical instruments to play as they marched their small military-style parade. The image set a patriotic tone for the pamphlet to follow, suggesting that American patriots would support the American capitalist system. Many of the other illustrations in the booklet were simply panels that added simple transitions to the layout: "There are a lot of things I don't understand," or "question number one." At the beginning of the section describing the various individual roles within a capitalist economy, Schulz included a group portrait of all the *Peanuts* characters, including Franklin, Snoopy, and Woodstock to emphasize the importance of each member of the group relying on the others for success. The pamphlet only included one full-length strip, a scene of Snoopy rushing over to aid Woodstock in a heavy snow. "Poor Woodstock doesn't know how to take care of himself in emergencies," the dog worried. "He's probably snowed under or frozen stiff." When Snoopy finally made it through the snow drift to Woodstock's nest, however, he found that the little yellow bird had built himself an igloo and had a fire going to keep warm. Within the context of the booklet, which had challenged readers to ask themselves whether a proposed program was "a proper one for government" and whether it could "be done better by the private sector," this strip seemed to minimize the need for a strong, activist federal government and endorse the skills and resourcefulness of the individual. Schulz's artwork in the pamphlet set a patriotic tone that championed the power of the individual and his or her role in the larger economy.[33]

"The American Economic System and Your Part in It" had its critics. Educators questioned how effective such campaigns could be. "Unless you have a captive audience," said Nobel Prize-winning economist Paul Samuelson, "these programs tend to speak to the converted. They have no cutting edge toward people on the margin." Others charged that the pamphlet was "simplistic and boring." Some challenged whether the pamphlet was as nonpartisan as the Ad Council claimed. Several groups demanded equal broadcast time from the networks because they argued that the Ad Council campaign was a violation of the Federal Communications Commission's (FCC) "fairness doctrine." Both ABC and CBS were reluctant to run the television advertisements. CBS even required the Ad Council to revise its television spots to remove the endorsement of the pamphlet. It contended that "the

American economic system is a topic about which there is debate and that the booklet offer would therefore require the network to grant time under the fairness provisions" of the FCC. The Public Media Center in San Francisco developed its own campaign called "Americans for a Working Economy" to offer ideas for equitable reforms to help the disadvantaged in the American economy. "The campaign is a sham," protested the center's director, Roger Hickey. "It represents the corporate interest, not the public interest." The Public Media Center went even further to petition the FCC to revise its regulations for public service announcements to disqualify the Ad Council because of its "inherent corporate-industry bias." Ultimately, CBS and ABC pulled the television ads for fear of political backlash and demands for equal airtime for opposing views. ABC, in particular, decided that the advertisements "would violate an internal policy we have had which prohibits offering time in the form of public service announcements or commercials for the discussion of controversial issues of importance which we think are more appropriately discussed in news or public affairs programs." Conversely, NBC—after an initial delay—joined over 400 newspapers and 500 radio stations from across the country and ran the pamphlet advertisements.[34]

Another group attracted a wave of media attention for its opposition to the Ad Council's economics campaign. The People's Bicentennial Commission (PBC), led by the young left-leaning economist Jeremy Rifkin, who had been deeply involved in Vietnam War protests, published its own opposing materials that did not reflect such a capitalist bias. "The Ad Council campaign is a direct attempt to propagandize their point of view," Rifkin believed. Like many who challenged the consequences of capitalist affluence, Rifkin wondered why the Ad Council's booklet ignored the negative effects of an economic system based on the continual pursuit of higher profits. "Nowhere do they raise the issues of pollution," he complained, "or the flight of capital. Nowhere do they discuss corporate policies that adversely affect the health and safety of workers." As PBC co-director Ted Howard put it, the Ad Council campaign was "advocacy by omission."[35]

Ad Council Vice President Lewis Shollenberger did his best to reassure the public that the pamphlet was unbiased. He asserted that the material had received the approval of both the council's internal policy-review committee and several government agencies. "We have done our level best to be neutral," Shollenberger claimed. "We believe we're representing the facts as they are." Another Council official stated that, "We have no philosophy." The only criteria they considered was "only whether free advertising is in the public interest." The Council's President Robert P. Keim agreed. "We're not talking advocacy or Marxism versus capitalism in this campaign," he asserted.

Going even further, he emphasized that "the word 'capitalism' I don't think even appears in [the booklet] and we're not even calling it 'the free enterprise system.'" Keim, however, showed his hand in this final statement by revealing that while he and his organization might think of the economy as a "free enterprise system," they had opted not to use such language. Talk of laissez faire economics still had strong connections to the pro-business 1920s that many Americans felt had shipwrecked the economy in the Great Depression. Since then the federal government had embraced a much more managed economy with social safety net programs like Social Security and Medicare. Even in the mid-1970s, free-market thought, while rising in esteem, was still not mainstream economic understanding. The businessmen of the Ad Council thus avoided such obvious markers of a partisan position. Campaign chairman and advertising executive Barton A. Cummings perhaps best explained the Council's goal when he said, "We think the product (the American economic system) is so good, all we have to do is get the people to understand it." The campaign would not "advocate capitalism" or be a "hip-hip-hooray for American business," he insisted.[36]

Whether the Council used the buzzwords or not, Rifkin was right in his assertion that "The American Economic System and Your Part In It" was a brochure promoting free-market capitalism. The *New York Times* certainly had no doubts that this was a campaign to educate Americans on the merits of "the free enterprise system." *Times* columnist Louis M. Kohlmeier wrote that "America's giant corporations, which have long advertised their products, have begun advertising their economic viewpoint."[37]

The Ad Council's was just one of many pro-business campaigns that experienced public backlash in the 1970s. In 1976, many US oil companies were fighting their own battle to redeem their industry's image in the midst of the oil crisis. Mobil Oil Corporation, for example, was spending $13 million on its own education program. The response from critics was sharp and direct. One activist collaborative, the Energy Action Committee, charged that Mobil Oil was presenting "a one-sided and misleading, if not fraudulent" perspective. Mobil also tried more subtle ways of improving its corporate brand, such as sponsoring respected public broadcast programs. The nation's largest collective labor union, the American Federation of Labor-Congress of Industrial Organizations, charged that corporations were abusing public television for commercial purposes. The union was "highly concerned that this thing will grow insidiously." Randall Meyer, president of the Exxon Company U.S.A., worried that the magnitude of protest represented a more fundamental shift in American economic understanding. He warned his fellow business leaders about the "growing volume of criticism equating bigness in business with badness." The *New York Times* recognized the tricky public climate in which business found itself in the 1970s. "Now the harder business tries to sell itself and its point of view," wrote columnist Louis M. Kohlmeier, "the more controversial the effort becomes."[38]

Nonetheless, "The American Economic System and Your Part in It" was largely a success. By late 1976 the Ad Council had received over 1 million requests for the pamphlet and officials were planning a second printing of 1 million additional copies. Many media commentators attributed a large portion of the success to the addition of Schulz's cartoons to the pamphlet. In June 1976, Schulz would even be awarded a special medal from Secretary of Commerce Elliot L. Richardson for "outstanding contributions to public understanding of the American economy." He was presented with the honor during a ceremony at the Bank of America building in San Francisco. Secretary Richardson told the media and dignitaries present that the cartoonist's illustrations "went a long way in brightening up the presentation of what is often termed the dismal science of economics." Schulz also received a letter from President Gerald Ford commending him for his "most effective public service contribution" to the project. "Because of this contribution," Ford continued, "the interests and needs of many Americans concerned with increased economic education will be particularly well served."[39]

This pro-capitalist pamphlet might have been the most publicly scrutinized project Schulz had ever participated in. Still, such a project revealed some of Schulz's own feelings about the government's role in both the economy and the environment. It also revealed his belief in "personal responsibility" in the economy, a principle that was becoming the core message of corporate America on pollution and a principle that Schulz would incorporate into his most important environmental works.

If Schulz's environmental ethos was informed by his capitalist sensibilities, it was also informed by his Christian faith. In Schulz's faith community, evangelical leaders were also talking about the Christian's role in caring for the environment. One such leader was an independent-minded Presbyterian missionary in Switzerland named Francis Schaeffer. Although Schaeffer would later be known among young evangelicals for his 1976 book *How Should We Then Live?*, which focused on the practical application of orthodox theology, in the early 1970s he was interested in the environmental crisis. Schaeffer's *Pollution and the Death of Man* (1970) was a call for a Christian ecological ethos. Following the lead of Rachel Carson, Schaeffer began with the example of the devastating effects of DDT and warned that humanity was in danger of losing the habitable world. Yet where Carson pled for public activism and government regulation, Schaeffer called Christians to spiritual repentance. "The distressing thing about this is that orthodox Christians often really have had no better sense about these things than unbelievers," he wrote in the pamphlet. Those who had been entrusted in the Bible to be caretakers of the earth, Schaeffer believed, had become derelict in their duties, blinded by mass consumption. "The death of 'joy' in nature," he diagnosed, "is leading to the death of nature itself." While Schaeffer wrote in explicitly religious terms, he certainly echoed the sentiments of the conservationists who had tried for much of the century to encourage environmental concern among their countrymen by preserving and celebrating the aesthetic beauty and "joy" of nature.[40]

Schaeffer was not alone among evangelicals calling for Christians to see spiritual calling in the looming disasters of overpopulation and environmental degradation. The bestselling nonfiction book of the 1970s was Hal Lindsey's *The Late Great Planet Earth*, which connected the Bible's apocalyptic prophecies to Cold War geopolitics, pointing to the rise of the U.S.S.R. and China and the turmoil in the Middle East over an Israeli state as markers of the end of times. Lindsey believed that all of these developments and the declining state of the global environment would culminate in the second coming of Jesus in 1988. By 1979, Lindsey's book was adapted as a popular film narrated by Orson Welles. The movie poster for the film showed Earth set ablaze, alone in the blackness of space. Historian Matthew Avery Sutton has argued that the mass appeal of *The Late Great Planet Earth* reflected the way that the many environmental concerns, from ecological disaster to overpopulation and nuclear proliferation, "all made apocalyptic evangelicalism palatable to the broader American public." But if evangelical pre-millennialism was influencing American culture, the growing environmental movement was also influencing American religion. Schulz's engagement with the Nixon and Carter administrations' environmental programs was just one example of a persistent evangelical environmental ethos that existed in the 1970s.[41]

Environmental degradation worried many Americans. In 1971, the Nixon White House found that a majority of them wanted to see the federal government increase spending on projects that would "enhance and restore our environment." Sixty-three percent of respondents believed this to be a "very important" issue. This sentiment ran high throughout most of the 1970s. The numbers were quite similar whether Americans were asked about the federal or state government's role. In fact, 70 percent of Americans felt that "a healthy physical environment" would be a "major contributor" to whether or not the United States would remain "great" over the next decade.[42]

While environmental issues had been present in Schulz's work in various ways, they had often been secondary to making a joke or developing a character. The environment would take center stage, however, when Schulz and his television production team of Lee Mendelson and Bill Melendez began brainstorming about a new *Peanuts* television special for 1976. Though Schulz would joke in a 1977 interview that he had only chosen the topic because he had run out of holidays, *It's Arbor Day, Charlie Brown* fit well with previous environmental concerns addressed in Schulz's work.[43]

The Arbor Day special focused on educating families about conservation and providing them with some ideas for getting involved in tree and forest conservation in local communities. The episode began when Sally Brown was unable to correctly define Arbor Day for her class. She was quite confident that it was the day "when all the ships come sailing into *arbor*," to which her classmates erupted in laughter. To address the child's misunderstanding, the teacher assigned Sally to write a report on Arbor Day. With a little help from her love interest Linus (unrequited, like most love in *Peanuts*), Sally discovered everything she needed to know about the history of the holiday at the local library. The first Arbor Day was celebrated on April 10, 1872 in Nebraska and was the product of the efforts of J. Sterling Morton, later Secretary of Agriculture under President Grover Cleveland. The "main idea of Arbor Day," she found, was "conservation." It was intended as a holiday to demonstrate "to both children and adults the need to maintain and protect certain areas of our natural forests and woodlands." Arbor Day, she learned, was a day to celebrate and enrich green spaces.[44]

"Other holidays repose upon the past," Sally quoted J. Sterling Morton, but "Arbor Day proposes for the future." *Peanuts* here was promoting a vision of a more responsible, more considerate, future-oriented consumer ethos to combat the narcissistic culture of instant gratification during the "Me" decade. This was the same critique Schulz had made about throw-away society twenty years earlier, only the idea had come to be connected to a larger national movement.[45]

Sally's research led her to action, another theme developed in this television special. "Every child can plant an orchard!" she bellowed with the conviction of a revolutionary. And like any young revolutionary, she was not content to go about her crusade alone. "Let us fly to the field to cultivate a few forest trees!" Sally charged her friends to take shovel and rake and join her green mission. Linus, Snoopy, and Woodstock all dutifully followed. But she also persuade the often skeptical Lucy to join her project and, in regular Lucy fashion, she was soon barking out orders to the rest of the children.[46]

To these newly awakened environmentalists, prior possession meant little in their crusade to make their town greener. They went straight to work on Charlie Brown's baseball field—without his knowledge, of course—planting trees, bushes, vines, flowers, and vegetables. As Lucy wrested leadership of the project from Sally's control, the world champion fussbudget demonstrated an almost religious zeal. "There is beauty in a well ordered orchard, which is a joy forever," she said, another quote from J. Sterling Morton on the first Arbor Day celebration that took on the tone of an Old Testament proverb. "Orchards are missionaries of culture and refinement," she pronounced, wedding Schulz's typical Christian rhetoric with the Bible's call to be a responsible caretaker for the earth. In Schulz's worldview, this type of conservation and community green activism should be the Christian, middle-class, suburban environmental ethic.

Of course, Charlie Brown was not too happy about the state of his field when he arrived for opening day of the neighborhood baseball season. When Lucy had assured him that she would take care of "sprucing up" the field, he had hardly imagined he would find an actual tree in the middle of his pitcher's mound. While Sally tried to explain to her panicking brother that the cultivated field was part of their Arbor Day celebration, Lucy bluntly reminded him that his baseball team had never been good anyway so he had not lost anything.

When Peppermint Patty and her team arrived for the game, she could hardly believe her eyes. Charlie Brown's "victory garden" had "everything here but sheep and cattle." Nonetheless, she would not miss an opportunity to crush an opponent in sports and decided to make the best of the situation. As the game proceeded, it quickly became clear that nature did not play a passive role in this story. Peppermint Patty struggled to strike batters out as she normally would because she kept getting hung up on the tree in the middle of the pitcher's mound. Similarly, when Snoopy hit one deep into the outfield he failed to make it to first base because the vine at the backstop, which he had earlier mishandled, reached out and tripped him. The flowers in the outfield distracted Lucy and Frieda from doing their jobs, while Peppermint Patty was unable to get on base because she could not find it underneath all the vegetation.[47]

By the end of the game, even the trees were making catches for Charlie Brown's team. After a chaotic eight and a half innings, the little boy who had never won a baseball game found himself one out away from winning the season opener. Though he had initially been horrified at the sight of an orchard on his baseball field, nature had given Charlie Brown a gift.[48]

Just as quickly as nature gave, nature took away. As Charlie Brown wound up to throw his final pitches and finish the game, a sudden storm flooded the field and ended the game short of victory. All the children but Charlie Brown scrambled for cover, leaving him standing there in sopping disbelief. The game's outcome left it unclear whether nature in *Peanuts* was to be interpreted as a positive force to be cultivated or a negative force to be feared. What was clear was that the environment in *Peanuts* was quite capable of caring for itself, as evidenced by Sally's consolation to her defeated brother: "At least it's good for the crops, Charlie Brown."[49]

As powerful, independent, and awe-inspiring as nature could be in *Peanuts*, there was a human message pervading *It's Arbor Day, Charlie Brown*. Quoting J. Sterling Morton a final time in her report to the class, Sally said that "every man, woman, and child who plants trees shall be able to say . . . 'If you seek my monument, look around you.' " Schulz's concept of environmentalism was one that still placed human beings and their needs and desires at the center of the narrative. While Sally's and Lucy's did conflict with Charlie Brown's interests, the children's horticultural endeavor did not seek to radically change or replace the existing capitalist systems that produced unprecedented levels of waste and pollution. Instead, Schulz advocated reasonable modifications to the consumer ethos, calling Americans to be more conscientious in their consumption and to balance progress with ordered green spaces. This centrist environmental message was well-received by Schulz's audience, critics, and activists. *It's Arbor Day, Charlie Brown* surprised even the artist, earning an Emmy nomination and winning the Arbor Day Award from the national Arbor Day Foundation.[50]

Newspapers across the country, from Atlanta to Los Angeles, promoted this latest Charlie Brown television special. It seemed an odd addition to the canon of *Peanuts* holiday specials, even to the artist himself. By the mid-1970s, Schulz and his producers had "covered practically every season and holiday." In his mind, Arbor Day was the bottom of the idea barrel. Sterling himself could hardly have imagined a more perfect moment for the 100th anniversary of his holiday than the 1970s, when people had been struck with concern over the human influence on the environment.[51]

In many ways, Schulz's *It's Arbor Day, Charlie Brown* reflected a major thrust of the Earth Day movement with its central theme of educating Sally about the history and importance of environmental action. While Earth Day 1970 connected old-school conservationists, ecologists, suburban housewives, and student activists with the institutional power of federal government through leaders like Senator Gaylord Nelson, perhaps its greatest achievement was a national grade school environmental education effort that created what historian Adam Rome has called "the first green generation." This approach to improving the future by educating school children was present as well when Schulz lent his talents to a national clean air project in the late 1970s.[52]

"Charlie Brown has become concerned," Schulz wrote in his script proposal to the American Lung Association in 1979. The concern that troubled America's most famous worrier was the declining state of the environment. At stake in this mounting crisis, Schulz asserted, was the prospect of a "better world for ourselves, our children and the future generations of our nation." The cartoonist insisted that he had "long been committed to doing what I can to help preserve our environment." But this level of direct social engagement was a new development for Schulz, who had been clear about Charlie Brown's philosophy for dealing with problems back in the 1950s: "You've just got to let things go along, ride them out and see how they turn out in the end." There was no sense in "swinging left and right and trying to solve all your problems in one day." Schulz had called this his "policy of moderation." But such a policy would no longer do. Charlie Brown and the American people could not sit by idle in the face of looming environmental catastrophe. "Concern leads to action," Schulz espoused.[53]

Schulz was writing as the new honorary Chairman of the American Lung Association's Christmas Seals Campaign. The annual program solicited artwork from kindergarteners through third graders from across the United States to adorn the organization's fifty-four commemorative Christmas seals—one for each state, plus the District of Columbia, Guam, Puerto Rico, and the Virgin Islands—decorative stamps sold to raise money for medical research. Each year, the American Lung Association reported, more than 60 million American households purchased sheets of seals. Schulz was a logical choice to be the face of the program since he had spent his career drawing children.[54]

Schulz would not, however, just be a figurehead. The American Lung Association also asked him to produce a short film to be shown in schools and community centers across the country about the role individuals had to play in combating air pollution, a leading cause of lung disease. In 1979, the Environmental Protection Agency (EPA) would find that lung disease caused by air pollution was costing Americans $1.3 billion each year. Furthermore,

Figure 6.4 During the 1970s, Schulz partnered with the Department of the Interior and Tennessee Valley Authority to promote an anti-litter campaign called Johnny Horizon for school-aged children. Courtesy of the Charles M. Schulz Museum and Research Center.

though air quality had generally improved across the country thanks to clean air regulations passed during the Johnson and Nixon administrations, by 1978 the EPA found that most Americans still lived in areas of elevated levels of carbon dioxide, sulphur monoxide, nitrogen dioxide, smog, and other air pollutants. The EPA, whose research and grants had raised awareness of environmental concerns considerably in the 1970s, would also be funding the *Peanuts* short film.[55]

"Our film alone is not the solution," Schulz admitted, "to the problem of air pollution and a totally improved environment." He did feel, though, that it was "a special way of involving young minds in seeing, understanding and taking upon themselves a sense of direct self-concern and self-responsibility for their environment." Schulz clearly articulated a message of personal responsibility for both environmental degradation and cleanup directed to young people.[56]

The storyboards for "Charlie Brown Clears the Air" were intended to pitch the message, major scenes, and dialogue to the folks at the American Lung Association. The credits to open the story pictured Pigpen, the messy *Peanuts* child who was always "covered in [the environment]," carrying a picket sign that read "Fight pollution!" (Since his introduction in 1954, Pigpen's presence in *Peanuts* had suggested some deeper connection between class and pollution that clearly unsettled the other characters.) From the beginning of the story, the message was not only that individuals should take personal responsibility for both the degradation and care of the environment. It was also a call to battle. The environmental problems facing Americans could not be overcome by simply modifying personal behaviors. Individuals would need to change the very culture of their communities.[57]

As the actual story began, the American Heart Association's executives found Charlie Brown, Linus, and Snoopy on a walk. Snoopy was in a particularly bad mood, essentially attacking Linus when he made a critical observation about dogs. Linus turns to the dog's owner to find out why Snoopy was not acting like himself. The cat owner next door, Charlie Brown explained, "keeps burning his leaves and trash in the backyard." But Linus did not understand the correlation. "It's causing soot and dirt all over Snoopy's house," Charlie Brown elaborated. Just then, the three arrived in front of the dog house. The typically vibrant red paint was layered with dark gray grime so thick Snoopy could barely wipe any away with his paw. Overhead hung a black cloud of soot emanating from the neighbor's backyard. Seeing Snoopy weeping against his filthy dog house, Linus finally understood. "Why don't you do something about it," he asked Charlie Brown, assuming the boy's personal responsibility for correcting the problem.[58]

The air pollution in this case was really the result of two different processes. First, the neighbor burned leaves because he viewed his environment through a widely shared suburban environmental ethic, valuing nature for its aesthetic beauty but intolerant of nuisances such as crabgrass, autumn leaves, or insects deemed hindrances to a fulfilling suburban life. Second, the neighbor burned trash that was the byproduct of the enormous consumer revolution that surged through post–World War II American life. Thus, the film implicitly suggested that air pollution was the product of both individual consumption and corporate production.[59]

Charlie Brown assured Linus that he had confronted his neighbor to say that "trash burning helps to pollute the air." The neighbor had replied, however, that "as soon as Snoopy tunes up his motorcycle, he'll stop burning brush." Immediately, Snoopy came tearing by on motorcycle, leaving a thick cloud in his wake. This exchange between Charlie Brown and his neighbor got to the real heart of Schulz's message. Air pollution was really a product of Americans shirking their own responsibility for their environment. Pollution was, then, ultimately a social problem more than even a scientific, political, corporate or cultural problem. Thus it required personal, not regulatory, solutions. This message would have been favorable both to Middle Americans, who already placed an enormous emphasis on individuality, and pro-business advocates who felt their interests were best served by modifying the status quo rather than drastically reforming a system through government activism.[60]

In the next scene, Charlie Brown and his friends play an afternoon baseball game. Above them, a dark smog cloud that never appeared in the regular *Peanuts* comic strip loomed as the children struggled to capture their first win in 900 games. Going into the ninth inning, they were leading by a single run, thanks to a home run from Snoopy. But as Charlie Brown tried his best to get the final strikeouts the team needed, the batter slammed a pop fly into the outfield. Linus, normally sure handed, rushed to make the catch but stumbled and slipped on the litter that cluttered the children's baseball lot. The scene of smog and litter bore a stark contrast to the typical pristine settings of the *Peanuts* suburb. On the very next pitch, another fly ball careened over Lucy's head because she could not see it through the smog. At this point, Charlie Brown's team mutinied. "I quit!" Lucy shouted between coughs, "This pollution is too much. I could get killed out here!" Linus quit, too. "It's no fun out there in all this litter," he complained. Even Snoopy threw down his hat and glove in protest and stormed off. "Now I'm losing games because of pollution," Charlie Brown grumbled in defeat.[61]

The next scene of the film found Charlie Brown sitting at Lucy's psychiatry booth for advice. "I'm depressed about all the polluting and littering," the boy confided. "Why don't you give a report on it at school," Lucy suggested. She then offered him an American Lung Association pamphlet with facts on addressing pollution before charging him 20 cents for her services (she generously threw in the pamphlet for free).[62]

Charlie Brown took the advice and presented his findings to his classmates at school. "Each of us breathes 35 pounds of air each day," more than a person's daily consumption of food or drink, he explained. "And yet we all pollute our air with over 150 million tons of aerial garbage each year," he continued. "That's terrible!" he exclaimed as he showed his audience a slide of cars puffing dark clouds of exhaust. Charlie Brown pointed to a number of causes for the nation's air pollution problem, most of them domestic sources. Cars without emissions regulating devices were a "major cause." Home heaters that were not properly maintained were another. As Snoopy had found, burning leaves and trash or driving untuned vehicles further harmed the air. Only in the last slide did Charlie Brown add that "large factories" could contribute to air pollution. Even then he appealed to the individual's sense of responsibility for the environment, calling on his classmates to "report violations yourself" and depicting an evil scientist with a toxic chemistry set rather than factories with smoke stacks. By charging the public with policing environmental criminals, the federal government could expand its enforcement powers without expanding infrastructure and costs.[63]

After the presentation, Linus was convinced that he must do something. But "what can we do about it," he wondered aloud. Charlie Brown and Snoopy were prepared for this question. Citizens could "report any air pollution violations you see." They could discourage their neighbors from burning leaves or trash. They could maintain their motorized vehicles through regular tune ups or avoid them altogether by utilizing public transportation options. They could even "support programs in your community that fight air pollution."[64]

According to the original storyboards for the film, the closing credits were intended to include a song written by Schulz. The song did not appear in the final video, but it did further reveal Schulz's understanding of environmental ownership. "You can help clean up the air," the song began, "all you have to do is care." Viewers should "fight pollution" and do it for "your health" and "for yourself." The message, once again, was one of individual responsibility.[65]

In demonstrating potential causes of air pollution, Schulz utilized some of the prominent imagery of the early environmentalist movement. One of those images was that of the Native American, a visual that seemed a bit out of place in a *Peanuts* television special. As Charlie Brown talked about the importance of maintaining home heating systems to avoid contributing to air pollution, he directed his audience to an image of a sad-looking Indian character in traditional dress, complete with a feather headdress, standing next to his teepee as black smoke billowed out the top. In the entire short film, this Indian character was the only non-*Peanuts* figure to appear. But in the context of 1970s culture most of the audience would have hardly viewed the character's appearance as disconnected from the program's theme.

Life magazine had announced the "Rediscovery of the Redman" in a 1967 cover story. The article pointed out how certain parts of popular understandings and misconceptions about the Native American past were becoming central to countercultural identity. Native Americans were "being discovered again—by the hippies." "Viewing the dispossessed Indian as America's original dropout, and convinced that he has deeper spiritual values than the rest of society," the article observed, "hippies have taken to wearing his costume and horning in on his customs." *Life* saw the link between the Indian and the hippie particularly in their shared attire (beads, headdresses, and moccasins) and their use of marijuana or hallucinogens like LSD.[66]

Romanticized images of Native Americans quickly became central to the iconography of environmentalism. In 1971, the antilitter organization Keep America Beautiful commissioned a television ad that featured a Native American character standing beside a highway as a passing driver tossed a bag of trash at his feet. "Some people have a deep abiding respect for the natural beauty that was once this country. And some people don't," the narrator announced as the camera zoomed in on a single tear running down the Native American's face. A print version of the ad sponsored by the Advertising Council stated that "People start pollution. People can stop it." This television commercial and its many iterations in both print and film became one of the most recognized images of environmentalism in the 1970s, winning many advertising awards, including two Clios. According to television scholar Robert Thompson, most Americans who viewed the television ad saw it as a representation of genuine emotions captured on camera. "The tear was such an iconic moment," wrote Thompson, "Once you saw it, it was unforgettable. It was like nothing else on television. As such, it stood out in all the clutter in the early '70s." The Indian in the commercial was, as historian Finis Dunaway has pointed out, "an anachronism who does not belong in the picture" of the modern world. He was the image of a more natural, innocent past mournfully critiquing the present—despite the fact that the actor was actually Sicilian.[67]

On Earth Day 1978, President Jimmy Carter met with the actor at the center of the crying Indian ad campaign, Iron Eyes Cody. Cody addressed the president as the "Great White Chief" and presented him with a handmade eagle feather headdress in a ceremony christened as Keep America Beautiful Day. The three television networks and newspapers from across the country covered the event.[68]

But the story of the crying Indian in the 1970s was more complicated than it seemed at face value. Keep America Beautiful was formed in 1951 by the American Can Company and the Owens-Illinois Glass Company. The organization would later include some of the largest corporate creators of garbage in the world, including Coca-Cola and the Dixie Cup Company. Keep America Beautiful also gained the support of the Advertising Council, the nation's leading public service advertiser and creator of the US Forestry Service's

Smokey Bear campaign that told Americans "Only You Can Prevent Forest Fires." Using the same message of individual responsibility, the Ad Council's campaign for Keep America Beautiful "framed litter as a visual crime against landscape beauty and an affront to citizenship values." According to David F. Beard, a Reynolds Metals Company advertising director and leader in Keep America Beautiful, this was a central part of the campaign's mission. In 1961 he wrote in a public memo that Keep America Beautiful would employ the media in "an accelerated campaign to help to curb the massive defacement of the nation by thoughtless and careless people." "The bad habits of littering," he continued, "can be changed only by making all citizens aware of their responsibilities to keep our places as clean as they do their own homes." The campaign absolved corporations of responsibility for pollution while also earning them good press coverage.[69]

On September 22, 1978, President Jimmy Carter wrote to thank Schulz for agreeing "to let Charlie Brown and his friends work with the Environmental Protection Agency and the American Lung Association on a project to make children and adults more aware of threats to our environment." This issue was, the president wrote, "one of my own great concerns, too." The two men would meet in the Oval Office the following year for a photo-op with some of the child artists who had illustrated the Christmas seals.[70]

The viewpoints represented in "Charlie Brown Clears the Air" certainly reflected popular opinion in the 1970s. In one 1971 survey, a majority of respondents claimed to have helped "protect" the environment by recycling used bottles. Another third claimed to have had their "automobile tuned up to reduce exhaust emissions." About 13 percent had either campaigned or voted for a political candidate who "supports the environment." Virtually every example respondents provided flowed out of a sense of personal responsibility for pollution. In fact, only 5 percent of respondents admitted to having "informed authorities of environmental violations." Early in the 1970s, corporate messages of individual responsibility for environmental protection had clearly taken a firm hold in popular understandings of the problem. While most Americans felt that the environment was in serious need of protection, they consistently opposed any new legislation that would either tax poor environmental behavior or prohibit manufacturers from selling products that were harmful for the environment, like large, gas-guzzling automobiles. They would, however, tolerate paying more in their consumer purchases to help companies cover the costs of raising corporate environmental standards. Thus, Americans believed that they had a personal responsibility in helping protect the environment but they wanted to exercise that responsibility voluntarily.[71]

Figure 6.5 Charles Schulz met President Jimmy Carter at the White House in 1979. Courtesy of the Charles M. Schulz Museum and Research Center.

When Americans were asked what the most serious environmental problem facing the country was, large majorities did point a finger at water and air pollution by plants and factories. But two-thirds also pointed to "litter of streets, parks, highways and countryside by careless people," and nearly half cited auto exhaust as a serious contributor to air pollution as well. Even more telling, when asked whether industrial pollution was a serious issue in their own local community, an overwhelming majority of respondents believed it was "practically no problem" at all. At the same time, more than a third saw consumer litter as a "major problem" in their local community. These survey results reveal that industrial waste was a more abstract problem in the minds of citizens while issues of litter or automobile smog were much more tangible, a fact that bolstered the personal responsibility argument. By January 1977, Americans tended to associate "big business" with job creation and helping "the nation and communities in which it operates to grow." Only 3 percent associated big business with polluting the environment.[72]

Perhaps the clearest instance of *Peanuts*' pro-capitalist environmental ethos came during the era's great energy crisis. In 1973, the Organization of Petroleum Exporting Countries (OPEC) declared an oil embargo on the United States in retaliation for its support of Israel in the Six Days War (1967) and the Yom Kippur War (1973). That fall, the Nixon administration tried to address the mounting oil shortage by encouraging voluntary consumption reductions, calling "for a full-scale effort to conserve energy" and warning that "we may face fuel shortages for the next few years." In a public presentation in early October, President Nixon tried to persuade Americans that reducing their energy consumption was in their economic interest. A family could save $74 a year, he asserted, by eliminating one trip for errands a week. The national savings would be about 2.9 billion gallons of oil or nearly 3 percent of yearly consumption. Likewise, families could save as much as $55 dollars by lowering their thermostats four degrees, Nixon suggested. Nationally, this change in consumption would cover the projected shortage of 400,000 barrels per day. These savings would only amount to about 1 percent of the average annual income a family in 1973 needed to maintain an "intermediate standard of living." But there were far more savings incentives outlined in the 62-page pamphlet the president promoted, "Citizen Action Guide to Energy Conservation," a resource prepared by the Citizen's Advisory Committee on Environmental Quality.[73]

The slogan for this energy saving campaign was "SavEnergy," and the mascot for the program was none other than Snoopy. The administration planned to print decals that featured him relaxing atop his doghouse, saying in his thought bubble, "I believe in conserving energy!" The decals would be distributed by local electric utilities to families that pledged to participate in the program and wanted to advertise their patriotic duty.[74]

The "Citizen Action Guide to Energy Conservation" that accompanied this program carried a similar theme to other public-private environmental collaborative programs: individual responsibility. "The White House points an accusing finger at Mr. and Mrs. America," reported the *New York Times*. It seemed to blame citizens for the pressures of the energy crisis without also considering corporate misconduct or foreign policy missteps. Americans, instead, needed to take personal responsibility by driving less, tempering their electric appliance purchases, never running the dishwasher or clothes dryer half-full, and cleaning their ovens by hand rather than relying on "self-cleaning" features.[75]

Still, the program did do some things to address concerns about government and corporate energy consumption as well. Federal agencies were under a mandate to cut energy consumption by 7 percent. Meanwhile, the Department of Commerce began work on a campaign to advise private corporations on the economic benefits of "reduced illumination, recycling wastes, [and] switching operations to off peak hours." Once again, environmental concerns were pitched to Americans as an issue of economics: wiser consumer habits, responsible uses of tax revenues, and more efficient corporate capitalism. Thus, environmentalism as a political initiative was conceived of as a capitalist reform, as an attempt to revitalize an aging system that had become bloated and stagnant three decades into the Cold War. *Peanuts*, of course, did not lead this reform or drastically transform it. It did, however, reflect the overlap of the environmental crisis and the crisis of capitalism in

Figure 6.6 By the 1970s, Snoopy was becoming an increasingly popular face of federal advertising initiatives to encourage personal responsibility concerning environmental issues, such as in this 1971 partnership with the Department of Agriculture. Courtesy of the Charles M. Schulz Museum and Research Center.

the 1970s. These two national concerns were not isolated and in some ways not even antagonistic to one another. They were, instead, part of a larger rethinking of the limits of postwar American affluence in the later decades of the twentieth century. And in a number of cases, *Peanuts* became the public face of this revitalization effort.[76]

The voluntary program was just one part of the Nixon administration's much larger plan for dealing with the energy crisis. The administration also announced a mandatory plan to allocate heating oil and jet fuel within industries. The rule would require refiners and wholesalers to disperse future reductions proportionately among their clientele, while the administration reserved the right to reallocate 10 percent of the national supply between regions to address shortages. The president also appealed to Congress for $115 million for alternative fuel techniques, raising federal research funds for energy to nearly $1 billion.[77]

There was sufficient evidence that President Nixon was personally a *Peanuts* fan. In October 1970, Nixon had written to Schulz's film producer, Lee Mendelson, to thank him for sending a copy of a special twentieth anniversary collection *Charlie Brown and Charlie Schulz*. "It seems that most of the members of the White House staff are also avid *Peanuts* fans," Nixon wrote to Mendelson. It was so popular in the Nixon White House, in fact, that he joked that "the book will probably have to be put on a 'lending library' basis." Nixon himself had "only had a chance to glance through the pages" because some other staffer would carry it off for reading and sharing. But Nixon's appreciation for *Peanuts* likely had little to do with why Snoopy was chosen as the face of this important energy conservation initiative. Just like having Merle Haggard and Johnny Cash play at the White House, shooting a photo-op with Elvis Presley, or inviting prominent evangelical ministers to preach chapel services he rarely attended, Nixon was most interested in public perception, not personal taste. Nixon had revealed the real reason that Snoopy appealed to him in his 1970 letter to Lee Mendelson: the strip's "enduring and international popularity." Schulz's mass appeal once again enabled his work to engage in important national policy issues, revealing the deep ties between the environmental and pro-business movements.[78]

7

"I Have a Vision, Charlie Brown"

Gender Roles, Abortion Rights, Sex Education, and *Peanuts* in the Age of the Women's Movement

"Why is Lucy so mean?" Mary Harrington Hall asked Schulz in a 1967 interview for *Psychology Today*. Schulz had thought a lot about his feelings on Lucy. "She is mean first because it is funny," he quickly replied, "and because it just follows the standard comic-strip pattern—that the supposedly weak people in the world are funny when they dominate the supposedly strong people." As always, Schulz was deliberate in using that term "supposedly," because he did not, in fact, believe that there was anything weak about Lucy at all.[1]

For a cartoonist who often avoided controversy in his public interviews, it is not surprising that Schulz chalked up Lucy's personality to a comic trope. "There is nothing funny about a little boy being mean to a little girl," he told *Psychology Today*. "But there is something funny about a little girl being able to be mean to a little boy." In this sense, *Peanuts* was a sort of vicarious fantasy, disruptive of traditional gender roles and yet nonthreatening since it was only imaginary children. Children thinking the thoughts typically reserved for adults, dogs dancing and fighting imaginary wars of their own, and little girls dominating their male counterparts were all commonplace in *Peanuts*. But Schulz also felt that his portrayal of childhood gender relations was accurate. "It's a true thing," he insisted. "Little girls do dominate little boys of their own age, and if you want to carry it further, the family generally goes in whichever direction the wife wants."[2]

"Do you like women?" Mary Harrington Hall asked Schulz. "Oh, yes," he replied, "I like women very much." Hall then pushed him further on his earlier comments about women directing the family. "Do you think families get run by women because men are kinder people than women are, or because women are raising the children, or what?" she questioned. Schulz then became more uncomfortable wading into the more controversial areas of this topic and returned to the security of his comic strip: "I don't know. I only draw pictures."[3]

Hall wondered if Schulz's wife, Joyce, minded his depictions of Lucy, since people might assume that these were reflections of her demeanor. "Oh, my wife is a very nice person," he assured Hall. In his mind, the issue at hand was not solely a Schulz family issue. It was an issue of societal norms. "I'm afraid that generally women never find the man who is ideal enough in their estimation so that they can continue to be dominated by him and accept his decisions and his leading all the time," he confided to Hall. In other words, Schulz believed that, while many women actually desired traditional gender roles, the realities of modern life fell far short of women's ideals and thus necessitated a more prominent role for women in society. "Plus the mere fact that women are not this much," he began before catching his subtle slide toward male chauvinism, "in fact, not at all inferior." Then, to be sure his point was not lost in his slip, Schulz added, "I think in many ways women are superior to men."[4]

The cartoonist probably was not saying that women were superior to men. Instead, he was articulating a popular trend within post–1960s evangelicalism that historian Bethany Moreton has referred to as "elevating domesticity," which emphasized the value of a woman's domestic roles and encouraged husbands not only to celebrate them but also to participate in them. Moreton has argued that this was a reaction to the perceived "feminization" of American men, especially in the last quarter of the twentieth century as the nation's labor force moved away from blue collar industrial jobs toward white-collar service jobs. Schulz had made this transition earlier than most, leaving the military in World War II to become a professional artist who labored with pen and paper in an office space, drove his children in the school carpool, and took off work early to play golf in the afternoons.[5]

At his heart, Schulz was a traditionalist when it came to gender roles. "It is quite obvious that women would prefer some sort of leading and domination, and when they don't get it, then they have to compensate for it in some way," he said. The prospects for correcting this perceived deficiency were not promising, Schulz said. "In their struggles to try to get their husbands to be stronger, they probably end up making him even worse than ever," he theorized. "This is a self-defeating thing which in most problems of this kind ends up being tragically depressing as the years go on."[6]

For all of Schulz's traditionalism he produced female characters who would push the mid-twentieth-century expectations of female roles. By the 1970s and 1980s, two of his characters, in particular, would become national symbols for the women's rights movement. Along the way, Schulz would wade into some issues of the women's movement like abortion rights and sex education. As was typical of him, Schulz's positions on these topics covered the broad center of the American political spectrum. Where Schulz might endorse traditional family gender roles and question birth control measures in some instances, he also championed gender equality and suggested support for more liberal public sex education programs in other instances. Once again, *Peanuts* voiced the broad range of opinion in Middle America, and his readers from across that spectrum responded passionately to his thoughts and suggestions all along the way.

Females asserted their dominance in *Peanuts* almost immediately. On the second day of the strip, October 3, 1950, a little girl named Patty strolled down the sidewalk reciting a classic nursery rhyme. "Little girls are made of sugar and spice," she chanted as she skipped along, "and everything nice." Just then she passed Charlie Brown and paused just long enough to give him a stiff right hook to the eye. Charlie Brown stood stunned as his eye instantly turned black and swelled shut. "That's what little girls are made of!" Patty continued as she went merrily on her way.

The following week, Patty swiped the boy Shermy's umbrella to shield herself from a sudden downpour. In another early strip, Snoopy strained to pull Shermy in a wagon. As Patty walked by she stopped to pet Snoopy. In the final frame, Shermy had been wrangled into pulling both Snoopy and Patty in the wagon. Patty even became a vocal defender of women. "Your mother is a girl!" she shouted at Shermy, "Your grandmother is a girl! Your wife will be a girl! And all your daughters will be girls, too! So there!" The stunned little boy was left with nothing to reply but, "Wow!" Schulz used another variation of this exchange when Patty silenced Shermy's claim that Washington, Jefferson, and Lincoln proved men's supremacy. "Your mother is a woman," she quickly replied, stopping Shermy in his tracks. Schulz regularly pointed out the absurdity of male chauvinism, as when Charlie Brown quoted statistics like

Figure 7.1 Patty shows Charlie Brown who is in charge on the second day of the new *Peanuts* comic strip. Charles Schulz, *Peanuts*, October 3, 1950. © 1950 Peanuts Worldwide LLC.

"sixty-eight percent of all men in this country are college graduates" and "seventy-four percent of all the men in the world are of an even temperament" to prove that "men are infinitely superior to women." When Patty calmly pressed him for his sources, the boy blushed ashamedly and confessed to making up the whole thing. A battle of the sexes was on in *Peanuts*, and the girls appeared well on the road to winning the war.[7]

Still, the *Peanuts* girls were also susceptible to childhood crushes on the boys. Patty wondered whether Shermy would "still love me when you're grown up and are rich and famous." Readers found that Patty loved Charlie Brown because he had the best comic book collection. Patty also looked to Charlie Brown for affirmations of her physical beauty. On February 2, 1951, Patty complained to Charlie Brown and Shermy that they made her feel unloved because they never fought one another for her attention. Even in their vulnerability, however, the female characters still often maintained an upper hand. In this case, the boys ended up fighting one another to prove their love for Patty. Patty was certainly satisfied: "That was fine . . . I feel much better now!" Schulz mocked chivalric bluster and Patty walked away the victor.[8]

Of course, there were plenty of examples of Schulz playing on more traditional stereotypes of girls as gossips or thorns in the side of the boys or incompetents at boys' war games. Patty cried because she was not born a boy. The girls kept hope chests and dreamed of being married someday. They criticized Charlie Brown's mother for not doing a better washing job on the boy's dingy bed sheet ghost costume. All of these characteristics were typical of popular culture in the 1950s and would have hardly seemed out of place.[9]

Though female domesticity, passivity, and dependence were certainly a dominant paradigm in 1950s America, scholars of the period have found numerous examples of a rising feminism during what was widely characterized as a conservative decade. Films like *Adam's Rib* (1949) and *Pat and Mike* (1952), books like Ashley Montagu's bestselling *The Natural Superiority of Women* (1953) and existentialist Simone de Beauvoir's *The Second Sex* (published in the United States in 1952), and popular television shows like *The Honeymooners* (1951–1955), *The Goldbergs* (1949–1951), and *I Love Lucy* (1951–1957) all "gave expression to the deep anxieties over who would wear the pants in postwar America," according to historian Susan Douglas.[10]

By far the most assertive female of the early *Peanuts* strip was a new character introduced two years in named Lucy Van Pelt. First appearing on March 3, 1952, Lucy was the fifth and youngest *Peanuts* child at the time she appeared. Initially a very naïve character who relied on Charlie Brown to help explain the world, she quickly developed the strongest and most powerful personality

Figure 7.2 Lucy refused to play along with traditional family roles. Charles Schulz, *Peanuts*, July 18, 1952. © 1952 Peanuts Worldwide LLC.

in the comic strip. Where the other characters seemed willing to settle into mock traditional societal roles, Lucy refused to play along.

Lucy's distinctive role in *Peanuts* was perhaps best displayed in a 1954 series where Lucy entered the women's state amateur golf championship with Charlie Brown as her caddie. The girls in *Peanuts* had been largely ineffective and uninterested in sports until Lucy had dazzled Charlie Brown with her golf skills in the spring of 1953. Lucy went off to compete among the adults, a feat that no other *Peanuts* character would ever attempt again. This strip was the only time that Schulz would ever picture adults in his comic strip, an anomaly further highlighting the special role here. Over the month of May 1954, Lucy took center stage in the Sunday strip, stringing together one great shot after another and coming within one hole of winning the state championship when she suddenly remembered that it was past her nap time. All the while Charlie Brown served as her faithful caddie and encourager. Lucy was not yet the self-confident, immovable force that she would become in the strip, but she was already pushing far beyond a typical female role. Unlike other popular female characters in 1950s popular culture—characters like Lucy Ricardo in *I Love Lucy*, one of the decade's most-watched television series—Lucy Van Pelt was not out of her league in the field of competition. In fact, Lucy was more capable than *Peanuts*' male characters in a historically male-dominated arena.[11]

Media descriptions of Lucy were not always flattering. In Schulz's first national interview, published in 1957, journalist Hugh Morrow described her as "the female critic incarnate, the disturber of mental peace." To some male journalists, Lucy's personality rang true with their personal experience with women they deemed too assertive. "Lord knows, we've all known, and maybe even married, a Lucy Van Pelt, a girl who shouts: 'I don't want any downs—I just want ups and ups and ups.'" *Penthouse* magazine called her the "severest critic." The *Los Angeles Times* went so far as to joke that "to know her is to loathe her." For some male journalists, Lucy clearly was coming to symbolize their negative feelings toward assertive females. But at least one commentator actually saw Lucy and *Peanuts* as a witty satire of gender traditionalism in

Figure 7.3 Lucy showed her superior athletic skills in a state amateur golf tournament while Charlie Brown served as her caddie. Charles Schulz, *Peanuts*, May 23, 1954. © 1954 Peanuts Worldwide LLC.

America. "Here's a perfect parody of what American life is supposed to be," said Walt Kelly, creator of another one of the twentieth century's most important comic strips (*Pogo*) and a former lead cartoonist for Walt Disney's studios. "The intellectual male and the domineering female." Whether for criticism or praise, the females in *Peanuts* were drawing considerable attention in the print media of the late 1950s and early 1960s.[12]

Even Schulz himself admitted to having a complicated relationship with Lucy. "Lucy is not a favorite," he told *Psychology Today*, "because I don't especially like her, that's all." The cartoonist understood, however, her integral role to *Peanuts* and its success. "She *works*, and a central comic-strip character is not only one who fills his [*sic*] role very well, but who will provide ideas by the very nature of his personality," he explained. Schulz also appreciated the fact that there was probably "a little of Lucy" in his own personality since he had created the character.[13]

Regardless of how male critics or even Schulz himself felt, Lucy quickly became quite a powerful force in the world of *Peanuts*. In the summer of 1954, he used her as the punchline for a gag about the Bikini Atoll hydrogen bomb tests. In that strip, Charlie Brown warned Patty that they were about to conduct their own "h-bomb test." Patty quickly covered her ears and closed her eyes as the boy threw his weight down on the detonator plunger. The following panels traced the detonator line to Lucy, who signaled the historic explosion with her own formidable "BWHAM!" When someone telephoned the Van Pelt residence in November 1952 asking for the head of household, Lucy declared with all seriousness, "Speaking." Lucy's personality would eventually become so aggressive that Schulz would have to dilute her character slightly to avoid making her unlikable. When film critic Leonard Maltin asked the cartoonist if he had ever consciously altered a character for his audience, Schulz replied that "the most conscious thing would be to tone Lucy down so she is not as mean as she might have been." Still, Lucy remained one of the most forceful female personalities in American popular culture in the late 1950s.[14]

Lucy took her ambitions to new heights in June 1960. Just a few weeks before the Democratic and Republican national conventions that would nominate John Kennedy and Richard Nixon, respectively, Lucy informed Charlie Brown that he "should start thinking about becoming president." As she spent the week grooming Charlie Brown for office (and destroying any small sense of pride he had remaining), Linus finally revealed Lucy's secret plan: she wanted to marry Charlie Brown and get him elected president for no other reason than that she wanted to be First Lady. But as the week had worn on, Lucy came to reconsider her endorsement. "Maybe I don't need you, Charlie Brown," she reasoned allowed. "Why should I settle for being just First Lady? Why shouldn't *I* be president *myself*?" Schulz's humor could play on multiple levels here, either celebrating this unusual young female for having daring in a society that typically looked to males for such and also mocking her bravado and moxie.[15]

Lucy also developed an annual ritual of ushering in autumn by pulling the football right as a hopelessly optimistic Charlie Brown went to kick it, sending him flying through the air and landing him flat on his back each time. This was a tradition that Schulz had begun in a Sunday strip in November 1952. On one such occasion in the fall of 1971, Charlie Brown tried to refuse, saying, "I can't believe that anyone would actually think I'm that stupid!" Lucy reassured him, however, that she was being genuine this time. "I represent an organization and I'm holding this ball as a representative of that organization," she claimed. "If she represents an organization," Charlie Brown reasoned, "then I guess she must be sincere." With that, the boy charged ahead at full speed and prepared to kick the ball. Just as he swung his weight to make contact, Lucy yanked the ball away and sent Charlie Brown sailing through the air. Stars spun around Charlie Brown's head as Lucy stood over him to announce her sponsor: "This year's football was pulled away from you through the courtesy of women's lib!" Lucy had proclaimed a year earlier in 1970 that she was part of the "women's liberation movement" and that "it's really the most important thing." This 1971 strip, though, seemed different. Like so many controversial issues, Schulz drew a scene that was open to some level of reader interpretation. A reader who felt positively about women's liberation might see this as a joke about a young woman taking the opportunity to show her dominance over a young man. But for an opponent of women's liberation, the scene could have seemed like a criticism of overbearing and vindictive feminism that had found an innocent victim in poor Charlie Brown.[16]

Lucy was embracing "women's liberation" at a moment of critical mass for the Women's Movement. The year 1970 had been, according to one scholar of gender studies, "feminism's pivotal year" because of the increased attention the movement received from major network news and national newsmagazines. Early in the decade, the American public "discovered the feminist movement." There had been earlier milestone moments for feminism in popular culture, most notably Betty Friedan's 1963 bestseller *The Feminine Mystique*. But by 1970, second-wave feminism was regularly addressed on the nightly news. Feminist leaders graced the cover of all the national magazines. *The Mary Tyler Moore Show*, a long-running, popular sitcom about the perseverance of

Figure 7.4 Lucy dedicated her 1971 pulling of the football to the cause of women's liberation. Charles Schulz, *Peanuts*, September 26, 1971. © 1971 Peanuts Worldwide LLC.

a single working woman in the male-dominated media world, first aired in the fall of 1970. In 1971, *Newsweek* presented feminist journalist and *Ms.* magazine editor Gloria Steinem as the face of "the new woman." By January 1972, Steinem was *McCall's* "Woman of the Year" because she was able to "bridge the gap between the early militants, whose vehemence frightened away the people they most wanted to reach, and the thoughtful dedicated women who understand that women's status must change." Similarly, by making Lucy an open supporter of the women's movement, Schulz was participating in the larger popularization of second-wave feminism. For many activists within the movement, this "proliferation of feminism" would ultimately undermine the more progressive goals as it diluted the impact of the movement by normalizing its least radical elements. As one scholar of the movement has written, by the early 1970s, the "movement had splintered, and fragmented; it was everywhere and nowhere."[17]

Elsewhere in graphic arts, comic books were taking a rather ambivalent approach to the rise of feminism. There had long been female superheroes in comic books, but these characters tended to target young male lust rather than attempting to reach new female readers. There was real confusion among comic book producers, though, about why most superheroes and most comic book readers were male. Stan Lee, head of Marvel Comics, wondered, "Do less females read comics because they seem to be aimed at a male audience, or are they aimed at a male audience because less females read them?" As much as white artists had been reluctant to write black characters for fear that they could not relate to the African American experience in the age of civil rights, some male artists worried that they could not accurately write female characters in the age of second-wave feminism. Nonetheless, with the increased attention to women's liberation in the media in the 1970s, the number of female characters in comics multiplied. Some of these characters were conservative caricatures of feminists like Thundra and Man-Killer in Marvel Comics, who hated all men. Even the most powerful of female superheroes, DC Comics' Wonder Woman, struggled to deal with the changing social and political trends of the 1970s. While praised by women's activist Gloria Steinem as a strong role model for girls, the Wonder Woman of the 1970s lost her superpowers, opened a fashion boutique, took to wearing white jumpsuits, and joined the decade's Kung Fu craze. *Wonder Woman* experienced only average circulation throughout the 1970s, despite the notoriety of a prime-time television series starring Lynda Carter that ran from 1975 to 1979.[18]

There were, however, some minor developments in female-oriented superhero comics. In 1972, Marvel Comics—which always prided itself on being a socially progressive brand under the leadership of Stan Lee—launched

Shanna the She-Devil, *Night Nurse*, and *The Cat*, which not only featured female lead characters, but also utilized the work of female writers and artists. Though these titles showed some initial promise, sales ultimately collapsed and all three were canceled within the year. While it had been difficult to get white readers to purchase comics with black characters, Marvel Comics editor-in-chief Roy Thomas explained, "it was even harder to get boys to buy comics about women."[19]

While Lucy was perhaps the strongest personality in *Peanuts*, she did, like the other female characters in the strip, have one vulnerability: her long-time crush on Schroeder. Lucy regularly lounged at the end of Schroeder's piano in a never-ending effort to distract his attention from his true love: the music of Beethoven. But even Lucy's devotion to Schroeder could be resisted for the sake of her new cause. In one 1972 *Peanuts* strip, Schroeder promised to give Lucy a kiss at home plate if she could hit a homerun. When Lucy succeeded in blasting the pitch out of the park, Schroeder dutifully waited for her to finish her jog around the bases. When she arrived home, she promptly rejected his offer and left him standing there with puckered lips. When she returned to the bench, she celebrated not her first homerun, but her "triumph for women's lib." This scene was featured verbatim four years later in the Emmy-nominated television special *It's Arbor Day, Charlie Brown*.[20]

Schulz was dealing in risky terms with such strips. "Women's liberation" did not always have the most flattering popular connotations. In one 1970 survey of women conducted by Louis Harris & Associates, while 38 percent associated the term with equal rights and opportunities for women, 40 percent believed that the movement was nothing more than "masculine-type women" who either wanted to take over men's roles or did not have anything better to do. In the words of some respondents, women's liberation was a "bunch of baloney." In the fall of 1971, 49 percent of women considered themselves "unsympathetic" to the women's liberation movement, while only 39 percent were

Figure 7.5 Lucy won another victory for women's lib by denying Schroeder a celebratory kiss after she hit a homerun. Charles Schulz, *Peanuts*, March 18, 1972. © 1972 Peanuts Worldwide LLC.

sympathetic to it. These attitudes, however, would change over the decade. By 1978, a full 60 percent of Americans surveyed were either "completely for" or "more for than against" women's liberation. While Schulz had associated one of his most popular characters with a controversial movement at the beginning of the 1970s, by the end of the decade Lucy's social politics were solidly in line with the trajectory of the women's movement, which had severed some of the more moderate economic and social status goals from the movement's most radical elements. By the 1980s feminism had become a normal part of American culture, though not the robust feminism that many activists had been advocating.[21]

Lucy Van Pelt was not the only strong female character in *Peanuts*. Peppermint Patty—different from the Patty in the earliest *Peanuts* strips—first appeared in the strip on August 22, 1966. She originally appeared as just another extra at the children's summer camp, and Schulz had little interest in making her much more. "I developed the character Peppermint Patty," he told one interviewer, "because I happened to be walking through our living room. I saw a dish of Peppermint Patties and I thought that would make a good name for a character, so I drew the face to match the name." Schulz had rushed to get the new character into the strip before some other enterprising cartoonist. "I put [Peppermint Patty] in because that's a great name and I didn't want to lose it," he told *Psychology Today*, "because another cartoonist might think of it." It quickly became clear that Peppermint Patty was not just another extra in *Peanuts*.[22]

Peppermint Patty was far from a typical girl in American popular culture. She felt most at home in sports, competing and often winning against the neighborhood boys. This was a rather new element in Schulz's comic strip, since he had made countless jokes in the 1950s about girls' ignorance and incompetence in sports. Even Lucy, who had competed for a state title in golf and could hit a homerun in baseball from time to time, was virtually incapable of catching a pop-fly in the outfield and struggled in other sports. Peppermint Patty was different. She excelled at every sport she played. In her first appearance in the *Peanuts* neighborhood, in fact, she was the manager and star pitcher of an opposing baseball team. As was usually the case, Peppermint Patty's team would go on to regularly defeat Charlie Brown's squad. She was a powerful running back in football, plowing over Charlie Brown and the other boys to score touchdowns. She was even an adept figure skater, much like Schulz's own daughter Jill, who would grow up to be a gold medal-winning professional figure skater and would perform the lead role in Knott's Berry Farm's holiday ice show "It's the Christmas Beagle, Charlie Brown."[23]

Conformity was not one of Peppermint Patty's characteristics. In the first week of January 1972, the school made a troubling announcement: a new dress code would be implemented that required all girls to wear a dress to school or face suspension. This was a problem for Peppermint Patty, who habitually wore a pinstriped polo shirt, shorts, and flip-flops. She was so bothered by the announcement that she confided to her friend Franklin that she was considering a transfer "to a new planet." By the end of the week, Peppermint Patty had reluctantly chosen to comply. "I never thought I'd see the day when I'd be wearing a dress to school," she grumbled as she walked to school with her shoulders slumped. Her biggest concern was that other kids might make fun of her traditionally feminine attire. "If anyone laughs at me," she told herself, "I'll pound him!" As soon as she stepped on the playground her fear came true as one of the boys called all the children to take a look at her dress. Peppermint Patty made good on her word and pounded the boy in the head, calling out to all others, "All right, who's next?!" This would be the last time that she would wear a dress.[24]

Of course, her resistance to the school dress code brought her into direct conflict with the school principal. When the principal ordered her suspension, she decided to fight the sentence. With her world-class defense attorney—none other than Snoopy, complete with bow tie, briefcase, and a long stream of legal jargon—by her side, Peppermint Patty went to face the student council and plead her case against the dress code. Though she had felt confident in her case, the student council ultimately ruled against her. Her sentence was that she must take her lunch hour to study the Constitution each day. But as she confessed to Charlie Brown one day, "The more I study it, the more I'm convinced I was right." Her defiance would continue. After a two-month hiatus from the strip while Schulz dealt with stories that utilized other characters, Peppermint Patty returned to school in her typical shirt, shorts, and flip-flops. This scene contradicted some of Schulz's own comments on controversial fashions. "I don't see anything wrong with miniskirts," he told the *Christian Herald* in 1967. "If a girl can wear one well, then I think it looks very nice. I am all for experimental changes in fashion if they make a person have a nice appearance." Here Schulz was commenting on women's fashion as something for male pleasure, to be judged by men like himself. Where Schulz supported Peppermint Patty's desire to dress as she pleased, he did not seem to have exactly the same attitudes in his personal life.[25]

Like Lucy, Peppermint Patty did have an attraction to the opposite sex. Where Lucy doted over Schroeder, Peppermint Patty secretly carried a flame for Charlie Brown. She affectionately referred to him as "Chuck." She would often take it easy when pitching to him on the baseball field. She would blush whenever his hand touched hers. While she regularly attempted to get Charlie Brown to see her as an attractive girl, these scenes often ended in frustration as the boy was either oblivious or too infatuated with his own love interest, the Little Red-Haired Girl, to notice Peppermint Patty's interest. Peppermint Patty always feared that her "unfeminine" personality would hinder her chances of ever having a boyfriend.[26]

Peppermint Patty's true feeling for Chuck became obvious during summer camp in 1972. That summer, Marcie informed Peppermint Patty that she had met a girl who knew Charlie Brown. As she described the girl, Peppermint Patty realized that it was the Little Red-Haired Girl. Struck with a sense of jealousy, Peppermint Patty stormed across camp to confront the girl. The ensuing episode caused such a stir that a bewildered Charlie Brown was sent home for causing trouble among the girls. Peppermint Patty explained the whole incident to Linus. As she faced the Little Red-Haired Girl, she confided, she suddenly "realized why Chuck has always loved her, and I realized that no one would ever love me that way." The heartbreaking confession revealed just

Figure 7.6 Peppermint Patty badly wants to be seen and admired as a girl, but Charlie Brown does not catch the hint. Charles Schulz, *Peanuts*, October 3, 1971. © 1971 Peanuts Worldwide LLC.

how much Peppermint Patty wanted to be viewed as an attractive and lovable girl. Schulz drew on the emotion of the reader to critique the vanity of a looks-obsessed society and how harmful it was to a child like Peppermint Patty. There were no comparable scenes in *Peanuts* with the unflappable Lucy Van Pelt.[27]

Peppermint Patty's emotions, though, did not prevent her from being a take-charge leader in *Peanuts*. In the mid-1970s, the Schulz family had taken an ill-fated vacation to Oregon. "In 1974, we took a trip down the Rogue River in rafts," recalled Schulz's second wife Jeannie. "It was a disastrous trip, because it rained a lot. But Sparky [as family called him] said, 'We should do a Charlie Brown.'" The resulting idea would become the storyline for *Peanuts*' third feature-length film, *Race for Your Life, Charlie Brown* (1977). On summer vacation at the secluded Camp Remote, Charlie Brown, Franklin, Linus, and Schroeder competed in a rafting race against a team of bullies and a third team of the girls, Lucy, Sally, Marcie, and their leader, Peppermint Patty. Wishy-washy Charlie Brown struggled to make decisions for his team. Peppermint Patty had no such problems. She repeatedly claimed that their team would be run democratically, but she always managed to steer the vote her way. Her leadership style was typically more authoritarian than inclusive. Though it would be Woodstock who would ultimately win the race at the last moment, Peppermint Patty was the strongest and most forceful of all the team leaders in the film.[28]

As with the larger struggle over women's rights, children and childbearing were often a central area of contention when it came to contests over *Peanuts*' public use during second-wave feminism. In 1971, Brandeis law professor and founding member of the National Organization for Women (NOW) Pauli Murray wrote to Schulz to express deep concern over a sign she had seen in downtown Cambridge, Massachusetts. "I do hope I am not being too myopic," she wrote in October, "when I call to your attention with some distress the use of your character, Lucy, of *Peanuts* in a way which may be at variance with your conception of your cartoon family." Passing through the popular downtown Cambridge shopping area near Harvard University, Murray had spotted an orange poster of "a Lucy, obviously close to term in pregnancy" in a store window. The caption on the poster, Murray reported, read "GOD DAMN YOU, CHARLEY [*sic*] BROWN!" Judging by the quality of the printed poster, Murray got the impression that it was "only one of a distribution of such a reproduction." She was so disturbed by the poster that she even stopped to closely examine it for any sign of a distributor she could contact to register a complaint, but she found none.[29]

Murray was not typically the kind of person to complain about such public displays. "I must disclose," she confessed to Schulz, "I am a member of the national board of the American Civil Liberties Union [ACLU] which is committed to freedom of expression under the First Amendment." While she was willing to allow such personally offensive expressions on the basis of constitutional principle, she was not so confident that Schulz would approve of such a usage of his characters. "It occurs to me," she reasoned, "that this type of reproduction may be without your knowledge or permission and represents an invasion of your copyright rights to your cartoon characters." In her estimation, this must be a case of infringement and "essentially, no question of civil liberties is involved."[30]

Murray was not, however, satisfied to leave it at that. Before closing the letter, she voiced her opinion of the display. "My personal view is that such a reproduction offends one's sense of innocence of delightful youngsters and its incomparable set of animal characters," she concluded. While Murray addressed the letter to Schulz, she also carbon-copied it for Al Reitman and Victor Gettner, two executive officers of the New York chapter of the ACLU.[31]

Schulz wrote back a few weeks later. He thanked Murray for her letter and acknowledged her concern. "This poster, of course, was a direct violation of the copyright laws," he replied. He made clear that he had contacted the syndicate's legal office and that the matter would be handled. He did not attempt to refute the offensive nature of the poster, but it was obvious in his response that he did not approve of such a use of his characters and would be willing to engage in litigation if necessary.[32]

Murray wrote back one last time to thank Schulz for his response. She had apparently been worried over how Schulz might receive her initial letter and found camaraderie in one of the cartoonist's characters. "Like Charley [*sic*] Brown," she confided, "one never knows when one is trying to be a good citizen whether it will be misinterpreted." Even though she had been confident of her evaluation of the legal implications of the case, Murray explained that she had copied the letter to the ACLU to double check her understanding. Victor Gettner, chairman of the ACLU's Free Speech/Free Association Committee, confirmed her assessment. She also confessed that she had gone back to the "horrible little store" and purchased the Lucy poster in order "to get it out of the window." The poster cost eighty-five cents and was, according to the store clerk, the last one in stock.[33]

Of course, Schulz did make his own comments on reproductive rights, such as in the July 20, 1970 strip where Linus asked Lucy about parents making family planning decisions. While some readers had read this controversial

Figure 7.7 This strip sparked heated discussion from *Peanuts* readers about abortion, birth control, and the population crisis. Charles Schulz, *Peanuts*, July 20, 1970. © 1970 Peanuts Worldwide LLC.

strip in the context of a larger environmental crisis, others viewed it within the context of political and moral debates over abortion. Like much of Schulz's most impactful work, the strip was open to interpretation. While some viewed this through the lens of overpopulation as an environmental issue, others saw this through the lens of the heated argument over abortion.[34]

To readers accustomed to the cartoonist's style of using the innocence of the *Peanuts* children to broach difficult subjects, it was clear that Linus's question was meant to trigger deeper reflection beyond childhood curiosity. Numerous readers responded in letters to this strip. Some were thankful for the strip because it seemed to promote their own pro-life worldview. "May I thank you from the bottom of a grateful heart for the message," wrote one reader who was requesting a new copy of the strip because she had "sent the other on to a 'talk' show host who recently touched on the subject of abortion—and limited families." Another mother of "six top notch children" wrote that she "loved and appreciated" this strip because "the reviews haven't been too good lately on families our size." Yet another reader commended Schulz and informed him that "a number of concerned citizens have formed a committee to fight the abortion trend of today." Playing on the wording of Linus's original question, the reader asserted that their group knew "only too well what happens to the beautiful babies when parents decide the two they have already are enough." Perhaps Marie Mocny, who agreed that Linus asked a good question, best spoke for this segment of *Peanuts* readers when she charged that "for this and other questions you (Schulz) must be our voice 'crying in the wilderness.'"[35]

A spokesperson for the San Francisco based pro-life organization Voice of the Unconceived wrote to show its support for Schulz's statement. "One picture is INDEED worth a thousand words," spokeswoman Mary Parsons praised. "You said it better than we *ever* could have." Parsons wrote that "in all this talk about 'ecology' and 'family planning,'" no one was speaking on behalf of the unborn. Voice of the Unconceived was a relatively new organization, but they were planning a campaign against "contraception on demand." Seeing Schulz as an advocate of their cause, Parsons asked him to join the organization as a co-chairman.[36]

Mary Hawblitzel, a Catholic, was so moved by the strip that she sent Schulz a six-page handwritten letter. "It must have taken a bit of nerve in this age of contraception and abortion to pen your cartoon," she praised Schulz. This was not the first time she had written a letter about "these antilife programs," she told the cartoonist. In her opinion, such programs were "philosophies of fear and demonstrate a lack of trust in the wisdom and providence of God." The problem was that "modern man is trying to play God." While she acknowledged the potential for a nuclear holocaust, she believed that "God scans the spans of the centuries and he knows best how many children we should have." "Poverty is not the worst affliction that can happen to man," she contended, suggesting that there were much worse spiritual consequences for abusing the innocent. Hawblitzel was upset that "a lot of people seem willing to disregard God's instructions to Adam and Eve to 'increase and multiply.'" She was even more shocked that "the [American Medical Association] is itself promoting liberalized or no abortion laws." "Most pediatricians and obstetricians agree," she insisted without citing any empirical evidence, "that a child in the womb is a *person* from the first moment of conception." In a postscript, Hawblitzel apparently wanted to clarify her position for Schulz, asserting that "abortion acts are the signs of a decadent civilization and in our society we have the barbarians already storming at the walls."[37]

Not all readers were happy with Linus's suggestion. Linus should instead ponder whether these "beautiful and highly intelligent" children should be born into a world where they are "unable to get food or water or an education because the world was overpopulated," asked one reader. "Overpopulation is a problem," he continued, "and if we don't solve it within the next several decades, it will become a crisis." He made clear that he supported Zero Population Growth, the population control organization founded by Paul Ehrlich and his colleagues, and the reader hoped that Schulz would "reconsider your position."[38]

Another *Peanuts* fan who had "heard [*Peanuts*] quoted from the pulpit many times" wrote to express her concern that Schulz had "lost sight of what happens to the unwanted child." He forgot this, she believed, because of his great wealth and personal success. "I have read of the way you live," she charged, "anything money can buy, you have." Given his elite financial status and celebrity, it might "come as a shock, but there are people in this country who can only afford two children." Similarly, Nancy Currier wondered "what Charlie Brown would have to say if he was one of the children starving or dying with one of the diseases of poverty." She was certain that "he would be all for having just two children in his family."[39]

One of the most prominent voices writing to discuss Schulz's July 20, 1970 strip was California's Governor Ronald Reagan. Reagan and Schulz had periodically corresponded over the years and had met at the governor's mansion in Sacramento when Reagan declared May 24, 1967 as "Charles Schulz Day." Writing a little over a week after Schulz's controversial strip ran nationally, Reagan could not get out of his mind the strip on unborn children. Reagan recounted the strip in his letter so that Schulz would know exactly to which one he was referring, though he mistakenly referred to Charlie Brown as the one questioning Lucy rather than Linus.[40]

This strip, he wrote, "continues to haunt me in a very nice way." He reflected that "perhaps my feeling for Charlie's [*sic*] question stems from the soul searching I had to do a few years ago with regard to the liberalizing of our abortion laws." In 1967, Reagan's first year in office, Anthony Beilenson, a liberal state senator from Los Angeles County, had sponsored one of the nation's most sweeping abortion laws, a piece of legislation he called the Therapeutic Abortion Act. "The author of the legislation," Reagan explained, "wanted to go all the way and simply make it a matter of personal choice and wide open." The new law legalized abortions when the pregnancy was deemed to "gravely impair physical or mental health of the prospective mother, or when a girl under 15 becomes pregnant as a result of rape or incest." The law was drafted partly in response to the case of nine San Francisco Bay area physicians who had been criminally charged for performing abortions on mothers with German measles, a disease that was known to cause birth deformities in children.[41]

This piece of legislation perplexed Reagan, in part because he had never before seriously considered his position on the topic. The governor confided to Schulz that "I probably did more studying on that subject at that time than on anything else before or since." This was a particularly difficult time for Reagan, "awful weeks," as he confided to reporter Lou Cannon. Reagan sincerely struggled over whether to support the bill saying, as the *Chicago Tribune* reported, that the "measure did not fully satisfy him but he sympathized with the effort to revise the statute in force [in California] for 106 years." Most concerning for Reagan were provisions that would have allowed for the abortion of deformed fetuses. "There is a very great question to me," he had stated at a news conference, "as to where we can actually stand, trying to judge in advance of a birth that someone is going to be born a cripple and whether we have the right to decide before birth what cripple would not be allowed to live." The implications, for Reagan, were nearly insurmountable.[42]

After much thought, Reagan notified Beilenson that he "would veto such a bill." There were, in his mind, only a few, clear cases where abortion should be allowed. "I could only reconcile abortion," he wrote to Schulz, "with the right of self defense, namely the right of the mother to protect herself and her health against even her own unborn child if the birth of that child threatened her." This was the only justification he could accept in good conscience. "Our religion does justify the taking of life in self defense," he told Schulz, but he could not "accept that simply on the whim even a mother has the right to take the life of her unborn child simply because she thinks that the child will be born less than perfect" or, even worse, because "she just doesn't want to be bothered." To get into the business of deciding whether a fetus with physical deformities should live, Reagan believed, "wouldn't be much different from what Hitler tried to do."[43]

Reagan was not the only one conflicted over this issue in the 1960s. Protestant denominations were surprisingly split over the new abortion laws. Some conservative leaders, like evangelist Billy Graham, insisted that abortion was sinful in most cases. Others were more open to "therapeutic" procedures. "Personally, I certainly do not condemn those who terminate a pregnancy to save the mother's life or when rape or incest is involved," wrote physician S. I. McMillen in his 1967 article for *Christian Life* magazine. The following year, the nation's leading evangelical publication *Christianity Today* held the Protestant Symposium on the Control of Human Reproduction, which concluded that "abortion-on-demand" was sinful, while "therapeutic" abortion could be acceptable in the right cases. In 1971, even the Southern Baptist Convention joined the growing debate with a resolution urging states to liberalize their abortion laws. Where Reagan and Protestants agreed was on the permissibility of abortion in cases where the life of the mother was at great risk. Because of their general agreement on this issue but growing conflict over degree, California evangelicals had largely left Reagan alone to make his decision in the 1967 law.[44]

While Protestant denominations tended to accept such new, liberal abortion laws as a necessary extension of access to legal birth control, most Catholics disagreed. For the Catholic Church, all abortion was morally wrong. Drawing on antiabortion teachings that dated back to the earliest centuries of the Christian faith and a series of papal papers (including Vatican II in 1964) that opposed abortion, church officials appealed not only to lay church members, but also to legislators. In fact, as Reagan had been debating whether to sign the California abortion law, some of Reagan's Catholic friends had arranged a weekend meeting with Cardinal Francis McIntyre, Archbishop of

Los Angeles, in an attempt to persuade the governor that this bill was morally wrong.[45]

Ultimately, Reagan signed the bill into law when the legislature eliminated the provision about fetuses with deformities. "I am satisfied in my own mind we can morally and logically justify liberalized abortions to protect the health of a mother," he told the press. Though he had been reluctant to endorse such a bill during the summer legislative session, when the assembly approved the new law by a margin of 48 to 30, Reagan felt it was time to move ahead. "I am confident that the people of California recognize the need and will support the humanitarian goals of the measure," he announced following the signing. Still, he warned that Californians "must be extremely careful to assure that this legislation does not result in making California a haven for those who would come to this state solely for the purpose of taking advantage of California's new law."[46]

It did not take very long for the governor's worst fears to come true. "I have discovered," he complained to Schulz, "some of our psychiatrists are particularly willing to declare an 'unwed mother-to-be' to have suicidal tendencies" as a medical excuse for an abortion. Reagan was especially distraught imagining that such a consequential decision might be made "on a five minute diagnosis." The governor could hardly believe the effects of the new law only three years later. "The result," he told Schulz, "is that our medical program will finance more than fifty thousand abortions of unwed mothers in the coming year on such flimsy diagnosis."[47]

Perhaps the reason that abortion played so prominently in his mind as he read that 1970 *Peanuts* strip was the fact that Reagan was dealing with a new proposal to further liberalize the state's abortion law. This time the governor and his allies in the assembly were successful in defeating the legislation. In a "Dear Citizen" letter, he wrote, "Those who summarily advocate a *blanket population control* should think carefully. Who might they be doing away with? Another Lincoln, or Beethoven, an Einstein or an Edison? Who shall play God?"[48]

Whether it was a population control advocate, a pro-life activist, a popular governor, or just an ordinary private citizen, readers from across the country took this conversation between Linus and Lucy very seriously. Though the Supreme Court's landmark decision in *Roe v. Wade* would not come for another three years, the issue of abortion rights was rapidly becoming a heated topic. Schulz had never mentioned the words, but in the context of the early 1970s, both supporters and opponents of the procedure could not help but read the strip as a comment on abortion and birth control. And as far as his readers were concerned, Schulz seemed decidedly pro-life.

The last week of October 1971, Schulz ran a five-day series of strips where Snoopy, acting as a boss, narrated the week of his secretary, Woodstock. During that week, Snoopy told a story of a secretary who was useless on Mondays, late from lunch on Tuesdays, extremely productive on Wednesdays, phoning in sick on Thursdays, and scrambling to get everything finished by closing time on Fridays. Over the weekend, Snoopy walked over to visit Woodstock's nest and found that "on Saturdays, secretaries sleep 'til noon." Though Woodstock had originally evolved from a nameless female bird in the 1960s, "she" had been redefined as male by the 1970s and owed his name to the 1969 music festival in rural New York. But while Woodstock might have been male, it was clear from the reader response that it was female secretaries who most directly related to this strip.[49]

Numerous secretary pools wrote to voice their affinity for the series. The female secretaries at Chief Francisco Solano Junior High in Vallejo, California wrote to thank Schulz for the series. "Our boss posted all of them on the bulletin board," they reported, admitting that "we have a suspicion he was trying to tell us something." As many others did, these women picked up the literary structure of Schulz's secretary series and repurposed it to produce their own office humor, documenting their minor rebellion against the principal's authority when they added in a handwritten postscript that "on Friday afternoons secretaries use school stationery to write personal letters." A secretary pool working for Governor Ronald Reagan's administration in Sacramento, California wrote to thank the *Peanuts* cartoonist for "brightening the week for us" and joked that at the Capitol secretaries typically called in sick on Fridays, but only "if it isn't payday!!!" Even Congressional secretaries sent their praises. Secretaries from the offices of both Congressmen Dan Kuykendall of Tennessee and Floyd Spence of South Carolina wrote requesting autographed originals for their Capitol Hill offices.[50]

Seven female secretaries of the Rawles, Golden and Hinkle law offices of Ukiah, California wrote to thank Schulz for the series and to share a clipping from their local newspaper reporting how the secretaries had taped large posters of "*Peanuts* characters on all the attorneys' doors, depicting characters they felt were appropriate to each of them." The photograph accompanying the article showed Newell Rowles, the head of the firm, laughing next to the poster intended to depict him: a large drawing of Lucy shouting, "If you can't be right, be wrong at the top of your voice." Just as Vietnam soldiers had sometimes used Snoopy the flying ace as a subversive image to undermine the authority of their commanders and US officials, so these women used *Peanuts* characters to playfully criticize the men in authority over them in the workplace. Another letter included two pages' worth of grievances against bosses that included their habit of calling in sick to play golf on a beautiful day, dictating letters only minutes before lunch or closing, having the secretary make excuses for why he is late to a board meeting, and forgetting to take her out for lunch during Secretaries' Week.[51]

Some employers, too, wrote to praise what they saw as a lighthearted series in the funny pages. Wayne E. Keith, a manager for a business services company in Hartford, Connecticut, wrote of the "joy and laughter you recently brought to me and my staff." Keith had long been a Snoopy fan, but "this particular sequence certainly captured the atmosphere of a business office from both the standpoint of the boss and the secretary." He was so impressed that he collected the entire series and framed it to hang on the office wall as "a subtle reminder for all of us to laugh at ourselves whenever we look at it." Of course, the laughs in this series came largely at the expense of the secretary, still a predominately female role in American business in the 1970s. In fact, the 1970 US Census reported that of the twenty-nine million women in the American workforce, a third of them were employed in clerical jobs. Such secretarial work was the most common career path for female workers in 1970.[52]

Beverly L. Walker of Clinton, Maryland, had a very different take on this series. "I want to complain," she began as she described how her "boss has been delighted over this week's series and generally [has] been giving me a terrible time." Since *Peanuts* had spent a week joking at the secretaries' expense, Walker "thought it only fair that you should print the other side." She included with her letter a reworked series that depicted female secretaries' complaints about their male bosses, adding in the postscript that "I still love Snoopy even though he's a rotten boss." On the next page, Walker attached five hand-drawn strips of her own where Woodstock narrated Boss Snoopy's week, explaining why each day of the week was a "bad day for bosses." On Mondays, "they see us youthful and beautiful secretaries come back from our weekends and think about what they should have been doing if they still could." On Wednesdays, "the week is half over and there is so much work to do and not enough secretaries to do it." And on Thursdays, "the janitors always clean and forget to leave the medicinal alcohol behind the toilet tank in the *executive* bathroom." Walker's humor was substantially more biting than other women that wrote to Schulz and was just one demonstration of the level to which everyday readers could transform *Peanuts* into a channel for their own personal satire.[53]

Audrey A. Fromnecht was equally concerned in her letter about Schulz's secretary series. The strip itself, she wrote, had been "excellent and [was] enjoyed by secretaries throughout the country." The strip "lost some of its humor," however, when one of her "sadistic bosses" circulated a copy of the Thursday, October 28, 1971 strip (which had asserted that on Thursdays secretaries call in sick) on a Thursday when Fromnecht had indeed been at home sick. "Since Snoopy exhibits an open-minded intelligence superior to your usual run-of-the-mill boss," she suggested, "I am sure he would wish to give equal time to the same situation from the secretary's viewpoint." Like Walker, Fromnecht included a series of *Peanuts* strips that she had reengineered using corrective liquid and a copy machine. On Mondays, bosses were worthless. On Tuesdays, they suffered from mental blocks. On Wednesdays, "they do everything they should have done on Monday and Tuesday." On Thursdays, Fromnecht recommended that bosses should call in sick because of their uselessness. And on Fridays, bosses threw loads of last minute assignments onto their exhausted secretaries. Fromknecht ended her letter with the valediction, "Yours for Equal Rights," a clear reference to the House of Representatives passage of the proposed Equal Rights Amendment in October, then on its way to the Senate.[54]

Some employers wrote in to report their secretary's revolts against them to Schulz. Charles R. Bergoffen, an attorney at Trubin, Stillcock, Edelman, and Knapp where Republican Jacob K. Javits had once been a partner, told the cartoonist that he had "foisted" the series of strips on his secretary with each new day of the week. He attached a copy of "her revenge," a reworked strip that proved "what a witty secretary, a compliant Xerox, and a disregard for the copyright laws can do." The strip depicted Woodstock frantically racing around the doghouse typing and rustling papers as Snoopy barked orders. "On Fridays," the secretary's punchline read, "bosses are impossible."[55]

Barbara Quackenbush, secretary to the president of Van de Kamp's bakery in Los Angeles, wrote that while she was "a regular follower of yours and have always really looked forward to reading *Peanuts*," this series on secretaries had "given us all a black eye." She recommended that Schulz "replace your secretary" because she had clearly given the cartoonist the wrong impression about the profession. "Some secretaries DO work and are kept pretty busy," Quackenbush asserted. "I could hardly believe my eyes," she wrote in disgust, "as each day progressed that week and not one good thing was said about secretaries." She felt that her own experience in the field was much more "representative of most secretaries." Each year she missed no more than three or four days of work (due to illness). Each day she began working fifteen minutes early and did not leave work until after five o'clock. Many lunches she spent part of her break running errands for her boss. Secretaries' work was hardly a joke, she made clear.[56]

Quackenbush's real problem with the series had as much to do with the medium as the message. People reading *Peanuts* naturally assumed, she supposed, that "you derive your material from real life [experience]" and, therefore, "almost everyone who reads *Peanuts* accepts what is said in it pretty much as truth." She understood the relationship between the audience and a comic strip as intrinsically different from that of an audience and a print article. "Anyone reading an *article* . . . on secretaries," she explained, "would automatically agree and disagree as he read." A cartoon, she believed, was different. A comic strip was "so subtle that there is almost no disagreement—just acceptance with no thought of evaluation." While she drastically generalized about comic strip readers, theorizing her own personal reception theory, Quackenbush invested Schulz's work with authority and authenticity, a sense that many other fans had cited over the years as a reason for their love for *Peanuts*. This acute level of genuineness gave Schulz, she believed, a special "responsibility for what you print." In the end, Quackenbush's letter was at least therapeutic, since she did not "expect this to change your low opinion of secretaries." She did, at least, sarcastically hope that the letter would make it to Schulz's desk for him to read: "If it gets by your secretary, if she happens to be around the office for an hour or two this week."[57]

Once again, Schulz had hit on a gendered issue that evoked strong feelings from his readers. Though Woodstock was male, his designation as a secretary had resonated with working women nationwide. Some took this weeklong series as a good-humored tribute to the efforts of female office workers. Others read it as a patronizing affront to their dignity as workers and women. Whether the cartoonist had intended to make a political statement or not, in the age of second-wave feminism it was certainly read with political overtones, either of chauvinism or feminist humor.

When Gloria Steinem's *Ms.* magazine hit newsstands in the winter of 1972 it almost immediately became synonymous with the women's rights movement. At its launch, *Ms.* was, according to one scholar, the "first commercial magazine in the United States to unambiguously claim a feminist perspective." Feminists would argue over whether the arrival of *Ms.* heralded a new age of awareness for women's rights or the commercialization of the movement. At its height, *Ms.* enjoyed a circulation of 400,000–500,000 and an estimated readership of three million. Over the 1970s and 1980s, the magazine would become an important publication in American culture, defining feminism for a broad popular audience and providing a much-needed point of unity and discourse for a diverse national movement.[58]

In 1976, Schulz got an opportunity to contribute to Gloria Steinem's magazine. His work had no relation to the ERA or any of the best-known elements of the feminist movement. Schulz drew an original cover for the April issue of *Ms.* The sky-blue cover showed Lucy relaxing behind her typical yard stand, except this time it was not her famous psychiatry booth. Instead, the sign overhead offered lemonade for five cents as part of "Lucy, Inc." The cover promoted an article meant to attract young women's attention: "How to Start Your Own Business!" Gloria Steinem and the rest of the magazine staff were so pleased with the finished cover that they presented Schulz with his very own copy autographed by the entire *Ms.* crew.[59]

The article bore a striking resemblance to the project Schulz was doing contemporaneously, promoting the capitalist system for the Department of Commerce. The article itself was "conceived, compiled, and edited" by Heidi Fiske and Karen Zehring, a business writer and entrepreneur, respectively, and both National Organization for Women officers. "The self-employed woman is an idea whose time has come," declared the sixteen-page cover article. According to the US Census Bureau, women-owned businesses were growing, numbering 402,025 and generating $8.1 million in 1972. But women-owned businesses still only made up 3.1 percent of the American economy. The purpose of this article was to give women tips based on the advice of successful female entrepreneurs on how to start and sustain a business.[60]

The article offered practical counsel to those new to the idea of starting a business. It gave advice on everything from making a business plan and securing licenses to dealing with lawyers, bankers, and accountants. The report directed women to the Small Business Administration and the Economic Development Administration of the US Commerce Department for assistance with small business loans and setting up a new business, including the contact information for major offices around the country. The cover story instructed women on how to raise capital, balance cash flow, and advertise their goods and services. The article also directed women to various private organizations that could provide support and networking specifically for females, like the Association of Women Business Owners in Washington, DC, the Feminist Financial Consultants in New York, or the Feminist Economic Network in Detroit. And the guest authors tried to prepare young women for their "first encounter with sex discrimination," and warned female entrepreneurs to be prepared to carry both the praise and the blame that came along with running a small business.[61]

In closing, the authors proposed what they called "a feminist business ethic," which would follow six basic principles to achieve "compassionate capitalism." First, the entrepreneur's product should fulfill a feminist need, advance a feminist cause, or improve the feminist life. Second, the product should be quality-made and fair-priced. Third, the business should only bring in what profit is needed for the business to survive in order to avoid profiteering. Fourth, wages and benefits to employees should be as generous as the employer can afford. Fifth, all business transactions should be performed in good faith. And, finally, the entrepreneurs should be personally involved in the feminist movement beyond their business connections. "We need both the Movement and our business," the authors claimed, "to ensure that our declaration of economic independence will last."[62]

Schulz's participation with this project represented an extension of the cartoonist's interests in the feminist movement of the 1960s and 1970s, but it was also consistent with his other advocacy work, especially his pro-capitalist campaign for the Department of Commerce. The authors of this article made a passionate case for the harmony of capitalism and progressive movements like second-wave feminism. By boldly placing Lucy on the cover of *Ms.*, Schulz clearly showed *Peanuts'* synchronicity with both resurgent capitalism and the women's rights movement. Schulz's sense of personal responsibility and social fairness blended in his support of this project.[63]

This article about uniting feminism and capitalism seemed a bit oddly timed for the headlines that surrounded it. Nineteen seventy-six was a particularly challenging season for the fight to ratify the ERA. In March 1976, feminist writer Lisa Cronin Wohl tried to explain "what the hell happened in New York" when the voters rebuffed the polling data and shocked feminists by rejecting the amendment by a margin of 400,000 votes. But many feminist thinkers and strategists believed that this was in fact a "400,000 vote misunderstanding," arguing that much of this margin was women who voted against "the media image of the Women's Movement." The battle to defeat that misconception, wrote feminist journalist Lindsy Van Gelder, was at the heart of the ERA's—and the women's movement's—fight for survival against a surprisingly powerful conservative opposition. The mortal enemies in this fight, some feminists believed, were not antifeminists like Phyllis Schlafly and her army of "misinformed" housewives, but corporate America. In May, *Ms.* magazine warned their readers that "big business is trying to defeat the ERA." In author Elinor Langer's estimation, while liberal feminists battled in campaigns against antifeminists of the right, "the beneficiaries of this old-fashioned diversion are the major business interests," what Langer referred to as the "corporate center." She reasoned that corporate motivation must come to the conclusion that "equality for women, coming on top of the decreasing flexibility in the hiring and firing of black people that has followed the civil rights movement, would introduce an inelasticity into the labor force that their profit margins cannot bear." Nonetheless, Schulz and the *Ms.* magazine contributors obviously believed that feminism was an important cause and that capitalism offered a clear path to progress women's rights.[64]

The issue of amateur women's sports was cropping up everywhere in American media by the late 1970s. In the summer of 1978, women's sports scored a *Time* magazine cover, complete with young women playing field hockey, softball, and rugby. This cover story discussed "the revolution that is taking place on the country's playing fields as, at all ages and levels, women have moved into the world of sport," wrote *Time* publisher Jack Meyers. B. J. Phillips, the female associate editor responsible for writing the cover story, had herself experienced a junior sports culture that sought to drive young women away from athletics toward dresses, make-up, and more "feminine" pursuits. The article argued that women's growing role in sports was "transforming American athletics." The story quoted numerous female athletes who could hardly believe the new opportunities provided by Title IX of the Education Amendments Act in 1972 though, ironically, few of the law's original architects had had the slightest idea that it would impact sports so dramatically. Nineteen-year-old Susan White, a hurdler for the University of Maryland, told *Time*, "When I was in high school, I never dreamed of competing in a national meet. People are finally accepting us as athletes." Another woman, golfer Carol Mann, said that "five years ago, little girls never walked up to tell me that they wanted to be a professional golfer. Now it happens all the time." Women athletes could all sense that they were entering a new era of access to athletics and popular support they had only dreamed of. And these opportunities were creating more optimistic attitudes among young women. "Women no longer feel that taking part in athletics is a privilege," wrote Joan Warrington, executive secretary of the Association for Intercollegiate Athletics for Women (AIAW). "They believe it is a right."[65]

The *Time* cover article saw this surge in women's sports at the confluence of three larger trends: the 1970s fitness craze, the feminist movement, and a stream of court rulings and congressional legislation. In this new climate, the progress was obvious. Where a mere 294,000 high school girls had participated in school sports in 1970, 1.6 million young women were playing them by 1977. The AIAW, which had launched in 1971 with 278 member schools, boasted 825 active members by 1978. That was 115 more than the men's collegiate organization, the National Collegiate Athletic Association. And by 1978, there were more than 100,000 women participating in intercollegiate sports, compared to 170,000 men.[66]

This rapid growth of women's sports had a marked economic impact. In 1978, Adidas, one of the world leaders in manufacturing athletic shoes, reported a 63 percent increase in women's shoe sales. This same trend continued with new lines of sporting equipment designed especially for women, from baseball catcher's masks to hockey skates. Women were coming to feel more at home on the sports field. And women athletes at all levels, the article found, were gaining a "refreshingly unapologetic pride" about themselves.[67]

Still, as women saw progress across the board in sports programs during the 1970s, there were considerable limits. For example, while the University of Georgia had made great strides to increase its 1973 women's athletics budget of $1,000, the 1978 budget of $120,000 lagged far behind the men's athletic budget of $2.5 million. At North Carolina State, the number of women's athletic scholarships went from zero to 49 in only four years, but that still trailed the 180 scholarships for men. In 1978, the nation's largest women's athletics budget was only $600,000 at Yale University. Perhaps University of Georgia coordinator of women's athletics Liz Murphey put it best when she said that "things are looking better, but it's very slow."[68]

The *Time* article covered one example after another of young women's personal experiences with this new wave of gender equality in athletics. After pages of sports photographs, statistics, and testimonials, in a closing section titled "The Weaker Sex? Hah!", *Time* associate editor B. J. Philips discussed psychologists' and physicians' research on the difference between the sexes as it related to sports. The closing piece reported that women were physically and mentally equipped to handle the same rigorous athletic training that men could. Though women might not currently record the same running and swim times as men, this gap was largely a byproduct of women's recent arrival to many of these competitive events. "You can train women as hard as you can train men," argued Dr. Jack Wilmore, "and the records will fall by the wayside." Assuaging apparent public concerns, it assured readers that athletics would not pose significant risk to their sexual organs or future pregnancies.[69]

Rather than illustrating this section with more photographs of female student athletes, however, *Time* selected a *Peanuts* strip. The strip they chose was from the summer of 1977 and depicted Lucy showing off her new baseball glove to Charlie Brown. Charlie Brown wanted to know which baseball player's autograph was printed on the mitt: "Hank Aaron? Pete Rose? Reggie Jackson?" He was likely unprepared for the answer. "Liv Ullmann," she replied smugly as she made her way back to the outfield. A famous actress who had won the Golden Globe award for best actress and an Academy Award nomination in 1972 for the film *The Emigrants*, Liv Ullmann was hardly the type of figure an athletics gear company would print on a baseball glove. But this comic strip used in the context of the *Time* cover story suggested that young women were not just engaging in sports like never before, they were also indelibly changing the culture of American sports to reflect their own perspectives. Still, it could also be read as a comment on the disparity between male and female celebrity in the 1970s.[70]

One of the most famous feminist episodes in *Peanuts* came as a result of Schulz's friendship with the professional tennis player Billie Jean King. King had joined a small group of women's amateurs who fought for a professional women's tennis league. They accomplished that goal in 1968. In 1973, former tennis champion and self-proclaimed male chauvinist Bobby Riggs agreed to play two matches, one against Margaret Court and a second against King. King intended the matches to highlight the importance of Title IX legislation passed the previous year. Riggs defeated Court rather easily, leaving Lucy Van Pelt angry for weeks before she wrote the victor a letter: "Dear Bobby Riggs, You were lucky!!!" King defeated Riggs four months later at the Houston Astrodome in three straight sets, earning a winner-take-all purse of $100,000. The stakes, however, had been much higher than money. The public dignity of women athletes was on the line. In the 1970s, King and Schulz developed a close friendship. They would periodically talk on the phone or exchange letters. King was a regular participant in the Women's Tennis Classics Tournament hosted by Schulz at the sports complex he built near his home. In 1979, King asked Schulz to join the Board of Trustees of her Women's Sports Foundation (WSF), an advocacy group for women's athletics. He also became a major donor to the cause.[71]

That same year, 1979, Schulz drew his series on Title IX in *Peanuts*. The two-week episode, which ran from September 24 through October 6, began with Peppermint Patty and Marcie pointing out to Linus the structural sexism in collegiate athletics, citing a 1978 statistic that showed that men's athletics received $717,000 on average, while women's athletics only received $141,000. In the final panel, the two girls walked away with Linus's football. Similarly, the girls noted that Charlie Brown's basketball is twice as nice as the one provided for the girls. "You're not against women's sports are you, Chuck?" They confiscated his basketball, too. These young ladies were on a crusade. "We've been silent for seventy years about the unfair treatment of women athletes," Peppermint Patty lectured Charlie Brown, "but now that unfair treatment is causing an uproar." As the girls expanded their crusade, they logically recruited the strip's greatest feminist, Lucy. "What's she going to do?" Charlie Brown wondered. "SPEAK OUT!!!" Lucy bellowed in his face, sending him tumbling backward.

The next week, Schulz continued his march of statistics. Women only received 21 percent of athletic scholarship budgets, and 14 percent of athletic operating budgets. But while Schulz was clearly championing equal opportunity and support for women's sports, some of the strip's humor poked fun at the effort as well. "What we're working toward," Peppermint Patty announced as she punted a football to Sally Brown, "is equality for women in sports. That's a good cause, don't you think?" Sally, distracted from the football falling from the sky, was unable to catch the ball as it pounded her in the head and sent her tumbling to the ground. When Peppermint Patty rushed over to be sure she was all right, Sally finally responded: "The sooner the better!" Here Schulz joked that while an athlete like Peppermint Patty might be ready for equal access to sports, girls like Sally had a long way to go to be able to compete, a reality that was, at least in part, likely a symptom of past discrimination. The next day, Schulz carried this mild critique even further. As Peppermint Patty worked to instill a greater passion for Title IX in her friend, Marcie, the glasses-wearing girl admitted, "Sports don't really interest me, sir, so what do I care?" Peppermint Patty was utterly shocked. "But what about women's rights?" she demanded. "I'm not a woman yet, either," Marcie snidely remarked as she sauntered away. Nonetheless, Peppermint Patty refused to stop her crusade for equality in sports. When the other children failed to listen, she recited her statistics to Woodstock. Her mission came from one clear inspiration. "I have a vision," she told Charlie Brown. "I can see the day coming when women will have the same opportunities in sports as men!" The final punchline of the

Figure 7.8 Peppermint Patty led a two-week crusade for public awareness of Title IX of the Higher Education Act of 1972. Charles Schulz, *Peanuts*, September 29, 1979. © 1979 Peanuts Worldwide LLC.

strip pushed the critique even further. By turning Charlie Brown down as unqualified for her team, Peppermint Patty mocked the essentialist certainties of male and female difference. In the world of *Peanuts*, at least, Charlie Brown would not be athletically skilled enough to make it on a team with the likes of Peppermint Patty.[72]

The seriousness of the issue to Schulz was evidenced in his persistence. Rarely did *Peanuts* stay on one particular issue for longer than a week, and here he had hammered his point for two. His commitment to the cause was also clear in the fact that he gave the WSF and other feminist organizations permission to freely reprint this series of Title IX strips in their magazines and newsletters. One example was a poster for the WSF that showed Lucy vigorously jumping rope in a green dress. "Thank goodness for sports," she said. "If they didn't exist, I don't know what I'd do with my tremendous natural ability." Another example was an interview with Peppermint Patty featured in Billie Jean King's own *womenSports* magazine, the first national publication to exclusively follow female athletics. But perhaps the most important usage of these strips came in 1980. That year the US Commission on Civil Rights released a multiyear study titled *More Hurdles to Clear: Women and Girls in Competitive Athletics*. In the one hundred-page report, the commission reviewed the long history of discrimination against women in publicly funded sports. The study found marked progress since the passage of Title IX in 1972, but laid out goals for greater progress in parity. The commission illustrated the report with the *Doonesbury* comic strip from the innovative comic artist and social critic Gary Trudeau. They also used a strip from Schulz's 1979 Title IX series. Peppermint Patty and Lucy found themselves at the apex of national policy discussion on issues of sexual equality they had long stood for in the comic strip. Schulz himself received national recognition in 1985 when the WSF awarded him their highest honor, the President's Award, for his contributions and support to the cause of girls' equal access to athletic programs.[73]

On November 24, 1986, Schulz contributed his artwork to a controversial *Time* magazine cover that dealt with an unusual topic for a cartoonist who had spent his career avoiding even the slightest suggestion of sexuality in his work. "Sex Education," read the headline in bold font. "What should children know?" and "When should they know it?" read the bulleted questions on the cover. In the artwork, Charlie Brown, Linus, Lucy, and Snoopy all looked uneasy as they surveyed a school poster that read, "Today in Room 301—'The birds and the bees' (and much much more!)." The cover article reported that the growing AIDS epidemic and recent comments by President Ronald Reagan's Surgeon General C. Everett Koop had intensified the long battle over sex education in public schools. "There is now no doubt," wrote the surgeon general in late October 1986, "that we need sex education in schools and that it must include information on heterosexual and homosexual relationships." The spread of dangerous sexually transmitted diseases as AIDS, Koop believed, was partly the result of the fact that "many people—especially our youth—are not receiving information that is vital to their future health and well-being because of our reticence in dealing with the subjects of sex, sexual practices, and homosexuality." Koop bluntly charged Americans that "the silence must end." He recommended that American public schools promptly implement sex education programs "at the lowest grade possible"—third grade, he suggested. The course would also need to be graphic. "We have to be as explicit as necessary to get the message across," Koop pleaded. "You can't talk of the danger of snake poisoning and not mention snakes."[74]

Such a course actually had considerable public support. In May 1981, 70 percent of respondents had told Gallup that all public high schools should have sex education programs. Seventy-one percent of women, in particular, agreed or strongly agreed that public grade schools should provide some form of sex education. But the opposition to public school sex education was highly vocal. Opponents often made moral arguments, *Time* reported, that "the recommendation to students that they use condoms as an anti-AIDS measure helps erode moral opposition to premarital sex and contraception." Koop's endorsement of sex education had come as a shock to many conservatives who had praised the Reagan administration's opposition to such programs in the past. They were especially offended when the surgeon general largely wrote off parents as a reliable source of sex education. "Most parents are so embarrassed and reluctant," he wrote, "you can't count on getting the message across at home." And there were other conservative complaints. Phyllis Schlafly, champion of the anti-ERA crusade, took up opposition to sex education as well. She believed that sex education particularly harmed young women. "The way sex education is taught in schools encourages experimentation," she warned. "It's the cause of promiscuity and destroys the natural modesty of girls."[75]

In much the same way that concerns over specific beliefs and differences had ultimately undermined the push for prayer in public schools, sex education had struggled for consensus throughout the twentieth century. "No matter what is written in the curriculum, there is not much going on out there," sex-education consultant Mary Lee Tatum informed *Time*. "Under 15 percent of U.S. children get really good sex education. We are only beginning to

Figure 7.9 Schulz became a major public supporter of many women's issues, especially women's sports. Courtesy of the Charles M. Schulz Museum and Research Center.

institute adequate programs." Studies of existing public school programs did very little to help build consensus between advocates and critics. The largest study by that time, a seven-year, six-volume 1984 analysis by Mathtech Inc. of nine programs around the country, found that the programs had almost no demonstrable effect on contraceptive use or premarital sex. The only positive finding of the study was that the most significant changes in behavior and attitude came in the two programs with the highest levels of parent and local community engagement. Birth control usage only changed when combined with access to a health clinic. Where the study showed the significance of the family and community in sex education, however, it also revealed that students who had completed a sex education program were only slightly less predisposed to premarital sex than their counterparts. Other studies found equally discouraging results. The Center for Population Options' study of 3,600 high school students in Indiana, Texas, and Mississippi found sex education made no discernable impact.[76]

The *Time* cover story documented the numerous public battles over sex education in the 1980s. The article was filled with colorful quotes of conservatives who worried that the gay community would use the AIDS epidemic as an opportunity to indoctrinate children with alternate lifestyles. "What's next?" asked Joseph Casper, an elected Boston school committee member. "Do we bring in people who want to talk about safe bondage, too? Chimps making it with chickens? It's insane." Equally concerned, liberals worried that this moment would be coopted by conservatives who wanted to impose puritanical abstinence principles on American youth, oppressing women and sexual minorities they deemed to be "deviant." And on the face of these heated debates taking place during Thanksgiving week in *Time* were Charles Schulz's famous cartoon children.[77]

Numerous readers responded to the *Time* editors about the November 24 cover story. In a Letters section two weeks later readers spoke their mind about the topic of sex education next to a reproduction of Charles Schulz's cover, once again suggesting an association between the comic strip and the sex education controversy to the minds of readers. "We should expand public education," wrote one reader from Cincinnati, "to include classes that will guide parents in clarifying their own sexual values and developing the skills they need to communicate these standards to their youngsters." A reader from Minneapolis, Minnesota wrote that "even if this knowledge has to come from outside the home, it is better than having parents give youngsters misinformation or no information at all." Another reader felt that public sex education was an "invasion and is a usurpation of parental rights." Discussions of sex with children was "something so intimate," Frank Kolk of Newark, New Jersey wrote that it "must be kept within the confines of the home and the church." In his opinion, "God never made a substitute for a mother." Kolk made no mention of a father's role in sex education. An Ohio teenager weighed in with her thoughts: "Most of the young people I know have developed liberal ideas about sex, even though the school programs have, if anything, discouraged promiscuous sex and so-called immoral sexual behavior." The young woman believed the reason for the discrepancy was that teenagers' "attitudes do not come from teachers; they come from society and our peers." She recommended that the best approach for teachers would be to give students "the biological facts, teach us about sexually transmitted diseases, then stand back and let us make our own decisions."[78]

Perhaps one of the most glaring omissions in Schulz's cartoon world was the presence of a prominent minority female in *Peanuts*. The cartoonist had made a considerable impact on American culture with the introduction of Franklin, but despite requests from those civil rights advocates who had written to him in the summer of 1968, Schulz never followed Franklin with a black female character. In fact, over the entire fifty-year history of *Peanuts*, Schulz never incorporated a black female in the strip. This omission was symbolically fitting for a post–World War II culture that had always valued racial equality over gender equality, even within civil rights groups. But as scholars have shown, there was a vibrant black feminist movement that tapped into both the civil rights movement and the global pan-African movement. Lawyer Pauli Murray worried about the disconnect within the feminist movement between women's rights and black rights. Murray would quickly become reluctant to support NOW because of its lack of diversity. "I saw no Catholic sisters, no women of ethnic minorities other than about five Negro women," she wrote to the organization's first chairwoman, Kathryn Clarenbach, of the initial meetings, "and obviously no women who represent the poor." In his handling of gender and feminism, Schulz did nothing to address these disparities within the movement.[79]

Still, *Peanuts* did make a real contribution to the visibility of gender and sexual issues in 1970s and 1980s America. Schulz had touched on many important social and political issues over his thirty-five celebrated years in comic arts. Just as Linus's personality had been directly tied to debates over Christianity and civil religion, Franklin embodied the battle for integration, and Snoopy symbolized the passionate emotions of many about the Vietnam War, Lucy and Peppermint Patty became pop-cultural ambassadors of second-wave feminism through *Ms.* magazine and the fight for Title IX. Of course, Schulz's characters were conflicted and imperfect representatives of the movement, but they were also helpful symbols in the fight for publicity and public awareness because their ubiquity in 1960s and 1970s popular culture raised awareness of alternate female types. This was especially important in the promotion of legislation like Title IX. Schulz joined national debates about abortion, women's equality in the workspace, and public school sex education, each time facilitating further discussion of these topics and increasing public awareness of such issues.

Peppermint Patty had a vision. Charles Schulz, while an imperfect spokesman, worked to make the world a little more amenable to her dream.

Epilogue

Snoopy Come Home

As Americans in the summer of 1980 prepared for one of the most consequential elections in modern history, the Republican candidate for president was privately joking not about his Democratic opponent but another "new candidate in the race": Snoopy.[1]

"If I'd only known of his political ambitions, I might have persuaded him to run on the ticket with me as vice president," Ronald Reagan quipped in a letter to Charles Schulz (with no mention of how his running mate George H. W. Bush might feel about the matter). Schulz had poked at his old friend that Snoopy was considering a run for the White House as a third-party candidate. Reagan was probably right in his desire to recruit Snoopy to his ticket given that arguably more Americans were Snoopy fans than registered Republicans (or Democrats, for that matter). Reagan hoped that he could dissuade such a popular candidate from stealing the race. "How would he feel about a cabinet post?" he offered.[2]

The *Peanuts* characters were some of the biggest icons in American culture. There were few comparable images in the world. The list was "Mickey Mouse, the Eiffel Tower, and *Peanuts*," as one advertising executive put it. Snoopy became an especially important figure, both in the strip and popular culture. When astronaut Eugene A. Cernan held a sketch of Snoopy that Schulz had drawn during a global telecast from Apollo 10, NASA estimated that as many as a billion people watched. This recognizability translated into a continued stream of historic licensing deals for Schulz and the *Peanuts* gang.[3]

These deals were massive. In 1983, *Peanuts* joined the Knott's Berry Farm theme park, the third largest park in the country. By the 1990s, more than 3.5 million tourists visited the theme park's Camp Snoopy each year. The bigger deal, however, was the advertising license Schulz signed in 1985 with MetLife, one of the world's largest insurers. By the turn of the century, MetLife would spend more than $30 million a year to reach 100 million customers. Snoopy overlooked the nation's major sporting events for decades from the side of the company's two famous blimps. Snoopy's notoriety was not just about advertising dollars, either. In 1990, the Paris Louvre hosted a pop art exhibit featuring Snoopy for *Peanuts*' fortieth anniversary.

Snoopy truly seemed to be an unstoppable force in American and even world culture.[4]

Yet that was only half of the story. These same years were also a period of declining influence for *Peanuts*. In the years following Ronald Reagan's election to the presidency, Schulz began to lose his hold on Middle America. Increasingly both readers and journalists alike viewed Schulz as conservative, traditional, and rightward-leaning, whereas just a few years before so many had been convinced that he and his work had been progressive, existential, and left of center. By the 1980s, America's mainstream political culture was shifting toward a more openly contentious partisan war over culture, part of the lingering and intensifying legacy of the 1960s. Where Schulz had once been the voice of the broad middle, he began to lose some of his cultural stature and appeal in a new era of open, televised partisanship.

During the last twenty years of the twentieth century, the "culture wars" brought a new contentiousness to American society. Americans on the Left, confident in the successes of the "rights revolution" of the late 1960s and 1970s, pushed for greater social and political openness in America for women, gays, and racial and ethnic minorities, where Americans on the Right, emboldened by their electoral and economic successes in the same period, sought to use their new political strength to "roll back" the advances of the Left. Politicians came to reflect this cultural warfare in their rhetoric, best exemplified in Patrick Buchanan's infamous speech at the 1992 Republican National Convention in which he proclaimed that the party was in "a war for the soul of America." But Buchanan's fiery speech was more a coming of age for the conflict than an origin. Commentators had already been noting this changing political culture for years. George Wallace and Spiro Agnew had received national attention for their verbal assaults on hippies, academics, bureaucrats, and other liberal-minded people, but in the 1970s they had been novel. By the 1980s, this sort of open, verbal partisanship was becoming commonplace not just in Washington, but in communities and school districts across the country. Simultaneously, many social conservatives sensed that artistic expression in television, film, and music was becoming more violent, crude, and sexualized. This was the new political culture rising as Schulz took Peanuts into the overt world of politicized history.[5]

Throughout the 1960s and 1970s, Schulz had addressed the contested social issues of the time through ambiguity, suggestion, and even fantasy. By the 1980s, with his friend Ronald Reagan in the White House, Schulz would start turning to the past to express his feelings about the nation. In 1980, Schulz wrote the fourth *Peanuts* feature film, *Bon Voyage, Charlie Brown (And Don't*

Come Back!), which showed the children traveling for a visit to France and ultimately discovering the story of Charlie Brown's grandfather who had fought in World War II. This seems to have been part of a growing personal nostalgia Schulz felt for the American past, a sense that only intensified following the quadruple bypass surgery he underwent in 1981. As the cartoonist recovered, he penned the screenplay for a new television special to follow immediately after the events of *Bon Voyage, Charlie Brown* and set the children exploring a D-Day cemetery and the battlefields of Omaha Beach and Ypres. *What Have We Learned, Charlie Brown* (1983) would become a meditation on the events and personal sacrifices of soldiers in both world wars. The special would climax with the children standing on the Ypres battlefield overgrown in poppies—a visual reference to the text of one of Schulz's favorite poems, Canadian Lieutenant-Colonel John McCrae's World War I-era "In Flanders Field," published in 1919—and Linus innocently asking, "What have we learned, Charlie Brown?" Much like Schulz's work during Vietnam, this was both a solemn salute to dutiful soldiers and a sober questioning of the benefits of war. Schulz would win the Peabody Award and receive another Emmy nomination for this television special.[6]

The success of the D-Day special also gave executives at CBS the idea to try creating more educational *Peanuts* programming. In the fall of 1988, the resulting project made television history. *This is America, Charlie Brown* was television's first animated miniseries. The opening episode, "The Mayflower Voyagers," premiered on CBS on October 21, 1988. This episode depicted the *Peanuts* children back in 1620 when they boarded the *Mayflower* for the New World. In one of many odd breaks from the *Peanuts* franchise's past, the children changed wardrobe to help them fit into seventeenth-century England. The girls bore most of the imprint of periodization. Peppermint Patty, Marcie, Sally, and Lucy all wore full-length dresses complete with apron and bonnet. Charlie Brown and Linus, however, got away much easier with clothes that were only slightly different from their usual. This program was the most overtly Christian production Schulz had put on television since 1965's *A Charlie Brown Christmas*. Despite the grave danger that faced the voyagers, Charlie Brown narrated in the opening minutes of the program, "their belief in God, their desire for freedom from religious persecution, and their dreams of creating a new world for future generations all make their life-threatening journey a risk worth taking." Both the *Peanuts* characters and the adult Pilgrims would openly pray to God throughout the episode, something that had never before occurred in a *Peanuts* program.[7]

The program was envisioned as a truly educational experience for children. Schulz's longtime producer Lee Mendelson assured the press that "all the statistics and historical references are accurate," going as far as to make sure "there were actually one or two dogs and a couple of birds on the *Mayflower* in 1620 before letting Woodstock and Snoopy on board." Yet the pursuit of historical accuracy quickly ran the program into some of the culture wars' controversies over public history. Concerned members of the American Indian Parents, a civil rights group based in Schulz's hometown of Minneapolis, Minnesota, had contacted the local CBS affiliate in the fall of 1988 with a "strong protest" against the use of the word "savage" in "The Mayflower Voyagers." A week before the premiere CBS vice president of program practices, Carol Altieri, made the public announcement that the word would be removed from the script. But, while the word "savage" was not used, the Native American characters in the program certainly embodied the "noble savage" stereotype. Dressed in little more than a loin cloth and feather headdress, Squanto played a docile servant to the *Peanuts* children and the Pilgrims as they took over land previously cleared by Native Americans. Some critics even questioned the accuracy of the opening episode altogether. "If 'The Mayflower Voyagers' represents a fair sampling of the series," wrote *Los Angeles Times* television critic Charles Solomon, "*This is America, Charlie Brown* is a well-intentioned effort to present history and humor that delivers little of either."[8]

So much of what had defined Schulz's successful career was criticized in this opening episode. The scriptwriting, for which Schulz had often been praised, was "far less seaworthy than the historic sailing ship," Solomon wrote. Charlie Brown and his friends were far removed from their comfortable suburban lives where adults had little say and the children were the philosophers, psychiatrists, and experts. *Peanuts* was "a poor match" for the Pilgrims and felt "bizarrely out of place in the grubby hold of a 17th Century sailing ship, surrounded by adults." Even more sympathetic critics found elements of the episode hard to swallow. The *New York Times*' Caryn James wondered why Peppermint Patty, who had famously protested when her school required her to wear a dress, joined the other girls in wearing a full-length dress, apron, and bonnet when Charlie Brown's only "concession to history is to go barefoot."[9]

Where Schulz had once been celebrated for his inclusivity and moderated approach to racial integration, his animated work in *This is America, Charlie Brown* was found by many to be lacking. Where "The Mayflower Voyagers" did briefly mention indentured servitude, there was no reference to slavery, which had arrived in Plymouth within the first few years. Consequently, Franklin was noticeably missing from the episode. This deficiency in ethnic diversity was obvious in the miniseries' advertising as well. One of the ads for the mini-series depicted Charlie Brown marching beneath the first national flag while playing a field drum. He was flanked on either side by Lucy happily playing a flute and Snoopy accompanying with a drum of his own. The editors of the *New York Amsterdam News*, an African American paper, were stunned. "This is America?" they demanded. "Gosh, artist Schultz [*sic*]," they wrote, "couldn't you let Franklin, the little African-American pal of Chuck's, beat the drum—or is America going to the dogs?"[10]

What was more, the Pilgrim story perfectly fit with the rise of evangelicalism and the Religious Right in the period. Billy Graham, Jerry Falwell, Pat Robertson, and Phyllis Schlafly were all leading personalities in the politicization of evangelicalism during the Reagan years. Ronald Reagan himself had even famously invoked the words of Puritan leader John Winthrop, calling America to embrace its manifest destiny to be a "shining city upon a hill" on the Cold War landscape during his reelection campaign in 1984. If anything, this episode was a parable for Reagan's America whose lesson was that America's foundations lay in Christian faith, racial cooperation, and white male leadership.[11]

Similarly, the second episode of the miniseries, titled "The Birth of the Constitution" and airing on October 28, 1988, reflected the political culture of the 1980s and provided a historical morality lesson for the day's political culture. In this episode, the *Peanuts* children sat in the room and watched as the fifty-five delegates of the Philadelphia Convention sought to save the legacy of the Revolution by reforming the young nation's government. The program highlighted the contentious debate over the various elements of the new government. Throughout, the children, especially Linus, worried whether the Founders would be able to secure a workable compromise to maintain the future union of the thirteen independent republics. Ultimately, the lesson was clear: while the Framers had been able to set aside their personal differences to secure the greater good of the nation, America in the 1980s would be wise to do the same. But where this episode presented a relevant lesson for the time, it also avoided some of the other obvious controversies surrounding this historical event. Like the first episode, Franklin was nowhere to be found and the other major compromise of the convention, the infamous Three-Fifths Compromise, never came up.[12]

There were noticeable changes by the fourth episode of *This is America, Charlie Brown*. In this episode, titled "The NASA Space Station," Lucy served as mission commander while Franklin made his first appearance in the miniseries as the crew's social scientist studying the odd behavior of the other characters. This episode presented some of Schulz's progressive causes. As the children looked down on Earth from the space station, Linus pondered the "unspoiled" appearance of the globe from their viewpoint. "Somehow, when we get back to Earth, we've got to convey this to the people," he expressed to the others. "Somehow, we've just got to work at keeping it undamaged, unspoiled." While Linus offered no practical solutions for his charge, he did articulate the general goal of Schulz's 1970s environmental ethos. Meanwhile, Sally noticed something peculiar about the continents below. "There are no boundary lines," she noted to Peppermint Patty. "Wouldn't it be nice to have maps with no boundaries?" It was becoming clear that the longer the program went on, the more daring Schulz was becoming in his presentation.[13]

The fifth episode, "The Building of the Transcontinental Railroad," offered perhaps the series' most direct acknowledgment of racial exploitation. In a history report to his class at school, Charlie Brown highlighted the fact that Central Pacific Railroad officials had brought in Chinese laborers to work on their section of the transcontinental line. Without reference to their pay or working conditions, Charlie Brown justified the commodity-like importation of over 10,000 low-wage Chinese by praising the workers as "excellent" and "the best workers the railroad officials had ever seen." Schulz used this story to show how Chinese immigrants had proven themselves to the American laborers through hard work, highlighting a quote from one of the railroad's officials who contended that "if these people could build the Great Wall of China, then I have no doubt that they can get through the Sierra Nevada." Much like the Native Americans in the opening episode, the Chinese were represented as undifferentiated small men with wide brimmed hats, ponytail hairstyles, and slanted eyes. There was a moment of honesty, however, when Charlie Brown directed the class to take a closer look at the famous photograph of the Union and Central Pacific railroads meeting in Promontory, Utah. "Ironically, although the Chinese were the backbone of the Central Pacific," he pointed out, "not a single Chinese worker appeared in this picture." Though he did use language to temper a bit of the impact of the truths he spoke, Charlie Brown was the most frank he had been in the series. "In a way," he concluded, "this was a symbol of the negative side of this unbelievable project. Throughout construction, workers on both sides were underpaid and overworked and many lost their lives." It was also, he asserted, "the beginning of the end of the lifestyle of the American Indian." Nonetheless, the engineering marvel and the migration of millions to the West apparently outweighed these negative consequences for Schulz.[14]

Franklin, the sole representative of racial diversity in the *Peanuts* cast, appeared only twice more in the miniseries, coming in the final two episodes. The children visited the Smithsonian Museum in the seventh episode, "The Smithsonian and the Presidents." Franklin did not get to travel back in time to meet Abraham Lincoln with Charlie Brown and Linus, though, and the president made no mention of slavery when he explained the causes of the Civil War to the boys. Franklin did chime in, however, in an extensive discussion of the Great Depression that ended with him, Lucy, Peppermint Patty, and Marcie witnessing Franklin Roosevelt's first inaugural address. But the final episode, "The Music and Heroes of America," was where Franklin finally got his moment. Here he talked about the origins of gospel and blues music in slavery ("where people were owned like property," he explained to the children watching). He went so far as to point out that slavery had begun in America at Jamestown in 1620. One flashback showed Franklin and a group of black children working in a field as a white overseer on horseback looked on. In many ways, the scenes resembled an animated version of the hit television miniseries *Roots* (1977). The narrative would move on to touch the history of segregation. With the help of the girls, Franklin continued to celebrate the achievements of black leaders like Booker T. Washington, George Washington Carver, and W. E. B. DuBois. The program would go on to emphasize the role of Schulz's hero Dwight D. Eisenhower and of Martin Luther King in the desegregation of the United States. In an emotionally charged montage, the children discussed "the turbulent 1960s," complete with newsreel footage of John Kennedy's funeral procession and American air raids and the combat wounded in Vietnam. As Franklin and the girls told the story of civil rights, shots of the audience showed numerous African American children who had never before appeared in the strip or other animated programs.[15]

The final two episodes also focused on a number of the issues that had interested the cartoonist over the years. Schulz highlighted conservationist John Muir and his relationship to Theodore Roosevelt. Charlie Brown singled out Roosevelt's work in securing the national parks system as one of his greatest achievements. In the final episode, Peppermint Patty, Lucy, and the other girls recognized the accomplishments of women like Susan B. Anthony, Clara Barton, Helen Keller, Amelia Earhart, and Margaret Mead. This episode celebrated the lives of immigrants and the importance of labor unions in improving the daily lives of the working class. The miniseries ended with optimism about America's ability to overcome adversity, but the historical interpretation by the end of the miniseries had shifted considerably from where it had begun. In this way, *This is America, Charlie Brown* reflected Schulz's ability throughout his career to shift left and right within the boundaries of mainstream American opinion. Nonetheless, by the late 1980s, Schulz's subtle shifting did not attract the same attention and praise it once had from the press. After the first episode, the miniseries garnered almost no media discussion.

Of course, there were many reasons that *Peanuts* had lost some of its luster by the late 1980s. One reason was that there was so much competition in television by that point. In 1965, *A Charlie Brown Christmas* only had to compete with the programming on the other two network channels. In the intervening twenty-five years, paid cable television had significantly expanded the available channel options for television watchers. The amount of children's animated programming on television had equally increased. Programs from *The Smurfs* and *The Care Bears* to *He-Man and the Masters of the Universe* and *Teenage Mutant Ninja Turtles* were presenting children with many more high-action alternatives to the more traditional formatting of the *Peanuts* specials. And while *Peanuts* was facing increased competition for its child audience, it was facing an equally, and perhaps more important, challenge for the adult audience it had long enjoyed. A new breed of adult-oriented cartoons stormed onto the landscape of American popular culture with the arrival of Matt Groening's *The Simpsons* in 1989, a program filled with overt social commentary and crude humor that was more in the mold of Gary Trudeau's *Doonesbury* than *Peanuts*. This cultural trend was perhaps the biggest challenge to *Peanuts*' dominance in American visual culture. Americans' tastes seemed to be changing. No longer did they look for voices of consensus, but rather they increasingly sought out more sharply opinionated spokespeople in their media. Schulz seemed old-fashioned, in part, because he would not clearly pick a side.[16]

In 1997, Charles Schulz gave one of his final lengthy interviews to the editor of the *Comics Journal*, Gary Groth. At one point, Groth decided to broach the topic of politics. "You don't like politics in strips," he began, noting that politics had been the shortest sections in his notes on the cartoonist. "My impression, based on various things I've read," Groth continued, "is that your bent is somewhat conservative." Schulz quickly butted in. "No," he asserted, "I'm very liberal." Groth was shocked. But Schulz had been "overjoyed to have dined with Ronald Reagan," an invitation that many liberals would have likely declined, Groth pointed out. "Well, so what?" Schulz demanded. "I mean, the man was governor." More than that, though, when Schulz said "liberal" he meant kind or generous, the artist claimed. But he also admitted that he had "always been Republican" like his father. He admired Dwight Eisenhower and Wendell Willkie, and later, Ronald Reagan.

Schulz seemed to sense that Groth was not following his explanation, so he turned to a story. He and his wife Jeannie went to an event for California gubernatorial candidate Kathleen Brown, the daughter of former Democratic Governor Pat Brown. At that event, Schulz claimed, he had a conversation with the candidate about taxes and government services. He demanded to know who planned to cap his income through taxes, because he used considerable amounts of that income, he asserted, to support local charities. "Who is going to support Canine Companions?" he asked about the local non-profit he had heavily supported in recent years. "We built that whole building over there," he admitted, "and we pay to keep it going so those people in wheelchairs can have dogs. . . . Is government going to pay for it?" He even went further to include the sitting president, whom he had met. "This is my only argument with Clinton's whole philosophy. He just thinks that government can do everything," he said. "I've never seen a president who wanted to run so many different things." Just as Groth had sensed, Schulz seemed to have become a conservative.[17]

But conservatives were not all happy with him in later years, either. Reviewing David Michaelis's *Schulz and Peanuts: A Biography* (2007), Southern Baptist thought leader, educator, and regular guest columnist in many of the nation's leading newspapers Russell D. Moore found in Schulz a morality lesson for evangelicals. Where Schulz had once experienced "a profound sense of the Christian moral ethic," his move to California in the late 1950s had drawn him out of the close knit Christian community he had participated in faithfully for a decade and the cartoonist then "slid slowly into doctrinal unorthodoxy and personal despair." Like many evangelical fans who read in later interviews that Schulz had stopped going to church and that he had come to consider himself a "secular humanist," Moore bemoaned the loss of faith of a cultural hero who had proclaimed Jesus to be the meaning of Christmas in his most famous television special. Basing his understanding on Michaelis's interpretation of Schulz—one that Schulz's family members have disputed—Moore surmised that "Schulz's deathbed was, to him, a pumpkin patch on the day after Halloween, haunted only by disappointment in a Being who never showed up."[18]

Moore, like most evangelicals, did not know that Schulz continued to read his Bible regularly and that he had secretly funded the construction of a new fine arts center for his original church's college, Anderson College (now Anderson University) in Anderson, Indiana—though he had refused to let his name go on the building. To them, Schulz had become too liberal, a sort of apostate. Moore still liked Schulz and enjoyed watching the Christmas special with his family each year. He just hoped that Linus had won Schulz over with his story of the Nativity before it was too late.[19]

No critics or fans who read *Peanuts* in its final years claimed to have come to hate Charles Schulz. They had simply begun to lose interest. In 1993, *Chicago*

Tribune columnist Eric Zorn made a plea for *Peanuts* to give up the ghost. Zorn was a longtime fan writing for a newspaper that had carried Schulz's comic strip from its very first day in the fall of 1950. It was time for Charlie Brown to finally hit a homerun, kick the football, and go home. This would be an "overdue exit," Zorn insisted. "*Peanuts* simply isn't amusing or relevant anymore." While this was, in Zorn's opinion, the normal position of most of the funny pages by that time, it was troubling for *Peanuts* because it had once been something spectacular. "In the 1960s and 1970s, when its characters were NASA mascots and featured on the covers of *Time*, *Newsweek*, and *Life*, the strip was a powerful and intriguing cultural force." But now it was over and Zorn hoped that Schulz could sense it, too.[20]

Schulz disagreed. As long as he went on, *Peanuts* would go on. And so it did. But the audience's passion began to fade. Zorn was right, in some ways. Schulz had mattered to millions in a time when everything was shifting and there were so few clear lines in society. By the late twentieth century the battle lines had hardened and *Peanuts* seemed to be a quaint relic from a bygone era. And so by the time that Charles Schulz died on February 12, 2000—the night before his final strip, prepared weeks earlier, ran in newspapers around the world—the artist had lost some of his mass appeal for the same reason he had once earned it: because his work was defined by "sort of a wishy-washiness."[21]

In 2016, MetLife decided the times had changed and officially ended their advertising deal with *Peanuts*. "People are indifferent," an executive told the *New York Times*. "They basically don't care." While Snoopy had been "brought in to connect emotionally with consumers," the property was "no longer relevant to its target audience." To add insult to injury, the deal did not end quickly enough to prevent Nobel Prize-winning economist Paul Krugman from labeling Snoopy "the destroyer" when MetLife fought the federal government in court to stave off new financial regulations passed after the Great Recession. After thirty years as the face of one of the world's largest insurance companies, Snoopy had been sent back to the doghouse.[22]

Still, there were signs of resilience in the franchise. ABC acquired the rights to the television specials from CBS in 2001. Beginning in 2004, a popular reprinting of the entire run of *Peanuts* comic strips became an indie hit in the United States and Europe. Blue Sky productions released a well-received relaunch of the franchise with *The Peanuts Movie*, which combined Schulz's drawing style with 3D computer graphics and attracted a nearly quarter billion dollar global box office. In November 2019, Apple launched a new cartoon

Figure E.1 Since Schulz's passing in 2000, some of the classic themes of *Peanuts* have become important tropes in political cartooning and commentary, such as in this Theo Moudakis cartoon about the 2020 coronavirus pandemic. Courtesy of the Charles M. Schulz Museum and Research Center.

series, "Snoopy in Space," to help drive subscriptions to their new television streaming service intended to compete with Netflix. These new ventures will undoubtedly draw new and renewed attention to Schulz's work.

It has been the classic themes of *Peanuts*, however, that have remained most enduring in American political culture. Charlie Brown's unrequited love from the little red-haired girl, Linus's security blanket, Peppermint Patty and Marcie's ambiguous relationship, and Lucy pulling away the football have all become mainstays of social commentary in the twenty-first century. One example from the 2020 COVID-19 pandemic best symbolizes Schulz's lasting resonance. *Toronto Star* editorial cartoonist Theo Moudakis depicted Lucy, her head shaped like the coronavirus, holding a football called "reopening" before a reluctant Charlie Brown. Moudakis, a long-time *Peanuts* fan, aptly captured the melancholy and quiet persistence of Schulz's chief character. And as long as Charlie Brown keeps trying to kick that football, *Peanuts* will live on as an indispensable metaphor in the politics of modern life.[23]

Notes

Introduction

1. *Washington Post*, Dec. 31, 1965.
2. Charles M. Schulz, *The Complete Peanuts: 1950 to 1952* (Seattle: Fantagraphics Books, 2004), 330, 334.
3. "Good Grief, $150 Million!" *Newsweek*, Dec. 27, 1971; "Why Million of Newspaper Readers Love Peanuts," United Feature Syndicate promotion, c. 1956, "1940s, 1950s, 1960 thru 1969" binder, Charles M. Schulz Museum and Research Center [hereafter CMSMRC]; *Newsweek*, Dec. 29, 1999.
4. "Schulz at 3 O'Clock in the Morning," *Comics Journal*, No. 200 (Dec. 1997); George Lockwood, *Peanuts, Pogo, and Hobbes: A Newspaper Editor's Journey through the World of Comics* (Syracuse, NY: Syracuse University Press, 2013), 69.
5. "Schulz of Peanuts Interviewed," *Penthouse*, Oct. 1971, reprinted in M. Thomas Inge, ed., *Charles M. Schulz: Conversations* (Jackson: University Press of Mississippi, 2000), 66.
6. Kelly D. Soper, *We Go Pogo: Walt Kelly, Politics, and American Satire* (Jackson: University Press of Mississippi, 2012), 12.
7. For more on the turn-of-the-century origins of American comic strips, see Ian Gordon, *Comic Strips and Consumer Culture, 1890–1945* (Washington, DC: Smithsonian Institution Press, 1998) and Lara Saguisag, *Incorrigibles and Innocents: Constructing Childhood and Citizenship in Progressive Era Comics* (New Brunswick, NJ: Rutgers University Press, 2019).
8. Zach O'Malley Greenburg, "The Top-Earning Dead Celebrities of 2019," Forbes, Oct. 30, 2019, https://www.forbes.com/sites/zackomalleygreenburg/2019/10/30/the-top-earning-dead-celebrities-of--2019/#79952ee34e5e.
9. Rheta Grimsley Johnson, *Good Grief: The Story of Charles M. Schulz* (New York: Pharos Books, 1989); David Michaelis, *Schulz and Peanuts: A Biography* (New York: HarperCollins, 2007); Stephen J. Lind, *A Charlie Brown Religion: Exploring the Spiritual Life and Work of Charles M. Schulz* (Jackson: University Press of Mississippi, 2015); Jared Gardner and Ian Gordon, eds., *The Comics of Charles Schulz: The Good Grief of Modern Life* (Jackson: University Press of Mississippi, 2017).

Chapter 1

1. Ann Shields, "You're a Good Man, Charles Schulz," *Los Angeles Times*, Jan. 2, 2000.
2. Ibid.; Sarah Boxer, "You're a Good Man, Charles Schulz," *New York Times*, Feb. 14, 2000.
3. Jim Phelan, "Penthouse Interview: Charles M. Schulz," *Penthouse*, Oct. 1971; Charles M. Schulz, *Peanuts Jubilee: My Life and Art with Charlie Brown and Others* (New York: Holt, Rhinehart and Winston, 1975), 11–36.
4. Phelan, "Penthouse Interview: Charles M. Schulz"; Schulz, *Peanuts Jubilee*, 11–36.

5. Schulz, *Peanuts Jubilee*, 11–36.
6. Charles M. Schulz, *The Complete Peanuts: 1950 to 1952* (Seattle: Fantagraphics Books, 2004), 306; Schulz, *Peanuts Jubilee*, 11–36; David Paul Nord Joan Shelley Rubin, and Michael Schudson, eds., *A History of the Book in America, Vol. 5: The Enduring Book: Print Culture in Postwar America* (Chapel Hill: University of North Carolina Press, 2009), 119.
7. Schulz later wrote, "The entire course came to approximately $170, and I remember my father having difficulty keeping up with the payments. I recall being quite worried when he received dunning letters, and when I expressed these worries to him he said not to become too concerned. I realized then that during those later Depression days he had become accustomed to owing people money. I eventually completed the course, and he eventually paid for it." Schulz, *Peanuts Jubilee*, 11–36. Mary Harrington Hall, "A Conversation with Charles Schulz, or The Psychology of Simplicity," *Psychology Today*, Jan. 1968; Stan Isaacs, "Charles Schulz: Comic Strips Aren't Art," *Newsweek*, Aug. 28, 1977; Eugene Griessman, "Atlanta Weekly Interview: Charles Schulz," *Atlanta Weekly*, Nov. 15, 1981; Leonard Maltin, "Good Grief! Charlie Brown is 35," *International Herald Tribune*, Oct. 2, 1985.
8. Charles M. Schulz, Address to the National Cartoonists Society Convention, May 14, 1994, reprinted in M. Thomas Inge, *Charles M. Schulz: Conversations* (Jackson: University Press of Mississippi, 2000), 126–39.
9. David Michaelis, *Schulz and Peanuts: A Biography* (New York: Harper Perennial, 2007), 127–29; Schulz, *Peanuts Jubilee*, 11–36.
10. Michaelis, *Schulz and Peanuts*, 129; Schulz, *Peanuts Jubilee*, 11–36.
11. "Army of 4,500,000 in 1942; Draft of Fathers Year Away," *The Christian Science Monitor*, Sep. 21, 1942; Schulz, *Peanuts Jubilee*, 11–36.
12. Schulz, *Peanuts Jubilee*, 11–36; Michaelis, *Schulz and Peanuts*, 143.
13. Charles Schulz's "Army Journal" can be found in the holdings of the Charles M. Schulz Museum and Research Center.
14. Hugh Morrow, "The Success of an Utter Failure," *Saturday Evening Post*, Jan. 12, 1957; Hall, "A Conversation with Charles Schulz"; Griessman, "Atlanta Weekly Interview"; Schulz, *Peanuts Jubilee*, 11–36.
15. Hall, "A Conversation with Charles Schulz."
16. Inge, *Charles M. Schulz*, xiv; Schulz, *Peanuts Jubilee*, 11–36; Derrick Bang, *Charles M. Schulz: Li'l Beginnings* (Santa Rosa: Charles M. Schulz Museum and Research Center, 2003), 1; Charles Schulz, *Peanuts: A Golden Celebration* (New York: Harper, 1999), 9.
17. Kenneth L. Wilson, "A Visit with Charles Schulz," *Christian Herald*, Sep. 1967; Charles M. Schulz, "Peanuts," *Collegiate Challenge*, 1963.
18. Brian Walker, *The Comics: The Complete Collection* (New York: Abrams Books, 2011), 76–77; Michael Tisserand, *Krazy: George Herriman, A Life in Black and White* (New York: Harper Perennial, 2016), 232.
19. Barnaby Conrad, "You're a Good Man, Charlie Schulz," *New York Times Magazine*, Apr. 16, 1967; Hall, "A Conversation with Charles Schulz"; Schulz, *Peanuts Jubilee*, 11–36.
20. Schulz, *Peanuts Jubilee*, 11–36; Walker, *The Comics*, 360, 374, 382.
21. Bang, *Charles M. Schulz*, 115, 143.
22. Ibid., 175.
23. Schulz, *Peanuts Jubilee*, 11–36; Rheta Grimsley Johnson, *Good Grief: The Story of Charles M. Schulz* (New York: Pharos Books, 1989), 21–22.
24. Phelan, "Penthouse Interview."

25. Schulz, *Peanuts Jubilee*, 11–36.
26. Ibid., 11–36; Bang, *Charles M. Schulz*, 6.
27. Schulz, *Peanuts Jubilee*, 11–36.
28. Ibid., 11–36; Johnson, *Good Grief*, 23–24.
29. Johnson, *Good Grief*, 24–25.
30. Ibid., 25; Walker, *The Comics*, 438.
31. Johnson, *Good Grief*, 25–26; Letter from Joseph R. Fawcett to James Hennessy, July 21, 1950, Correspondence 1950, UFS Records, 1950–1959, Box 1, SC2002/2, CMSMRC; Letter from Benjamin M. Schankman to United Features Syndicate, Oct. 30, 1950, Correspondence 1950, UFS Records, 1950–1959, Box 1, SC2002/2, CMSMRC. The abruptness of the change in title helps to explain Schulz's career-long disdain for the *Peanuts* title. See Jane McMaster, "UFS Signs 'Li'l Folks,' 'Howdy Doody' Page," newspaper clipping, "1940s, 1950s, 1960 thru 1969" archive binder, CMSMRC.
32. Schulz, *The Complete Peanuts*, 316, 318.
33. Promotional Brochure and United Feature Syndicate invoice, Nov. 20, 1950, Correspondence 1950, UFS Records, 1950–1959, Box 1, SC2002/2, CMSMRC.

Chapter 2

1. Cynthia Gorney, "The Peanuts Progenitor," *Washington Post*, Oct. 2, 1985, reprinted in *Charles M. Schulz: Conversations*, ed. M. Thomas Inge (Jackson: University Press of Mississippi, 2000), 134.
2. *Denver Post*, Oct. 2, 1950; David Halberstam, *The Fifties* (New York: Random House, 1993), 69; George H. Gallup, *The Gallup Poll: Public Opinion, 1935–1971, vol. 2* (New York: Random House, 1972), 933. For more on the conduct of the Korean War, see the first two volumes of Allan R. Millett's projected trilogy *The War for Korea* (Lawrence: University Press of Kansas).
3. *Washington Post*, Oct. 2, 1950; *Seattle Times*, Oct. 2, 1950; *Denver Post*, Oct. 2, 1950.
4. "Fallout Shelters," *LIFE* (Sep. 15, 1961), 96; J. Ronald Oakley, *God's Country: America in the Fifties* (New York: Dembner Books, 1986), vii.
5. *Denver Post*, Oct. 2, 1950, 1; *Seattle Times*, Oct. 2, 1950, 1; *Washington Post*, Oct. 2, 1950, A3.
6. David Michaelis, *Schulz and Peanuts: A Biography* (New York: Harper Perennial, 2007), 206.
7. *Chicago Daily Tribune*, Oct. 2, 1950, 1.
8. Oakley, *God's Country*, 6; Rheta Grimsley Johnson, *Good Grief: The Story of Charles M. Schulz* (New York: Pharos Books, 1989), x.
9. "Through the Looking-Glass with Charles M. Schulz," *Yale Daily News*, no. 97, Feb. 21, 1958; Sarah Boxer, "The Exemplary Narcissism of Snoopy," *The Atlantic*, Nov. 2015.
10. Hugh Morrow, "The Success of an Utter Failure," *Saturday Evening Post*, Jan. 12, 1957; Richard Pitnick, "Charles Schulz: Good Grief," *Coast Weekly*, date unknown.
11. Grace Elizabeth Hale, *A Nation of Outsiders: How the White Middle Class Fell in Love with Rebellion in Postwar America* (New York: Oxford University Press, 2011), 3.
12. *Washington Post*, Oct. 17, 1954. Schulz later confessed that he did not anticipate how widely the security blanket would resonate with his audience. Had he known, he might have introduced the concept differently. "It wasn't plotted very carefully at first because I think even Charlie Brown had a blanket in one or two sequences," Schulz told one interviewer. Stan Isaacs, "Charles Schulz: Comic Strips Aren't Art," *Newsday*, Aug. 28, 1977, reprinted

in *Charles M. Schulz*, ed. Inge, 91; Stan Isaacs, "Charles Schulz: Comic Strips Aren't Art," *Newsday*, Aug. 28, 1977, reprinted in *Charles M. Schulz*, ed. Inge, 91.

13. *Dothan Eagle*, Sep. 4, 1944; Don Whitehead, "Hodges' Tanks Race on Toward Berlin at Will," *Los Angeles Times*, Mar. 27, 1945; Ray Robinson, "Australia Tense on Eve of A-Tests," *Christian Science Monitor*, Sep. 17, 1952; "A-Bomb Security Blanket Held Curb on Propulsion," *Christian Science Monitor*, Nov. 7, 1956; Ray Vicker, "Atom Sharing: U.S. Readies Glimpse Under Security Blanket for Foreign Friendlies," *Wall Street Journal*, Feb. 10, 1955. In some isolated instances, the term "security blanket" was also used to refer to the Social Security Act, such as in "Vandenberg Shifts, Asks Wider Security Blanket," *Atlanta Constitution*, Mar. 13, 1944, and "Ike Asks Broader Security Blanket," *Atlanta Constitution*, Jan. 15, 1954, though it does not appear that the largest national papers adopted this usage.
14. Letter from D. W. Winnicott to Editor, *New York Herald Tribune*, Sep. 19, 1955, Correspondence 1955, UFS Records 1950–1959, UFS Records, Box 1, CMSMRC; Letter from Laurence Rutman to D. W. Winnicott, Sep. 30, 1955, Correspondence 1955, UFS Records 1950–1959, UFS Records, Box 1, CMSMRC; Letter from Timothy Leary to Charles M. Schulz, Dec. 23, 1954, Correspondence January 1955, UFS Records 1954–1961, Box 1, Schulz Correspondence, CMSMRC; Letter from James Hennessy to Timothy Leary, Jan. 6, 1955, Correspondence January 1955, UFS Records 1954–1961, Box 1, Schulz Correspondence, CMSMRC; Letter from Timothy Leary to United Feature Syndicate, Nov. 13, 1956, Correspondence November 1956, UFS Records 1954–1961, Box 2, Schulz Correspondence, CMSMRC.
15. "The Play for High Stakes in the Summit Game," *LIFE*, Mar. 30, 1959. Even today, *Peanuts* fans find deep comfort and reassurance in reading about Charlie Brown's mental health struggles. See, for example, Deborah DeClementi, "Charlie Brown's Existential Crisis Saved My Life," The Coffeelicious, Medium, Mar. 25, 2017, https://medium.com/the-coffeelicious/charlie-browns-existential-crisis-saved-my-life-a9053a90d732.
16. Richard Slotkin, *Gunfighter Nation: The Myth of the Frontier in Twentieth-Century America* (New York: Atheneum, 1992), 347, 350–52.
17. While the first year or so of *Peanuts* was clearly set in an urban space (like the one Schulz knew in Minneapolis-St. Paul), the strip quickly and quietly moved to the suburbs for the rest of the strip's publishing run. This suburban space, the home of unprecedented home-building and strip mall developments, was in a sense a frontier of its own, making the use of Wild West metaphors apt. For more on the creation of this "crabgrass frontier," see Kenneth T. Jackson's *Crabgrass Frontier: The Suburbanization of the United States* (New York: Oxford University Press, 1987). Two such examples appeared in the same week in November 1951. On November 6, Violet played an Indian princess, while on November 7, she was a cowgirl gunfighter, though her gunshot sounds were not authentic enough to impress the boys.
18. Letter from Richard G. Axt to Charles M. Schulz, Jan. 22, 1955, Correspondence 1955, UFS Records 1950–1959, UFS Records, Box 1, CMSMRC.
19. Roy J. Dunlap, "When the A-Bomb Bursts on St. Paul," *St. Paul Pioneer Press*, Jan. 8, 1950.
20. *Washington Post*, Jan. 5, 1958.
21. Tom Engelhardt, *The End of Victory Culture: Cold War America and the Disillusioning of a Generation* (Amherst: University of Massachusetts Press, 1995), 7.
22. Murray Illson, "Atomic Neurosis Feared for Young," *New York Times*, Sep. 5, 1953, 12.
23. Lara Saguisag, "Consuming Childhood: *Peanuts* and Children's Consumer Culture in the Postwar Era," in *The Comics of Charles Schulz: The Good Grief of Modern Life*, ed. Jared

Gardener and Ian Gordon (Jackson: University Press of Mississippi, 2017), 73–74. For more on the backlash against comic books and the creation of the Comics Code, see Carol L. Tilley, "Seducing the Innocent: Frederic Wertham and the Falsifications That Helped Condemn Comics," *Information & Culture* 47, no. 4 (2012): 383–414 and Amy Kiste Nyberg, *Seal of Approval: The History of the Comics Code* (Jackson: University Press of Mississippi, 1998).

24. Saguisag, "Consuming Childhood," 75.
25. "Peanuts Artist Awarded Top Cartoon Prize," *Minneapolis Star Tribune*, undated clipping, "1940s, 1950s, 1960 thru 1969" binder, CMSMRC; "Schulz Wins NCS Reuben for Peanuts," *Editor & Publisher*, Apr. 28, 1956; "J. Walter Thompson Company News," vol. 14, no. 40 (Oct. 7, 1959), Box MN12, 1951–1970 *J. Walter Thompson Company News*, J. Walter Thompson Company, Newsletter Collection, 1910–2005, RL.00733, David M. Rubenstein Rare Book and Manuscripts Collection, Duke University; Letter from Robert D. McMillen to Laurence Rutman, Mar. 4, 1955, Correspondence 1955, UFS Records 1950–1959, UFS Records, Box 1, CMSMRC; Letter from Charles M. Schulz to James Hennessy, Aug. 22, 1954, Correspondence 1955, UFS Records 1950–1959, UFS Records, Box 1, CMSMRC.
26. Booklet: "The Brownie Book of Picture Taking" Kodak, 1955, 2011.110.004, CMSMRC; Letter from John Schnapp to Laurence Rutman, Apr. 29, 1955, Correspondence 1955, UFS Records 1950–1959, UFS Records, Box 1, CMSMRC.
27. "J. Walter Thompson Company News," vol. 14, no. 40 (Oct. 7, 1959), Box MN12, 1951–1970 *J. Walter Thompson Company News*, J. Walter Thompson Company, Newsletter Collection, 1910–2005, RL.00733, David M. Rubenstein Rare Book and Manuscripts Collection, Duke University; "J. Walter Thompson Company News," vol. 15, no. 21 (May 25, 1960), Box MN12, 1951–1970 *J. Walter Thompson Company News*, J. Walter Thompson Company, Newsletter Collection, 1910–2005, RL.00733, David M. Rubenstein Rare Book and Manuscripts Collection, Duke University.
28. "J. Walter Thompson Company News," vol. 17, no. 8 (Feb. 21, 1962), Box MN12, 1951–1970 *J. Walter Thompson Company News*, J. Walter Thompson Company, Newsletter Collection, 1910–2005, RL.00733, David M. Rubenstein Rare Book and Manuscripts Collection, Duke University.

Chapter 3

1. "A Charlie Brown Christmas Coca-Cola Company Correspondence Scrapbook," (hereafter Coca-Cola Scrapbook) Peanuts Licensing Archives, 2015.004, Charles M. Schulz Museum and Research Center (hereafter CMSMRC); "Roy Burns, Former Judge, Dead," *Argus Leader* (Sioux Falls, SD), May 15, 1980, Papers of Lorene Genevieve Burns and Roy David Burns, RG 02.0009.016, University Archives, University of Iowa Libraries.
2. David Michaelis, *Schulz and Peanuts: A Biography* (New York: Harper Perennial, 2007), 359; Coca-Cola Scrapbook, CMSMRC.
3. "Peanuts on TV: More than a Christmas Present," *Christianity Today*, Dec. 3, 1965; Stephen J. Whitfield, *The Culture of the Cold War* (Baltimore: Johns Hopkins University Press, 1996), 83; for more on the fragmentation of American religious culture in post–World War II America, see Peter Manseau, *One Nation, Under Gods: A New American History* (New York: Little, Brown, 2015).

4. Kenneth L. Wilson, "A Visit with Charles Schulz," *Christian Herald*, Sep. 1967; Rick Marschall, "An Interview with Charles Schulz," *NEMO: The Classic Comics Library*, Jan. 1992, reprinted in M. Thomas Inge, *Charles Schulz: Conversations* (Jackson: University Press of Mississippi); Charles M. Schulz, "Peanuts," *Collegiate Challenge*, 1963; Charles M. Schulz, "Knowing You Are Not Alone," *Decision*, Sep. 1963.
5. "Why Million of Newspaper Readers Love Peanuts," United Feature Syndicate promotional brochure, c. 1956, CMSMRC; *Time*, Apr. 9, 1965.
6. Charles M. Schulz, "Happiness Is a Lot of Assignments," *Writer's Yearbook*, 1965 edition, 44–46, 153.
7. *Writer's Yearbook*, 44–46, 153; *Time*, Apr. 9, 1965; *Collegiate Challenge*, 1963.
8. Michelle M. Nickerson, *Mother of Conservatism: Women and the Postwar Right* (Princeton, NJ: Princeton University Press, 2012), 148; Darren Dochuk, *From Bible Belt to Sunbelt: Plain-Folk Religion, Grassroots Politics, and the Rise of Evangelical Conservatism* (New York: Norton, 2011), 181–82; "Twixt Twelve and Twenty," *Washington Post*, Apr. 12, 1959.
9. Michaelis, *Schulz and Peanuts*, 294; Grant Wacker, *America's Pastor: Billy Graham and the Shaping of a Nation* (Cambridge, MA: The Belknap Press of Harvard University, 2014), 15; "In the Garden," *Christian Century*, May 15, 1957, quoted in William Martin, *A Prophet with Honor: The Billy Graham Story* (New York: Morrow, 1991), 225–38; *Los Angeles Times*, Sep. 1, 1957.
10. Charles M. Schulz, "Knowing You Are Not Alone," *Decision*, Sep. 1963; Michaelis, *Schulz and Peanuts*, 294.
11. Wilson, "A Visit with Charles Schulz."
12. *Washington Post*, Dec. 21, 1958.
13. *Salt Lake Tribune*, Dec. 20, 1959; *Abilene Reporter News* (Abilene, TX), Dec. 11, 1960.
14. *Joplin News Herald* (Joplin, MO), Jan. 29, 1960; *Berkshire Eagle* (Pittsfield, MA), July 6, 1960; *Los Angeles Times*, Feb. 24, 1961 *Charleston Daily Mail* (Charleston, WV), Aug. 1, 1960; *Washington Post*, Aug. 14, 1960.
15. *Christian Herald*, Sep. 1967.
16. "Dead Sea Scrolls to Be at '64 Fair," *New York Times*, Aug. 1, 1962.
17. *Chicago Tribune*, Dec. 23, 1962; "Dead Sea Scrolls Stir Growing Controversy," *New York Times*, Feb. 12, 1956.
18. For more on *Engel v. Vitale* and *Abington School District v. Schempp*, see Kevin M. Kruse, *One Nation Under God: How Corporate America Invented Christian America* (New York: Basic Books, 2015), 165–201, and Bruce J. Dierenfield, *The Battle Over School Prayer: How Engel v. Vitale Changed America* (Lawrence: University Press of Kansas, 2007); *Chicago Daily Tribune*, June 27, 1962; *Chicago Daily Defender*, July 9, 1962; Harris poll, Nov. 1966, iPoll Databank, Roper Center for Public Opinion Research, University of Connecticut, ropercenter.uconn.edu.libdata.lib.ua.edu/data_ access/ipoll/ipoll.html (Oct. 4, 2015).
19. *Corpus Christi Caller Times* (Corpus Christi, TX), Oct. 20, 1960.
20. *Time*, Apr. 9, 1965; Charles M. Schulz, *Peanuts: A Golden Celebration* (New York: HarperCollins, 1999), 50.
21. "Correspondence: Fan Letters re: specific strips" binder, CMSMRC.
22. M. Thomas Inge, ed., *My Life with Charlie Brown* (Jackson: University Press of Mississippi, 2010), 162; "Correspondence: Fan Letters re: specific strips" binder, CMSMRC.

23. "Correspondence: Fan Letters re: specific strips" binder, CMSMRC.
24. "Correspondence: Fan Letters re: specific strips" binder, CMSMRC. Another important example was a letter from the publicity chairman of the Altadena Americanism Center in Southern California. Beginning in 1960, at least thirty-six different conservative bookstores and educational centers, like the Altadena Americanism Center, opened across the greater Los Angeles region. These stores were filled with John Birch Society pamphlets, anti-communist literature, and bestselling books like Whittaker Chambers's *Witness* and Herbert Philbrick's *I Led Three Lives*. This network of independent stores worked to inform their communities of the dangers of communism on the home front, sharing inventory when necessary to meet urgent demands. The storeowners often referred to their establishments as "patriotic" bookstores in order "to reflect the self-perception among founders that they inculcated core American principles into the community rather than political ideology." The Altadena bookstore requested the original artwork for the October 20 strip, a request that was denied. "Correspondence: Fan Letters re: specific strips" binder, CMSMRC; Nickerson, *Mother of Conservatism*, 142–47. For more on New Right grassroots politics in Southern California, see Lisa McGirr, *Suburban Warriors: The Origins of the New Right* (Princeton, NJ: Princeton University Press, 2001).
25. Harold E. Achor, "Is This Concept Good for America?" *Vital Christianity*, Sep. 27, 1964, 7–8, 10, Nicholson Library Archives, Anderson University; "Removing Religious Practices," *Vital Christianity*, Oct. 11, 1964, 16, Nicholson Library Archives, Anderson University (hereafter NLA).
26. Charles M. Schulz, "No Government Approval Needed," *Vital Christianity*, Nov. 1, 1964, 16, NLA.
27. "Correspondence: Fan Letters re: specific strips" binder, CMSMRC.
28. "Schulz at 3 O'clock in the Morning," *Comics Journal*, No. 200 (Dec. 1997), reprinted in Inge, *Charles Schulz*, 254.
29. This is a central part of Kevin M. Kruse's argument in *One Nation Under God*.
30. "Correspondence: Fan Letters re: specific strips" binder, CMSMRC; see Kruse, *One Nation Under God;* "A Visit with Charles Schulz," *Christian Herald*, Sep. 1967; *Clearfield Progress* (Clearfield, PA), Sep. 11, 1963.
31. *Washington Post*, Sep. 27, 1964.
32. *Altoona Mirror* (Altoona, PA), Nov. 3, 1959; *Oneonta Star* (Oneonta, NY), Oct. 29, 1960; *Morning Herald* (Hagerstown, MD), Oct. 28. 1963.
33. *Time*, Apr. 9, 1965.
34. Robert L. Short, *The Gospel According to Peanuts* (Atlanta: J. Knox Press, 1965), 123; *The Andersonian* (Anderson College), Sep. 23, 1966; "Peanuts on TV: More than a Christmas Present," *Christianity Today*, Dec. 3, 1965; Michaelis, *Schulz and Peanuts*, 352; *Time*, Jan. 1, 1965; *Dayton Daily News and Journal Herald Magazine*, May 3, 1987; Review of "The Gospel According to Peanuts," *Young Calvinist*, Apr. 1965.
35. Lee Mendelson, *A Charlie Brown Christmas: The Making of a Tradition* (New York: HarperResource, 2000), 14–15.
36. Mendelson, *A Charlie Brown Christmas*, 17–23.
37. Inge, *My Life with Charlie Brown*, 162; Charles M. Schulz, *A Charlie Brown Christmas* (1965).
38. *A Charlie Brown Christmas* (1965).

39. Charles M. Schulz, Commencement Address at Saint Mary's College of California, delivered June 11, 1966, reprinted in Inge, *My Life with Charlie Brown*, 26–31, 138; "A Christmas Miracle: The Making of *A Charlie Brown Christmas*," (New York: United Feature Syndicate, 2008) in *A Charlie Brown Christmas*, DVD, directed by Bill Melendez (1965; Burbank: Warner Home Video, 2008); Lee Mendelson, *Charlie Brown and Charlie Schulz* (New York: New American Library, 1971), 156; Stephen J. Lind, "Christmas in the 1960s: *A Charlie Brown Christmas*, Religion, and the Conventions of the Television Genre," *Journal of Religion and Popular Culture* 26 (Spring 2014), 1–22.
40. *Advertising Age*, Jan. 10, 1966; *Variety*, Dec. 15, 1965; *Time*, Dec. 10, 1965.
41. Coca-Cola Scrapbook, CMSMRC.
42. Stephen J. Lind, *A Charlie Brown Religion: Exploring the Spiritual Life and Work of Charles M. Schulz* (Jackson: University Press of Mississippi, 2015), 69–70; Inge, *My Life with Charlie Brown*, 137–38.
43. Lind, *A Charlie Brown Religion*, 69; Coca-Cola Scrapbook, CMSMRC.
44. Coca-Cola Scrapbook, CMSMRC.
45. Coca-Cola Scrapbook, CMSMRC.
46. Newspaper clipping, "The Saga of Charlie Brown," Dec. 22, 1965, Coca-Cola Scrapbook, CMSMRC.
47. "Correspondence: Fan Letters re: specific strips" binder, CMSMRC.

Chapter 4

1. Derrick Bang, *Charles M. Schulz: L'il Beginnings* (Santa Rosa: Charles M. Schulz Museum and Research Center, 2003), 243.
2. In February 1968, crime and lawlessness (a reference to the looting and rioting that had taken place in cities across the United States over recent years and were inseparable from racial tensions) and civil rights were the two most concerning issues for Americans, according to the Gallup Poll. This reflected the trend throughout the 1960s. See *Los Angeles Times*, Feb. 28, 1968. See also *Hartford Courant*, Oct. 11, 1964; *Los Angeles Times*, Oct. 13, 1965; and *Washington Post*, Dec. 20, 1967.
3. Langston Hughes, *Vintage Hughes* (New York: Vintage Books, 2004), 12; *Washington Post*, Mar. 15, 1953.
4. For more on the cultural significance of mealtime during Jim Crow, see Angela Jill Cooley, *To Live and Dine in Dixie: The Evolution of Urban Food Culture in the Jim Crow South* (Athens: University of Georgia Press, 2015).
5. For more on the course of the civil rights movement in the 1960s, see Robert J. Norrell, *The House I Live In: Race in the American Century* (Oxford: Oxford University Press, 2005); James T. Patterson, *Brown v. Board of Education: A Civil Rights Milestone and Its Troubled Legacy* (Oxford: Oxford University Press, 2001); Danielle L. McGuire, *At the Dark End of the Street: Black Women, Rape, and Resistance-a New History of the Civil Rights Movement from Rosa Parks to the Rise of Black Power* (New York: Vintage Books, 2011); Charles W. Eagles, *The Price of Defiance: James Meredith and the Integration of Ole Miss* (Chapel Hill: University of North Carolina Press, 2014); Taylor Branch's *America in the Years of King* trilogy; Raymond Arsenault, *Freedom Riders: 1961 and the Struggle for Racial Justice* (Oxford: Oxford University Press, 2011); Julian Zelizer, *The Fierce Urgency of Now: Lyndon Johnson, Congress, and the Battle for the Great Society* (New York: Penguin Books, 2015);

Thomas J. Sugrue, *The Origins of the Urban Crisis: Race and Inequality in Postwar Detroit* (Princeton, NJ: Princeton University Press, 1996).

6. Fredrik Strömberg, *Black Images in the Comics: A Visual History* (Seattle: Fantagraphics Books, 2003), 131, 141; Bradford W. Wright, *Comic Book Nation: The Transformation of Youth Culture in America* (Baltimore: Johns Hopkins University Press, 2001), 219. Also see Adilifu Nama, *Super Black: American Pop Culture and Black Superheroes* (Austin: University of Texas Press, 2011) and Sheena C. Howard and Ronald L. Jackson II, eds., *Black Comics: Politics of Race and Representation* (London: Bloomsbury, 2013). Pre-Comics Code, publisher EC Comics did challenger some of the stereotypes of their era as documented in Qiana Whitted, *EC Comics: Race, Shock, & Social Protest* (New Brunswick: Rutgers University Press, 2019). As for the Black Panther, while he was introduced in *The Fantastic Four* 52 (Marvel Comics, July 1966), he did not receive a regular role in the Marvel universe until "Death Calls for the Arch-Heroes," *The Avengers* 52 (Marvel Comics, May 1967). The first black bystanders began appearing in *The Amazing Spider-Man* in 1965. The first major African American supporting character was the *Daily Bugle*'s city editor Joe Robertson, who first appeared in "The Tentacles and the Trap," *The Amazing Spider-Man* 52 (Marvel Comics, Sep. 1965). Meanwhile, DC Comics, the leading comic book publisher of the period, published books that "were the image of affluent [white] America" (Wright, *Comic Book Nation*, 184).
7. Kevern Verney, *African Americans and US Popular Culture* (London: Routledge, 2003), 51–57, 70; Mike O'Connor, "Liberals in Space: The 1960s Politics of Star Trek," *The Sixties* 5, no. 2 (2012): 185–203. The case of *Amos "n" Andy* was especially complicated by the fact that the television program had been adapted from an earlier radio program performed in the minstrelsy tradition by white actors in black face. For more context *Amos "n" Andy*, see Melvin Patrick Ely, *The Adventures of Amos "N" Andy: A Social History of an American Phenomenon* (Charlottesville: University of Virginia Press, 2001). For more on the "mammy" type in American popular culture, see Grace Elizabeth Hale, *Making Whiteness: The Culture of Segregation in the South, 1890–1940* (New York: Pantheon Books, 1998), 85–120.
8. Charles M. Schulz, *Peanuts Jubilee: My Life and Art with Charlie Brown and Others* (New York: Holt, Rinehart and Winston, 1975), 81.
9. Letter from Harriet Glickman to Charles M. Schulz, Apr. 4, 1968, Glickman Papers, SC2002.003, CMSMRC; Interview with Harriet Glickman, conducted by Patty Jackson, "Fireside Chat with Harriet Glickman", 106th Annual NAACP Convention, Philadelphia, PA, July 13, 2015; Interview with Harriet Glickman, conducted by Corry Katzenberg, Santa Rosa, CA, Oct. 29, 2014.
10. King's presence on behalf of striking laborers was part of his and the Southern Christian Leadership Conference's larger initiative known as the Poor People's Campaign, which was scheduled to hold a national march in the summer of 1968. This campaign represented a larger shift in the demands of the civil rights movement as black leaders expanded their attention to include not just legal equality, partially addressed in the Civil Rights Act of 1964 and Voting Rights Act of 1965, but also to economic equality. For more on the expansion of the civil rights movement to address economic inequality, see Taylor Branch, *At Canaan's Edge: America in the King Years, 1965–68* (New York: Simon & Schuster, 2006); *Washington Post*, Apr. 5, 1968; *Washington Post*, Nov. 29, 2015; Interview with Harriet Glickman, conducted by Corry Katzenberg, Santa Rosa, CA, Oct. 29, 2014; Letter from Harriet Glickman to Charles M. Schulz, Apr. 4, 1968, Glickman Papers, SC2002.003, CMSMRC.

11. Letter from Harriet Glickman to Charles M. Schulz, Apr. 4, 1968, Glickman Papers, SC2002.003, CMSMRC; for more on the "suburban housewife" in postwar American grassroots politics, see McGirr, *Suburban Warriors*, Nickerson, *Mothers of Conservatism*; Moreton, *To Serve God and Walmart*; Matthew D. Lassiter, *The Silent Majority: Suburban Politics in the Sunbelt South* (Princeton, NJ: Princeton University Press, 2006); Dochuk, *From Sunbelt to Bible Belt: Plain-Folk Religion, Grassroots Politics, and the Rise of Evangelical Conservatism* (New York: Norton, 2011); Donald T. Critchlow, *Phyllis Schlafly and Grassroots Conservatism: A Woman's Crusade* (Princeton, NJ: Princeton University Press, 2005).
12. Letter from Harriet Glickman to Charles M. Schulz, Apr. 4, 1968, Glickman Papers, SC2002.003, CMSMRC.
13. Letter from Charles M. Schulz to Harriet Glickman, Apr. 26, 1968, Glickman Papers, SC2002.003, CMSMRC.
14. Ann N. Ridgeway, "Allen Saunders," *Journal of Popular Culture* 5 (Fall 1971), 385–420; M. Thomas Inge, ed., *My Life with Charlie Brown* (Jackson: University Press of Mississippi, 2010), 4; Brian Walker, *The Comics: The Complete Collection* (New York: Abrams ComicArts, 2011), 382–87.
15. National Opinion Research Center SRS Amalgam Survey, Apr. 1968, iPOLL Databank, Roper Center for Public Opinion Research, University of Connecticut, ropercenter.uconn.edu.libdata.lib.ua.edu/data_ access/ipoll/ipoll.html (Jan. 14, 2016); Gallup Poll, Apr. 1968, iPOLL Databank, Roper Center for Public Opinion Research, University of Connecticut, ropercenter.uconn.edu.libdata.lib.ua.edu/data_ access/ipoll/ipoll.html (Jan. 14, 2016); Gallup Poll, May 1968, iPOLL Databank, Roper Center for Public Opinion Research, University of Connecticut, ropercenter.uconn.edu.libdata.lib.ua.edu/data_ access/ipoll/ipoll.html (Jan. 14, 2016); Gallup Poll, Sep. 1968, iPOLL Databank, Roper Center for Public Opinion Research, University of Connecticut, ropercenter.uconn.edu.libdata.lib.ua.edu/data_ access/ipoll/ipoll.html (Jan. 14, 2016).
16. Letter from Harriet Glickman to Charles M. Schulz, Apr. 27, 1968, Glickman Papers, SC2002.003, CMSMRC; Letter from Charles M. Schulz to Harriet Glickman, May 9, 1968, Glickman Papers, SC2002.003, CMSMRC. For more on the treatment of the black image in American popular culture see Hale, *Making Whiteness* and W. Fitzhugh Brundage, ed., *Beyond Blackface: African Americans and the Creation of American Popular Culture, 1890–1930* (Chapel Hill: University of North Carolina Press, 2011).
17. Letter from Harriet Glickman to Charles M. Schulz, June 11, 1968, Glickman Papers, SC2002.003, CMSMRC.
18. Letter from Kenneth C. Kelly to Charles M. Schulz, June 6, 1968, Glickman Papers, SC2002.003, CMSMRC.
19. Letter from Monica Gunning to Charles M. Schulz, June 8, 1968, Glickman Papers, SC2002.003, CMSMRC.
20. Letter from Charles M. Schulz to Harriet Glickman, July 1, 1968, Glickman Papers, SC2002.003, CMSMRC.
21. Letter from Harriet Glickman to Charles M. Schulz, July 7, 1968, Glickman Papers, SC2002.003, CMSMRC
22. *Newsweek*, Dec. 27, 1968; *Newsweek*, July 29, 1968.
23. *Hartford Courant*, Jan. 9, 1968; Lassiter, *The Silent Majority*, 121–22; for more on Ronald Reagan's racial politics, see Joseph Crespino, *In Search of Another Country: Mississippi and*

the Conservative Counterrevolution (Princeton, NJ: Princeton University Press, 2007) and Dochuk, *From Bible Belt to Sunbelt*; for more on public and media responses to busing across the United States, see Matthew F. Delmont, *Why Busing Failed: Race, Media, and the National Resistance to School Desegregation* (Berkeley: University of California Press, 2016).

24. *Newsweek*, July 29, 1968.
25. While Minneapolis-St. Paul had only 1 percent African American population in the 1930s, the 8,916 African Americans living in the metropolitan area made up nearly 90 percent of Minnesota's total African American population during that decade. U.S. Census Bureau, *Sixteenth Census of the United States: 1940*, Volume II, Part 4 (Washington, DC: Government Printing Office, 1943); by the 1950 U.S. Census, Minneapolis-St. Paul's 12,570 African Americans made up just 1.1 percent of the cities' populations. U.S. Census Bureau, *A Report of the Seventeenth Census of the United States, Census of the Population: 1950*, Volume II, Part 23 (Washington, DC: Government Printing Office, 1952); James T. Patterson, *Grand Expectations: The United States, 1945–1974* (New York: Oxford University Press, 1996), 19; U.S. Census Bureau, *1970 Census of Population*, Volume 1, Part 1 (Washington, DC: Government Printing Office, 1973); *Newsweek*, July 29, 1968.
26. Letter from Morrie Turner to Charles M. Schulz, July 26, 1968, "Correspondence: Fan Letters re: specific strips" binder, CMSMRC.
27. Robert O. Self, *American Babylon: Race and the Struggle for Postwar Oakland* (Princeton, NJ: Princeton University Press, 2003), 48, 52; *Atlanta Constitution*, Mar. 2, 1981; Interview with Morrie Turner, conducted by Scott Nichol, Santa Rosa, CA, Aug. 7, 2010.
28. Interview with Morrie Turner, conducted by Scott Nichol, Santa Rosa, CA, Aug. 7, 2010; *Hartford Courant*, Nov. 2, 1972.
29. *Hartford Courant*, Nov. 2, 1972; Interview with Morrie Turner, conducted by Scott Nichol, Santa Rosa, CA, Aug. 7, 2010.
30. Self, *American Babylon*, 42, 47; Interview with Morrie Turner, conducted by Scott Nichol, Santa Rosa, CA, Aug. 7, 2010 *Washington Post*, Nov. 29, 2015.
31. Walker, *The Comics*, 493; Interview with Morrie Turner, conducted by Scott Nichol, Santa Rosa, CA, Aug. 7, 2010.
32. Interview with Morrie Turner, conducted by Scott Nichol, Santa Rosa, CA, Aug. 7, 2010.
33. *Glens Falls Times* (New York), July 31, 1968. Michelle Ann Abate has argued that Schulz used a very similar shading method for Franklin's skin that he had used in depicting dirt on the character Pig-Pen, thus perpetuating a longstanding racial stereotype. Given Schulz's intent in presenting Franklin as a sort of black exemplar, it is unlikely that Schulz consciously made this connection. Still, as Abate points out, the similarities in the two characters' shading demonstrated "the gap that often emerges between a person's intentions and their [potential] impact." See Michelle Ann Abate, "Drawing Racial Lines: The Aesthetics of Franklin in *Peanuts*," *Inks: The Journal of the Comic Studies Society*, Vol. 3, Iss. 3 (Fall 2019), 227–48.
34. *Chicago Tribune*, July 5, 1963; *Los Angeles Times*, Jan. 14, 1971; *Washington Post*, Sep. 7, 1969; Andrew W. Kahrl, "Fear of an Open Beach: Public Rights and Private Interests in 1970s Coastal Connecticut," *Journal of American History*, Vol. 102, No. 2 (Sep. 2015), 450–51. Also see Andrew W. Kahrl, *The Land War Ours: How Black Beaches Became White Wealth in the Coastal South* (Cambridge, MA: Harvard University Press, 2012).
35. *Newsweek*, July 1, 1968; *Newsweek*, July 15, 1968; *Newsweek*, July 22, 1968; *Los Angeles Sentinel*, Aug. 15, 1968; for an "informal history" of the 1968 conventions, see Norman

Mailer, *Miami and the Siege of Chicago: An Informal History of the Republican and Democratic Conventions of 1968* (New York: World Publishing, 1968).

36. *Athens Messenger* (Ohio), Aug. 2, 1968.
37. Harris Survey, Feb. 1971, iPOLL Databank, Roper Center for Public Opinion Research, University of Connecticut, ropercenter.uconn.edu.libdata.lib.ua.edu/data_ access/ipoll/ipoll.html (Feb. 9, 2016).
38. Charles M. Schulz, *Peanuts: A Golden Celebration* (New York: HarperCollins, 1999), 93.
39. Letter from James Hennessy to Charles M. Schulz, Oct. 4, 1968, "Correspondence: Fan Letters re: specific strips" binder, CMSMRC.
40. Letter from Harriet Glickman to Charles M. Schulz, Aug. 20, 1968, Glickman Papers, SC2002.003, CMSMRC; *Los Angeles Sentinel*, Feb. 8, 1968.
41. "Correspondence: Fan Letters re: specific strips" binder, CMSMRC.
42. Letter from Jordan Rossen to Charles M. Schulz, undated, "Correspondence: Fan Letters re: specific strips" binder, CMSMRC.
43. Letter from Franklin R. Freeman to Charles M. Schulz, Oct. 30, 1968, "Correspondence: Fan Letters re: specific strips" binder, CMSMRC.
44. Sketch by Ric Hugo, undated, "Correspondence: Fan Letters re: specific strips" binder, CMSMRC.
45. Letter from "An Admirer" to Charles M. Schulz, undated, "Correspondence: Fan Letters re: specific strips" binder, CMSMRC; *Newsweek*, Dec. 27, 1971.
46. Letter from Mary Emily Peck to Charles M. Schulz, Sep. 8, 1968, "Correspondence: Fan Letters re: specific strips" binder, CMSMRC.
47. Letter from H.H. Houston to Charles M. Schulz, Nov. 5, 1968, "Correspondence: Fan Letters re: specific strips" binder, CMSMRC.
48. Letter from Spurgeon Cameron to Charles M. Schulz, Oct. 20, 1968, "Correspondence: Fan Letters re: specific strips" binder, CMSMRC.
49. *Middlesboro Daily News* (Kentucky), Oct. 18, 1968.
50. *Farmington Daily Times* (New Mexico), Oct. 20, 1968; Letter from Kenneth C. Kelly to Charles M. Schulz, June 6, 1968, Glickman Papers, SC2002.003, CMSMRC.
51. *Charleston Daily Mail* (West Virginia), Nov. 12, 1969.
52. Schulz, *Peanuts*, 144; *Washington Post*, Nov. 6, 1969; *Atlanta Constitution*, Nov. 7, 1969; for more on the politics of obstruction, see Kevin Kruse, *White Flight: Atlanta and the Making of Modern Conservatism* (Princeton, NJ: Princeton University Press, 2005), Joseph Crespino, *Strom Thurmond's America* (New York: Hill and Wang, 2012), and Dan T. Carter, *The Politics of Rage: George Wallace, the Origins of the New Conservatism, and the Transformation of Modern Politics* (Baton Rouge: Louisiana State University Press, 2000).
53. "Lessons of Leadership: Charles M. Schulz," *Nation's Business*, Aug. 1988.
54. *Sikeston Daily Standard* (Missouri), Nov. 6, 1974.
55. David Michaelis, *Schulz and Peanuts: A Biography* (New York: Harper Perennial, 2007), 84, 86; *Los Angeles Times*, Aug. 28, 1973.
56. *Chicago Daily Defender*, Jan. 22, 1958; *Washington Post*, July 25, 1974; *Baltimore Sun*, July 25, 1981.
57. "Correspondence: Fan Letters re: specific strips" binder, CMSMRC.
58. Letter from Charles M. Schulz, Dec. 23, 1986, private collection.
59. Schulz, *Peanuts*, 93.

60. "Lessons of Leadership: Charles M. Schulz," *Nation's Business*, Aug. 1988; Letter from Charles M. Schulz to Joel Lipton, Nov. 9, 1970, CMSMRC.
61. Letter from Harriet Glickman to Charles M. Schulz, Apr. 4, 1968, Glickman Papers, SC2002.003, CMSMRC.

Chapter 5

1. "It's Magic, Even in Vietnam," *Los Angeles Times*, June 9, 1968.
2. Ibid.; "Inept Heroes, Winners at Last," *Life*, 1967, clipping from "1940s, 1950s, 1960 thru 1969" binder, CMSMRC.
3. Quoted in Michael S. Sherry, *In the Shadow of War: The United States since the 1930s* (New Haven, CT: Yale University Press, 1995), 289; Tom Engelhardt, *The End of Victory Culture: Cold War America and the Disillusioning of a Generation* (Amherst: University of Massachusetts Press, 1995); Christian G. Appy, *American Reckoning: The Vietnam War and Our National Identity* (New York: Viking, 2015); *Time*, Jan. 5, 1970; for more on the discovery of the "Middle Americans," see Penny Lewis, *Hardhats, Hippies, and Hawks: The Vietnam Antiwar Movement as Myth and Memory* (Ithaca, NY: ILR Press, 2013), 163–72; See also Robert Coles, *The Middle Americans: Proud and Uncertain* (Boston: Little, Brown, 1971); for more on popular opinions about the war, see Melvin Small, *Antiwarriors: The Vietnam War and the Battle for America's Hearts and Minds* (Lanham, MD: SR Books, 2002) and George C. Herring, *America's Longest War: The United States and Vietnam, 1950–1975* (Boston: McGraw-Hill, 2002).
4. Mitchell K. Hall, *Crossroads: American Popular Culture and the Vietnam Generation* (Lanham, MD: Rowman & Littlefield, 2005), 104; Andrew J. Huebner, *The Warrior Image: Soldiers in American Culture from the Second World War to the Vietnam Era* (Chapel Hill: University of North Carolina Press, 2008), 241–43; Bradford W. Wright, *Comic Book Nation: The Transformation of Youth Culture in America* (Baltimore: Johns Hopkins University Press, 2001), 235; see also Matthew J. Costello, *Secret Identity Crisis: Comic Books & the Unmasking of Cold War America* (New York: Continuum, 2009); Brian Walker, *The Comics: The Complete Collection* (New York: Abrams ComicArts, 2011), 454–55.
5. Susan D. Moeller, *Shooting War: Photography and the American Experience of Combat* (New York: Basic Books, 1989), 387; this narrative of the rise and fall of popular support for the war can be found in books like Ron Kovic's *Born on the Fourth of July* (1976) and Philip Caputo's *A Rumor of War* (1977), films like *Apocalypse Now* (1979) and *Full Metal Jacket* (1987), and even in the design of the Vietnam Veterans Memorial dedicated in 1982; Huebner, *The Warrior Image*, 174–75.
6. David Michaelis, *Schulz and Peanuts: A Biography* (New York: Harper Perennial, 2007), 394, 418–19; Michael Stewart Foley, "A Politics of Empathy: Johnny Cash, the Vietnam War, and the 'Walking Contradiction' Myth Dismantled," *Popular Music and Society* 37, no. 3 (June 2013): 338–59.
7. For more on the pragmatics theory of audience reception, see Warren Buckland, ed., *The Film Spectator: From Sign to Mind* (Amsterdam: Amsterdam University Press, 1995) and Rick Altman, *Film/Genre* (London: British Film Institute, 1999).
8. *Chicago Tribune*, May 3, 1954.
9. *Washington Post*, June 5, 1965.
10. Michaelis, *Schulz and Peanuts*, 129–51.

11. Herring, *America's Longest War*, 182; "III. Draft to Double: Illinois Draft to Be Doubled," *Chicago Daily Defender*, Aug. 5, 1965; "Draft Call Seen for Married Men: Induction of Those Without Children is Under Study," *New York Times*, Aug. 19, 1965.
12. *Chicago Tribune*, Oct. 10, 1965.
13. Quoted in Robert C. Harvey, *The Art of the Funnies: An Aesthetic History* (Jackson: University Press of Mississippi, 1994), 219; Gallup Poll, Aug. 1964, iPOLL Databank, Roper Center for Public Opinion Research, University of Connecticut, ropercenter.uconn.edu.libdata.lib.ua.edu/data_ access/ipoll/ipoll.html (May 13, 2014); Gallup Poll, Jan. 1965, iPOLL Databank, Roper Center for Public Opinion Research, University of Connecticut, ropercenter.uconn.edu.libdata. lib.ua.edu/data_ access/ipoll/ipoll.html (May 13, 2014); Gallup Poll, Sep. 1965, iPOLL Databank, Roper Center for Public Opinion Research, University of Connecticut, ropercenter.uconn.edu/data_access/ipoll/ipoll.html (Sep. 22, 2014).
14. "The War No One Wants—Or Can End," *Newsweek*, Aug. 9, 1965; James Landers, *The Weekly War: Newsmagazines and Vietnam* (Columbia: University of Missouri Press, 2004), 3; "Our G.I.'s Fight a 'Private War' in Vietnam," *New York Times*, Nov. 4, 1962.
15. *Los Angeles Times*, Jan. 9, 1966; quoted in Harvey, *The Art of the Funnies*, 219.
16. *Huron Daily Plainsman* (South Dakota), Feb. 13, 1966; "Long Haul for Vietnam," *New York Times*, Feb. 13, 1966.
17. *Wellsville Daily Reporter* (New York), Feb. 21, 1966; *Joplin Globe* (Missouri), Apr. 2, 1966; *Washington Post*, May 12, 1966.
18. *Arizona Republic* (Phoenix, AZ), Mar. 13, 1966; Michael Stewart Foley, *Dear Dr. Spock: Letters about the Vietnam War to America's Favorite Baby Doctor* (New York: New York University Press, 2005), 52; George Gallup, *The Gallup Poll: Public Opinion, 1935–1971*, Vol. III (New York: Random House, 1971), 2010.
19. *Somerset Daily American* (Pennsylvania), Aug. 10, 1966; Canvas Bunk Bottoms, Museum Object Numbers 1574c0141, 1574c0119, 1574c0007, undated, USNS General John Pope Collection, The Vietnam Center and Archive, Texas Tech University (hereafter VCA); "Combat Fatigue Grips Carrier Ranger's Pilots," *Los Angeles Times*, July 31, 1966; Michaelis, *Schulz and Peanuts*, 387–88.
20. *Appleton Post Crescent* (Wisconsin), July 24, 1966.
21. Christian G. Appy, *Patriots: The Vietnam War Remembered from All Sides* (New York: Penguin Books, 2003), 29–30; Foley, *Dear Dr. Spock*, 22.
22. "Supporting 'Our Boys,'" *Los Angeles Times*, May 13, 1966; "Parade to Back Vietnam G.I.'s Will Be Held on 5th Ave. Today," *New York Times*, May 13, 1967; *Time*, Oct. 27, 1967.
23. "Charlie Brown & Co. Bewitching on TV," *Chicago Tribune*, Oct. 28, 1966; "Bonanza and Peanuts Head Nielsen Ratings," *Los Angeles Times*, Nov. 22, 1966; *Lake Charles American Press* (Louisiana), Dec. 11, 1966.
24. "U.S. Call on P.O.W.'s Rejected by Hanoi," *New York Times*, Dec. 9, 1966; "News Capsule: In the World," *Baltimore Sun*, June 28, 1971.
25. *Salt Lake Tribune* (Utah), May 11, 1967; Gallup Poll, May 1967, iPOLL Databank, Roper Center for Public Opinion Research, University of Connecticut, ropercenter.uconn.edu/data_access/ipoll/ipoll.html (Sep. 24, 2014); *Salina Journal* (Salina, KS), May 14, 1967.
26. *Kingsport Times* (Tennessee), June 12–13, 1967; Harris Survey, Apr. 1967, iPOLL Databank, Roper Center for Public Opinion Research, University of Connecticut, ropercenter.uconn.edu/data_access/ipoll/ipoll.html (Sep. 23, 2014); Gallup Poll, Oct. 1967, iPOLL Databank,

Roper Center for Public Opinion Research, University of Connecticut, ropercenter.uconn.edu/data_access/ipoll/ipoll.html (Feb. 27, 2015).

27. *Washington Post*, Oct. 27, 1967; Letter from Herbert Block to Charles M. Schulz, Nov. 29, 1968, CMS corresp., 1968, CMS Papers, 1956–1998, Box 1, SC2004.008, CMSMRC.
28. *Toledo Blade*, Oct. 31, 1967, "Correspondence: Fan Letters re: specific strips" binder, CMSMRC; Letter from Dorothy C. Haase to Charles M. Schulz, Oct. 27, 1967, "Correspondence: Fan Letters re: specific strips" binder, CMSMRC.
29. "Counting the Dead in Vietnam," *New Journal and Guide*, Aug. 19, 1972; Small, *Antiwarriors*, 60; in one of Martin Luther King Jr.'s 1967 speeches he pointed out the reality that in the first three years black casualties were more than 20 percent of all casualties—nearly double their proportion of the American population. See Christian G. Appy, *Working-Class War: American Combat Soldiers & Vietnam* (Chapel Hill: University of North Carolina Press, 1993), 19–21.
30. Letter from Major General Charles H. Gingles to Charles M. Schulz, "1940s, 1950s, 1960 thru 1969" binder, CMSMRC; see Huebner, *The Warrior Image*, 198–203.
31. Gallup Poll, Jan. 1969, iPOLL Databank, Roper Center for Public Opinion Research, University of Connecticut, ropercenter.uconn.edu.libdata.lib.ua.edu/data_access/ipoll/ipoll.html (Nov. 4, 2014); Gallup Poll, Jan. 1969, iPOLL Databank, Roper Center for Public Opinion Research, University of Connecticut, ropercenter.uconn.edu.libdata.lib.ua.edu/ data_access/ipoll/ipoll.html (Nov. 4, 2014); *Panama City News* (Florida), Dec. 24–25, 1968; Michaelis, *Schulz and Peanuts*, 419; Julian Bond and T. G. Lewis's *Vietnam: An Anti-War Tale* (1967), The Sixties Project, http://www2.iath.virginia.edu/sixties/HTML_docs/Exhibits/Bond/Bond.html. For more on the effects of media coverage and popular memory of the 1968 Tet Offensive, see David F. Schmitz, *The Tet Offensive: Politics, War, and Public Opinion* (Lanham, MD: Rowman & Littlefield, 2005).
32. *Independent Recorder* (Helena, MT), June 1, 1969; M. Thomas Inge, ed., *Charles M. Schulz: Conversations* (Jackson: University Press of Mississippi, 2000), 219.
33. Foley, *Dear Dr. Spock*, 47; *Washington Post*, Sep. 15, 1969; Gallup Poll, Jan. 1969, iPOLL Databank, Roper Center for Public Opinion Research, University of Connecticut, ropercenter.uconn.edu/data_access/ipoll/ipoll.html (Sep. 24, 2014); for more on popular attitudes about the draft see Appy, *Working-Class War*, 34–37 and Michael Stewart Foley, *Confronting the War Machine: Draft Resistance during the Vietnam War* (Chapel Hill: University of North Carolina Press, 2003).
34. Huebner, *The Warrior Image*, 275–76; Todd DePastino, *Bill Mauldin: A Life Up Front* (New York: Norton, 2008), 290–96.
35. *Pharos-Tribune and Press* (Logansport, IN), Apr. 16–17, 1970; *Sandusky Register* (Ohio), May 7, 1970.
36. *Paris News* (Texas), May 13, 1970.
37. Letter from Ronald Reagan to Charles M. Schulz, July 6, 1970, Schulz 952, Ronald Reagan Library; *Playground Daily News* (Fort Walton Beach, FL), July 2, 4, 6–10, 1970.
38. *Florence Morning News* (South Carolina), Jan. 10, 1971; *Times Herald Record* (Middletown, NY), July 19, 1971.
39. "Correspondence: Fan letters re: specific strips" binder, CMSMRC.
40. Appy, *American Reckoning, xvi*; *Washington Post*, Sep. 1, 1974.
41. "Correspondence: Fan letters re: specific strips" binder, CMSMRC.
42. Harvey, *The Art of the Funnies*, 215.

43. "Wife to Greet Vet with Sign," *Hartford Courant*, Dec. 23, 1971; see Lizbeth Cohen, *A Consumers' Republic: The Politics of Mass Consumption in Postwar America* (New York: Vintage Books, 2003).
44. Letter from Glen Goodson to Charles M. Schulz, "Veterans' Tributes" Binder, CMSMRC; Pleasant Eugene Davis, interviewed by author, Northport, AL, Feb. 23, 2015; David Larsen interview, July 1, 2009, item #OH0701, David Larsen Collection, VCA.
45. Joe Holden interview, ca. Oct. 1998, item #13550301002, Folder 01, Box 03, Jan Churchill Collection, VCA; Albert G. Rampone, II, interviewed by author, Knob Noster, MO (by phone), Feb. 22, 2015.
46. "GI Holiday Mood Turns Pessimistic," *Hartford Courant*, Dec. 24, 1972; "When the GIs Go Home," *Washington Post*, Apr. 21, 1974.
47. "Man and Woman of the Year: The Middle Americans," *Time*, Jan. 5, 1970.
48. Albert G. Rampone, II, interview by author, Knob Noster, MO (by phone), Feb. 22, 2015.

Chapter 6

1. *Charleston Gazette* (West Virginia), Mar. 9, 1951.
2. Finis Dunaway, *Seeing Green: The Use and Abuse of American Environmental Images* (Chicago: University of Chicago Press, 2015), 83; "Charles Schulz: 'Comic Strips Aren't Art,'" *Newsday*, Aug. 28, 1977.
3. Adam Rome, *The Bulldozer in the Countryside: Suburban Sprawl and the Rise of American Environmentalism* (Cambridge: Cambridge University Press, 2001), 149.
4. *Corpus Christi Caller Times*, Jan. 5, 1958. For more on the widespread cultural fear of the atomic and nuclear ages, see Paul Boyer, *By the Bomb's Early Light: American Thought and Culture at the Dawn of the Atomic Age* (Chapel Hill: University of North Carolina Press, 1994); William M. Tuttle Jr., "America's Children in an Era of War, Hot and Cold: The Holocaust, the Bomb, and Child Rearing in the 1940s," in Peter J. Kuznick and James Gilbert, eds., *Rethinking Cold War Culture* (Washington, DC: Smithsonian Institution Press, 2001); and Elaine Tyler May, *Homeward Bound: American Families in the Cold War Era* (New York: Basic Books, 1988). For more on the environmental experience the atomic and nuclear ages, see Kate Brown, *Plutopia: Nuclear Families, Atomic Cities, and the Great Soviet and American Plutonium Disasters* (New York: Oxford University Press, 2013) and Kristen Iverson, *Full Body Burden: Growing Up in the Nuclear Shadow of Rocky Flats* (New York: Crown, 2012).
5. Gallup poll, Apr. 1958, iPOLL Databank, Roper Center for Public Opinion Research, University of Connecticut, ropercenter.uconn.edu.libdata.lib.ua.edu/data_ access/ipoll/ipoll.html (Apr. 15, 2016); "Fallout Could Kill Everyone Inside Area of 7000 Square Miles," *Los Angeles Times*, Feb. 16, 1955; "Expert Views on Peril of Fallout Given," *Chicago Tribune*, Aug. 26, 1957; "Fallout Radiation is Concentrated in Food," *Hartford Courant*, Sep. 9, 1957; "Fallout Now Dooms 26,000–150,000, Expert Says," *Washington Post*, July 2, 1958; "Test Fallout Deadlier Than the Bomb," *Washington Post*, May 8, 1958.
6. Margot A. Henriksen, *Dr. Strangelove's America: Society and Culture in the Atomic Age* (Berkeley: University of California Press, 1997), 194; Nevil Shute, *On the Beach* (New York: Vintage, 2010; orig. pub. 1957), title page.

7. Rachel Carson, *Silent Spring* (Cambridge, MA: Riverside Press, 1962), 1–3; for more on the life and career of Rachel Carson, see William Souder, *On a Farther Shore: The Life and Legacy of Rachel Carson* (New York: Broadway Books, 2012).
8. *Great Bend Daily Tribune* (Kansas), Nov. 12, 1962.
9. *Joplin News Herald* (Missouri), Feb. 20, 1963; Philip D. Beidler, *Scriptures for a Generation: What We Were Reading in the '60s* (Athens: University of Georgia Press, 1994), 58.
10. *Altoona Mirror* (Pennsylvania), May 28, 1959; Malthus famously argued that there was a mathematical limit to global population growth. Once the world's population exceeded the world's food supply, growth would necessarily stagnate. Even more, overpopulation would lead to a sort of diminishing returns as less productive soil was farmed to address food shortages and economies would experience high unemployment rates. John Stuart Mill presented a different case against overpopulation in his 1848 book *Principles of Political Economy*, which argued in part that population growth was a threat to "quality of life," an idea that found widespread discussion during baby boom as Americans considered the cost of providing amenities for a historically large and young population. Later neoconservative economists, like William Godwin, contended that Malthus and Mill underestimated human ingenuity and the productive capacity of capitalism. The market, Godwin contended, would decide the optimal population size and encourage wise management of resources or the discovery of alternatives. For more on the population debate and American political economy, see Derek S. Hoff, *The State and the Stork: The Population Debate and Policy Making in US History* (Chicago: Chicago University Press, 2012), 111–12; "Overpopulation Deadlier Killer than A-Bomb," *Atlanta Daily World*, Mar. 13, 1952; "Overpopulation Called Threat to World Peace," *Los Angeles Times*, Feb. 14, 1956.
11. Paul Sabin, *The Bet: Paul Ehrlich, Julian Simon, and Our Gamble over Earth's Future* (New Haven, CT: Yale University Press, 2013), 23–24; Lyndon B. Johnson, "Two Threats to World Peace," Omaha, NE, June 30, 1966, American Presidency Project, University of California, Santa Barbara, http://www.presidency.ucsb.edu/index.php (July 20, 2016).
12. Lyndon Johnson, "Annual Message to the Congress on the State of the Union," Washington, DC, Jan. 4, 1965, Lyndon Baines Johnson Presidential Library, http://www.lbjlib.utexas.edu (July 23, 2016); "Population Crisis: Hearings before the Subcommittee on Foreign Aid Expenditures of the Committee on Government Operations," First Session on S.1676, United States Senate, 89th Congress (Washington, DC: Government Printing Office, 1966), 5–6, 9–11; for more on Senator Ernest Gruening, see Claus-M Naske, *Ernest Gruening: Alaska's Greatest Governor* (Fairbanks: University of Alaska Press, 2004); Robert David Johnson, *Ernest Gruening and the American Dissenting Tradition* (Cambridge, MA: Harvard University Press, 1998); and Ernest Gruening, *Many Battles: The Autobiography of Ernest Gruening* (New York: Liveright, 1973).
13. *Griswold v. Connecticut*, 381 U.S. 479, June 7, 1965; "Population Crisis: Hearings before the Subcommittee on Foreign Aid Expenditures of the Committee on Government Operations," First Session on S.1676, United States Senate, 89th Congress (Washington, DC: Government Printing Office, 1966), 9.
14. "Population Crisis: Hearings before the Subcommittee on Foreign Aid Expenditures of the Committee on Government Operations," First Session on S.1676, United States Senate, 89th Congress (Washington, DC: Government Printing Office, 1966), 11.

15. "Population Crisis: Hearings before the Subcommittee on Foreign Aid Expenditures of the Committee on Government Operations," First Session on S.1676, United States Senate, 89th Congress (Washington, DC: Government Printing Office, 1966), 463. Gruening pulled the three strips he entered in the record from Charles M. Schulz, *Go Fly a Kite, Charlie Brown* (New York: Holt, Rinehart, & Winston, 1959). Beginning in 1952, Rinehart Publishing played an integral part in *Peanuts*' rise to national prominence by reprinting collections of the strip in enormously popular paperback volumes. The strips Gruening cited here originally appeared in newspapers on June 5 and 18, and July 8, 1959.
16. "'Negroes Suspicious of Parenthood Movement,' says Dr. Alan Guttmacher," *Pittsburgh Courier*, Nov. 6, 1965; "Letters to the Editor: Planned Parenthood," *Baltimore Sun*, Sep. 25, 1965.
17. "Population Crisis: Hearings before the Subcommittee on Foreign Aid Expenditures of the Committee on Government Operations," First Session on S.1676, United States Senate, 89th Congress (Washington, DC: Government Printing Office, 1966), 13, 464.
18. "Population Crisis: Hearings before the Subcommittee on Foreign Aid Expenditures of the Committee on Government Operations," First Session on S.1676, United States Senate, 89th Congress (Washington, DC: Government Printing Office, 1966), 472.
19. "A Green Revolution?" *Washington Post*, Apr. 15, 1968; "'Famine 1975' is Discussed," *Washington Post*, June 17, 1967.
20. "Sees Riots, Famine, War: Death Answers Human Increase, Biologist Says," *Los Angeles Times*, Mar. 28, 1968; "Crisis Predicted by 1975: World Has No Way to Avert Long Famine, Biologist Says," *Los Angeles Times*, Nov. 17, 1967; "The Fight Against Famine is Already Lost," *Washington Post*, Mar. 10, 1968; "The Food Squeeze," *Washington Post*, Sep. 19, 1968; Sabin, *The Bet*, 1–2, 11, 16. See also, Matthew Connelly, *Fatal Misconceptions: The Struggle to Control World Population* (New York: Oxford University Press, 2008).
21. "Correspondence Fan Letters re: specific strips" binder, CMSMRC; for more on Zero Population Growth, see Sabin, *The Bet*, 36–41, 119–21.
22. "Correspondence Fan Letters re: specific strips" binder, CMSMRC.
23. "Correspondence Fan Letters re: specific strips" binder, CMSMRC.
24. Opinion Research Corporation, July 1971, iPOLL Databank, Roper Center for Public Opinion Research, University of Connecticut, ropercenter.uconn.edu.libdata.lib.ua.edu/data_ access/ipoll/ipoll.html (Mar. 28, 2016).
25. Sabin, *The Bet*, 2, 68–70; for more on the economic theory of Friedman and Hayek, see Daniel Stedman Jones, *Masters of the Universe: Hayek, Friedman, and the Birth of Neoliberal Politics* (Princeton, NJ: Princeton University Press, 2012).
26. Sabin, *The Bet*, 4–5. Many recent scholars have come to appreciate environmentalism in the context of larger global economic systems and American capitalism, in particular. The central example is Cronon, *Nature's Metropolis*. Other examples include Bartow J. Elmore, *Citizen Coke: The Making of Coca-Cola Capitalism* (New York: Norton, 2015), Richard Tucker, *Insatiable Appetite: The United States and the Ecological Degradation of the Tropical World* (Berkeley: University of California Press, 2000), and John Soluri, *Banana Cultures: Agriculture, Consumption, and Environmental change in Honduras and the United States* (Austin: University of Texas Press, 2005).
27. For more on business leaders' long campaign against the New Deal, see Kim Phillips-Fein, *Invisible Hands: The Businessman's Crusade Against the New Deal* (New York: Norton, 2009), Kevin M. Kruse, *One Nation Under God: How Corporate America Invented*

Christian America (New York: Basic Books, 2015); Bethany Moreton, *To Serve God and Wal-Mart: The Making of Christian Free Enterprise* (Cambridge, MA: Harvard University Press, 2009); Darren Dochuk, *From Bible Belt to Sunbelt: Plain-Folk Religion, Grassroots Politics, and the Rise of Evangelical Conservatism* (New York: Norton, 2011); Benjamin C. Waterhouse, *Lobbying America: The Politics of Business from Nixon to NAFTA* (Princeton, NJ: Princeton University Press, 2013).

28. Phillips-Fein, *Invisible Hands*, 151–52. For more on the extent of Bank of America protests, see "Bank of America Hit for the 35th Time," *Washington Post*, May 2, 1971.
29. Moreton, *To Serve God and Wal-Mart*, 146; "Why Johnny Q. Public can't understand economics," *Chicago Tribune*, Aug. 22, 1977.
30. Moreton, *To Serve God and Wal-Mart*, 145, 160; "Ad Council's Campaign Draws Counterattack: 'Peanuts' Is There, Too," *Christian Science Monitor*, Sep. 21, 1976; The Advertising Council, *National Survey on The American Economic System: A Study of Understanding and Attitudes of the American People* (New York, 1975), 9; Gallup Poll, Aug. 1974, iPOLL Databank, Roper Center for Public Opinion Research, University of Connecticut, ropercenter.uconn.edu.libdata.lib.ua.edu/data_ access/ipoll/ipoll.html (May 21, 2016); Time/Yankelovich, Skelly & White Poll, Sep. 1974, iPOLL Databank, Roper Center for Public Opinion Research, University of Connecticut, ropercenter.uconn.edu.libdata.lib.ua.edu/data_ access/ipoll/ipoll.html (May 21, 2016).
31. The Advertising Council, *National Survey on The American Economic System*, 13–19; the Compton Advertising pollsters defined the consumer's role as twofold: 1) to influence production through demand and 2) to stimulate competition. Their pro-capitalist, pro-business definition assumed the merits of the free market and did not consider possible negative roles such as over-consumption or stimulating increased wastefulness or pollution. One-fifth of respondents, however, did say that the biggest change they hoped to see among consumer behavior was that they learn to "limit consumption, don't waste, or buy only what you need" (75).
32. Ad Council, *National Survey on The American Economic System*, 15; "Ad Council's Campaign Draws Counterattack"; "NBC-TV to Run Economics Ads," *New York Times*, July 30, 1976; "Ad Council Hopes to Sell Americans on America," *Los Angeles Times*, Mar. 5, 1976; "Can Business Teach How Economic System Works," *Christian Science Monitor*, Aug. 20, 1976; *Mainliner*, Feb. 1978, 102.
33. "The American Economic System . . . and Your Part in It," *Mainliner*, Feb. 1978, 103.
34. "Can Business Teach How Economic System Works"; "NBC-TV to Run Economic Ads," *New York Times*, July 30, 1976; "Ad Council's Campaign Draws Counterattack"; "Counterads Asked: Economic Ads Stir Trouble," *Los Angeles Times*, July 30, 1976; "The Babel of Economic Advertising," *New York Times*, Sep. 19, 1976.
35. "Ad Council's Campaign Draws Counterattack"; "Counterads Asked"; "Economic Drive Spurs Conflict," *New York Times*, Apr. 22, 1976; in the midst of this controversy with the Ad Council, the Peopes' Bicentennial Commission, which had tried unsuccessfully to stage a demonstration to oppose the federal government's bicentennial Independence Day celebration, elected to change its name to the Peoples' Business Commission.
36. "Ad Council's Campaign Draws Counterattack"; "Counterads Asked"; "Ad Council Hopes to Sell Americans on America."
37. "2 Views of Economic System," *New York Times*, Mar. 15, 1976; "The Babel of Economic Advertising," *New York Times*, Sep. 19, 1976.

38. "The Babel of Economic Advertising."
39. *Christian Science Monitor*, Sep. 21, 1976; "The Babel of Economic Advertising"; *Washington Post*, July 30, 1976; United States Department of Commerce, "Outstanding Contributions to Public Understanding of the American Economy" award, 2002.027, Charles M. Schulz Award Collection, CMSMRC; Letter to Charles M. Schulz from Gerald R. Ford, June 14, 1976, Executive File, Gerald R. Ford Library; "U.S. Honors Creator of the 'Peanuts' Strip," *New York Times*, June 5, 1976.
40. Quoted in Barry Hankins, *Francis Schaeffer and the Shaping of Evangelical America* (Grand Rapids, MI: William B. Eerdmans, 2008), 118; for more on the work and influence of Francis Schaeffer, see Hankins, *Francis Schaeffer and the Shaping of Evangelical America* and Daniel K. Williams, *God's Own Party: The Making of the Christian Right* (Oxford: Oxford University Press, 2010), 137–43.
41. Matthew Avery Sutton, *American Apocalypse: A History of Modern Evangelicalism* (Cambridge, MA: The Belknap Press of Harvard University Press, 2014), 345–46.
42. Nixon Poll, Opinion Research Corporation, May 1971, iPOLL Databank, Roper Center for Public Opinion Research, University of Connecticut, ropercenter.uconn.edu.libdata.lib.ua.edu/data_ access/ipoll/ipoll.html (Mar. 28, 2016); National Opinion Research Center, University of Chicago, Feb. 1973, iPOLL Databank, Roper Center for Public Opinion Research, University of Connecticut, ropercenter.uconn.edu.libdata.lib.ua.edu/data_ access/ipoll/ipoll.html (Mar. 28, 2016); Gallup Poll, July 1973, iPOLL Databank, Roper Center for Public Opinion Research, University of Connecticut, ropercenter.uconn.edu.libdata.lib.ua.edu/data_ access/ipoll/ipoll.html (Mar. 28, 2016); National Opinion Research Center, University of Chicago, Feb. 1974, iPOLL Databank, Roper Center for Public Opinion Research, University of Connecticut, ropercenter.uconn.edu.libdata.lib.ua.edu/data_ access/ipoll/ipoll.html (Mar. 28, 2016); Roper Report, Dec. 1976, iPOLL Databank, Roper Center for Public Opinion Research, University of Connecticut, ropercenter.uconn.edu.libdata.lib.ua.edu/data_access/ipoll/ipoll.html (Mar. 28, 2016). Harris Poll, Aug. 1973, iPOLL Databank, Roper Center for Public Opinion Research, University of Connecticut, ropercenter.uconn.edu.libdata.lib.ua.edu/data_ access/ipoll/ipoll.html (Mar. 28, 2016).
43. Charles M. Schulz, *It's Arbor Day, Charlie Brown* (1976).
44. Ibid.
45. Ibid.
46. Ibid.
47. Ibid.
48. Ibid.
49. Ibid.
50. Ibid.
51. "A Charlie Brown Special Slated," *Atlanta Constitution*, Mar. 16, 1976; "Charlie Brown, March 16 on CBS," *Los Angeles Times*, Mar. 8, 1976; Jud Hurd, "Charles Schulz," *Cartoonist Profiles*, No. 44 (Dec. 1979), 46–55, reprinted in M. Thomas Inge, ed., *Charles M. Schulz: Conversations* (Jackson: University Press of Mississippi, 2000), 106; "A Day for Trees," *Atlanta Constitution*, Feb. 15, 1976.
52. Adam Rome, *The Genius of Earth Day: How a 1970 Teach-In Unexpectedly Made the First Green Generation* (New York: Hill and Wang, 2013), *xi*.
53. "The Success of an Utter Failure," *Saturday Evening Post*, Jan. 12, 1957; American Lung Assoc., "Charlie Brown Clears the Air" Storyboard Pamphlet (1979), 2003.101, Peanuts Licensing Archives: Ephemera Box 1 (c. 1952–1999), Schulz Correspondence, CMSMRC.

54. Jean K. Smith, "Christmas Seals 1978," *Art Education* 31, no. 7 (Nov. 1978): 4–5<.
55. "Air Pollution Disease Costs Set at $1 Billion," *Chicago Tribune*, Dec. 23, 1979; "EPA Says Most People Breathe Dirty Air Despite Reduction in Pollution Since '70," *Wall Street Journal*, Feb. 24, 1978; American Lung Assoc., "Charlie Brown Clears the Air."
56. American Lung Assoc., "Charlie Brown Clears the Air."
57. Ibid.
58. Ibid.
59. Ibid. For more on the development of a suburban environmental ethic, see Rome, *The Bulldozer in the Countryside*; this suburban environmental ethic played an important role in the sorts of federal environmental legislation passed in postwar America, as demonstrated in Samuel P. Hays, *Beauty, Health, and Permanence: Environmental Politics in the United States, 1955–1985* (Cambridge: Cambridge University Press, 1989); for more on the rise of consumer capitalism and consumer politics, see Lizabeth Cohen, *A Consumers' Republic: The Politics of Mass Consumption in Postwar America* (New York: Vintage Books, 2003).
60. American Lung Assoc., "Charlie Brown Clears the Air."
61. Ibid.
62. Ibid.
63. Ibid. For more on the expansion of federal reach through the strategic shifting of powers to the private sector, see Brian Balogh, *The Associational State: American Governance in the Twentieth Century* (Philadelphia: University of Pennsylvania Press, 2015).
64. American Lung Assoc., "Charlie Brown Clears the Air."
65. Ibid.
66. "Rediscovery of the Redman," *Life*, Dec. 1, 1967; Dunaway, *Seeing Green*, 87; for more on the counterculture's appropriation of the Indian, see Philip J. Deloria, *Playing Indian* (New Haven, CT: Yale University Press, 1998).
67. American Lung Assoc., "Charlie Brown Clears the Air"; Dunaway, *Seeing Green*, 79–80, 89; while national media developed a new popular image of Native Americans that combined the old "noble savage" stereotype with this message of personal responsibility for the environment in the late 1960s and early 1970s, many real Native Americans were fighting very public battles over the representation of Native American peoples and their future role in the United States. For more on this, see Sherry L. Smith, *Hippies, Indians, and the Fight for Red Power* (New York: Oxford University Press, 2014). For more on the use of Native American imagery and stereotyping in American pop culture, see Chad A. Barbour, *From Daniel Boone to Captain America: Playing Indian in American Popular Culture* (Jackson: University Press of Mississippi, 2016).
68. Dunaway, *Seeing Green*, 176.
69. For more on Keep America Beautiful see Heather Rogers, *Gone Tomorrow: The Hidden Life of Garbage* (New York: The New Press, 2005); for more on the Advertising Council see Robert Griffith, "The Selling of America: The Advertising Council and American Politics, 1942–1960," *Business History Review* 57.3 (Autumn 1983), 388–412; quoted in Dunaway, *Seeing Green*, 82.
70. Letter from President Jimmy Carter to Charles M. Schulz, SC2004_008_124a-072, Schulz Correspondence, CMSMRC; *Washington Post*, Oct. 24, 1979.
71. Opinion Research Corporation, July 1971, iPOLL Databank, Roper Center for Public Opinion Research, University of Connecticut, ropercenter.uconn.edu.libdata.lib.ua.edu/

data_ access/ipoll/ipoll.html (Mar. 28, 2016); Roper Report, Sep. 1973, iPOLL Databank, Roper Center for Public Opinion Research, University of Connecticut, ropercenter.uconn.edu.libdata.lib.ua.edu/data_ access/ipoll/ipoll.html (Mar. 28, 2016); Opinion Research Corporation, May 1975, iPOLL Databank, Roper Center for Public Opinion Research, University of Connecticut, ropercenter.uconn.edu.libdata.lib.ua.edu/data_ access/ipoll/ipoll.html (Mar. 28, 2016).

72. Roper Report, Sep. 1973, iPOLL Databank, Roper Center for Public Opinion Research, University of Connecticut, ropercenter.uconn.edu.libdata.lib.ua.edu/data_ access/ipoll/ipoll.html (Mar. 28, 2016); Roper Report, June 1975, iPOLL Databank, Roper Center for Public Opinion Research, University of Connecticut, ropercenter.uconn.edu.libdata.lib.ua.edu/data_ access/ipoll/ipoll.html (Mar. 28, 2016); Cambridge Reports/National Omnibus Survey, Jan. 1977, iPOLL Databank, Roper Center for Public Opinion Research, University of Connecticut, ropercenter.uconn.edu.libdata.lib.ua.edu/data_ access/ipoll/ipoll.html (Mar. 28, 2016).
73. "If Supplies Fail, Try Demand," *New York Times*, Oct. 14, 1973; "Nixon Asks Households to Save Heat by Lowering Thermostat 4 Degrees," *New York Times*, Oct. 10, 1973; "Average Income," *Atlanta Daily World*, June 26, 1973; Pamphlet; "Citizen Action Guide to Energy Conservation"; folder Conservation Statements (Oct. 9, 1973); Box 23; White House Central Files: Staff Member and Office Files: Energy Policy Office: Charles J. DiBona Subject Files; Richard Nixon Presidential Library and Museum, Yorba Linda, CA; for more on the tremendous economic and political changes wrought by the energy crisis, see Meg Jacobs, *Panic at the Pump: The Energy Crisis and the Transformation of American Politics in the 1970s* (New York: Hill and Wang, 2016); for more on President Nixon's handling of the energy crisis during this period, see J. Brooks Flippen, *Nixon and the Environment* (Albuquerque: University of New Mexico Press, 2000), 200–12.
74. "Snoopy Gets Federal Job," *Minneapolis Star Tribune,* Oct. 10, 1973, "Misc. Articles and Star Tribune collection of articles, 1952–1994" binder, CMSMRC.
75. "If Supplies Fail, Try Demand," *New York Times*, Oct. 14, 1973; Pamphlet; "Citizen Action Guide to Energy Conservation"; folder Conservation Statements (Oct. 9, 1973); Box 23; White House Central Files: Staff Member and Office Files: Energy Policy Office: Charles J. DiBona Subject Files; Richard Nixon Presidential Library and Museum, Yorba Linda, CA.
76. "If Supplies Fail, Try Demand."
77. Ibid.
78. Letter from Richard Nixon to Lee Mendelson, Oct. 16, 1970, SC2004.008.053-072, CMSMRC; Bruce J. Schulman, *The Seventies: The Great Shift in American Culture, Society, and Politics* (Cambridge, MA: Da Capo Press, 2002), 39; Michael Stewart Foley, "A Politics of Empathy: Johnny Cash, the Vietnam War, and the 'Walking Contradiction' Myth Dismantled," *Popular Music and Society*, 37:3, 338–59; Elizabeth Drew, *Richard M. Nixon* (New York: Times Books, 2007), 28.

Chapter 7

1. Mary Harrington Hall, "A Conversation with Charles Schulz or The Psychology of Simplicity," *Psychology Today*, Jan. 1968, reprinted in M. Thomas Inge, ed., *Charles M. Schulz: Conversations* (Jackson: University Press of Mississippi, 2000), 45.
2. Ibid., 45–46.

3. Ibid., 46.
4. Ibid., 46.
5. Bethany Moreton, *To Serve God and Wal-Mart: The Making of Christian Free Enterprise* (Cambridge, MA: Harvard University Press, 2009), 112. Moreton cites the work of Colombian historian Elizabeth E. Brusco who found a similar trend within working-class evangelicals and Pentecostals in Colombia. Brusco discovered what she called the "reformation of machismo" which, while it was a product of feminism was "not attempting to gain access for women to the male world; rather, it elevates domesticity, for both men and women, from the devalued position it occupies as the result of the process of proletarianization. It does serve to transform gender roles, primarily by reattaching males to the family." Elizabeth Bruscoe, *The Reformation of Machismo: Evangelical Conversion and Gender in Columbia* (Austin: University of Texas Press, 1995), 3.
6. Hall, "A Conversation with Charles Schulz," 46.
7. *Seattle Times*, Oct. 3, 1950; *Chicago Tribune*, Oct. 5, 1950; *Denver Post*, Oct. 12, 1950; *Chicago Tribune*, Dec. 7, 1950; *Washington Post*, Feb. 27, 1953. These early episodes in *Peanuts* reflect a larger conflict in American culture over the nature of masculinity after World War II, a debate that took place in much of the literature and speeches of the day, especially evangelical literature and sermons. For more on this battle over American masculinity, see James Burkhart Gilbert, *Men in the Middle: Searching for Masculinity in the 1950s* (Chicago: University of Chicago Press, 2005).
8. *Chicago Tribune*, Oct. 9, 1950; *Seattle Times*, Nov. 29, 1950; *Denver Post*, Jan. 22, 1951; *Chicago Tribune*, Feb. 3, 1951.
9. *Washington Post*, Nov. 15, 1950; *Seattle Times*, Mar. 22, 1951; *Denver Post*, July 2, 1951.
10. Susan J. Douglas, *Where the Girls Are: Growing Up Female with the Mass Media* (New York: Three Rivers Press, 1994), 49–51.
11. *Washington Post*, May 9, 16, 23, and 30, 1954; Schulz would later admit that one of the primary reasons he did not draw adults in the comic strip after that May 1954 series was because adults did not easily fit into the comic strip frame next to his child characters. In adults' first appearance in the strip—May 16, 1954—the adults could only be shown from the knee down if Lucy and Charlie Brown were to be shown in their regular proportions. Schulz explained this practical concern to one interviewer: "My strip, when it was given to me was about the size of four air-mail stamps. Well, you remember Fritzi Ritz and Nancy, Fritzi Ritz could never stand in the same room as Nancy because she was too tall. So Ernie Bushmiller always had to fake it. This is what is done in so many strips. There's just no room for adults to stay. . . . But size is very important. I just didn't have the room to draw kids—with the result that I brought the camera right down on level with the kids. I have never drawn the kids from an adult viewpoint, looking down on them"; for more on *I Love Lucy* see Karal Ann Marling, *As Seen On TV: The Visual Culture of Everyday Life in the 1950s* (Cambridge, MA: Harvard University Press, 1994), 38–39, 131–32 and Thomas Patrick Doherty, *Cold War, Cool Medium: Television, McCarthyism, and American Culture* (New York: Columbia University Press, 2003), 49–59.
12. Inge, *Charles M. Schulz:*, 6, 63, 76; "Comment in the Comics," *Time*, Apr. 9, 1965.
13. Inge, *Charles M. Schulz*, 47, 66.
14. *Lubbock Morning Avalanche* (Texas), June 18, 1954; in 1955, one of the directors at the National Science Foundation would write requesting a strip featuring Lucy, promising that it "would be most warmly received here and would be proudly displayed next to a large photo of the first H-bomb explosion!"; Letter from Richard G. Axt to Charles M. Schulz,

Jan. 22, 1955, Correspondence February 10, 1955, UFS Records 1954–1961, Box 1, CMSMRC; Inge, *Charles M. Schulz*, 131; *Washington Post*, Nov. 15, 1952.

15. *Abilene Reporter News* (Texas), June 11, 1960.
16. *Los Angeles Times*, Sep. 26, 1971; *Washington Post*, June 30, 1970.
17. Bonnie J. Dow, *Watching Women's Liberation 1970: Feminism's Pivotal Year on the Network News* (Urbana: University of Illinois Press, 2014); for more on the social and cultural impact of *The Mary Tyler Moore Show*, see Jennifer Keishin Armstrong, *Mary and Lou and Rhoda and Ted: And All the Brilliant Minds Who Made The Mary Tyler Moore Show a Classic* (New York: Simon and Schuster, 2013); "The New Woman: A Liberated Woman Despite Beauty, Chic, and Success," *Newsweek*, Aug. 16, 1971; "Woman of the Year," *McCall's*, Jan. 1972; Ruth Rosen, *The World Split Open: How the Modern Women's Movement Changed America* (New York: Penguin Books, 2000), 263.
18. Stan Lee, *The Superhero Women* (New York: Simon and Schuster, 1977), 7; Bradford W. Wright, *Comic Book Nation: The Transformation of Youth Culture in America* (Baltimore: Johns Hopkins University Press, 2001), 250–51.
19. Lee, *The Superhero Women*, 7; Wright, *Comic Book Nation*, 250–51. For more on Wonder Woman and her cultural role in the women's movement, see Jill Lepore, *The Secret History of Wonder Woman* (New York: Knopf, 2014). For more on the rise of Marvel Comics and their socially progressive philosophy, see Sean Howe, *Marvel Comics: The Untold Story* (New York: Harper, 2012) and Matthew J. Costello, *Secret Identity Crisis: Comic Books and the Unmasking of Cold War America* (New York: Continuum, 2009).
20. Charles M. Schulz, *It's Arbor Day, Charlie Brown* (1976).
21. Louis Harris & Associates, Virginia Slims American Women's Poll 1970, Aug. 1970, iPOLL Databank, Roper Center for Public Opinion Research, University of Connecticut, ropercenter.uconn.edu.libdata.lib.ua.edu/data_access/ipoll/ipoll.html (Dec. 3, 2016); Harris Survey, Oct. 1971, iPOLL Databank, Roper Center for Public Opinion Research, University of Connecticut, ropercenter.uconn.edu.libdata.lib.ua.edu/data_access/ipoll/ipoll.html (Dec. 3, 2016).
22. Inge, *Charles M. Schulz*, 47–48, 151.
23. "Ice-Skating Star Has Link to Charlie Brown," *Los Angeles Times*, Jan. 4, 1985.
24. *Chicago Tribune*, Jan. 5, 7, 1972.
25. *Los Angeles Times*, Jan. 19–20, 1972; Inge, *Charles M. Schulz*, 41.
26. Some fans and commentators have argued that Charlie Brown might have just been a cover—a "beard"—for Peppermint Patty's true love: her glasses wearing, bookish sidekick, Marcie. Highlighting Peppermint Patty's unusual love for sports and Marcie's insistence on referring to her as "sir," this interpretation presents Peppermint Patty as a closeted, butch-type lesbian. The fact that Peppermint Patty and Marcie became almost inseparable in the 1970s and that both girls came to express having an odd crush on Charlie Brown—expressed most overtly in the strip on July 21–22, 1979—has only fed rumors that these characters were secretly in love. Peppermint Patty would become a symbol of pride within lesbian communities. In the 2000s, the relationship between the two characters was parodied in many of the leading satirical programs of the period, such as *Saturday Night Live, The Simpsons,* and *Family Guy*. Of course, Marcie's "sir" references make more sense when one considers that Schulz had long conflated summer camp for Charlie Brown with his own loneliness after being drafted into the military in World War II. *Peanuts*' annual summer camp scenes were typically replete with militaristic references, as previously

demonstrated in chapter 5. Even more, the characters were only eight years old. Some fans have suggested, then, that the two girls might be "pre-lesbian." For more on this debate over Peppermint Patty and Marcie's sexual orientation, see Laura Bradley, "*Peanuts*' Most Fascinating Relationship Has Always Been Between Peppermint Patty and Lucy," *Slate*, Nov. 12, 2015, http://www.slate.com/blogs/browbeat/2015/11/12/peppermint_patty_and_marcie_s_relationship_in_peanuts.html. Also see David Michaelis, *Schulz and Peanuts: A Biography* (New York: Harper Perennial, 2007), 223, and Ben Saunders, "Peppermint Patty's Desire: Charles Schulz and the Queer Comics of Failure," in *The Comics of Charles Schulz: The Good Grief of Modern Life*, ed. Jared Gardner and Ian Gordon (Jackson: University Press of Mississippi, 2017), 13–28.

27. *Washington Post*, June 22, 1972. Comics scholar Ben Saunders has made a compelling argument that Peppermint Patty's core conflict is the frustration and repression of desire. This is why, he argues, that Peppermint Patty's relationship has always been such a powerful symbol for queer and transgender identification and a subject of considerable speculation in adult pop culture since the 1990s. For much more on this subject, see Saunders, "Peppermint Patty's Desire," 13–28.
28. Charles Solomon, *The Art and Making of Peanuts Animation: Celebrating Fifty Years of Television Specials* (San Francisco: Chronicle Books, 2012), 100; Charles M. Schulz, *Race For Your Life, Charlie Brown* (1977).
29. Letter from Pauli Murray to Charles M. Schulz, Oct. 25, 1971, Box 106, Folder 1903, "Oct. 14–31, 1971," Pauli Murray papers 1868–1985 (MC 412), Arthur and Elizabeth Schlesinger Library on the History of Women in America, Radcliffe Institute for Advanced Study, Harvard University, Cambridge, MA (Hereafter: SL). For more on Pauli Murray, see Rosalind Rosenberg, *Jane Crow: The Life of Pauli Murray* (New York: Oxford University Press, 2017).
30. Letter from Pauli Murray to Charles M. Schulz, Oct. 25, 1971, Box 106, Folder 1903, "Oct. 14–31, 1971," Pauli Murray papers 1868–1985 (MC 412), SL.
31. Ibid.
32. Pauli Murray Papers, Nov. 16, 1971, SL.
33. Ibid.
34. *Washington Post*, July 20, 1970.
35. "Correspondence: Fan Letters re: specific strips" binder, CMSMRC.
36. Ibid.
37. Ibid.
38. Ibid. For more on Zero Population Growth, see Sabin, *The Bet*, 36–41, 119–21.
39. Ibid. To be fair to Schulz, there *were* only two children in Charlie Brown's family. The Van Pelt family, however, would ultimately have a third child, Rerun, who first appeared in the strip on March 26, 1973.
40. "Charles Schulz Day" press release, May 24, 1967, Press Releases, May 1967 (5-19-67 thru 5-30-67), Ronald Reagan Presidential Library, Simi Valley, California [Hereafter RRPL]; Letter from Ronald Reagan to Charles M. Schulz, July 30, 1970, "Schul 952" folder, RRPL.
41. Letter from Ronald Reagan to Charles M. Schulz, July 30, 1970, "Schul 952" folder, RRPL; Lou Cannon, *Governor Reagan: His Rise to Power* (New York: Public Affairs, 2003), 208–209, 211.
42. H. W. Brands, *Reagan: The Life* (New York: Doubleday, 2015), 160, 260; Letter from Ronald Reagan to Charles M. Schulz, July 30, 1970, "Schul 952" folder, RRPL; Cannon, *Governor*

Reagan, 213; "Gov. Reagan to Sign New Abortion Bill," *Chicago Tribune*, June 14, 1967; California's bill to liberalize abortion was actually the third in the nation. The first had been signed into law early in 1967 by Colorado's Republican Governor John Arthur Love. For more, see Daniel K. Williams, *God's Own Party: The Making of the Christian Right* (New York: Oxford University Press, 2010), 112–13.

43. Letter from Ronald Reagan to Charles M. Schulz, July 30, 1970, "Schul 952" folder, RRPL; Brands, *Reagan*, 161.
44. Williams, *God's Own Party*, 114–15.
45. Ibid., 113; Cannon, *Governor Reagan*, 211. The evangelical's and Catholic's fight against at-will abortion laws has long history in the United States. For the battle over abortion before *Roe v. Wade* (1973), see Daniel K. Williams, *Defenders of the Unborn: The Pro-Life Movement before* Roe v. Wade (New York: Oxford University Press, 2016) and Donald T. Critchlow, *Intended Consequences: Birth Control, Abortion, and the Federal Government in Modern America* (New York: Oxford University Press, 1999). For the battle over abortion since, including the culture wars, see Williams, *God's Own Party*, Neil J. Young, *We Gather Together: The Religious Right and the Problem of Interfaith Politics* (New York: Oxford University Press, 2016), and Andrew Hartman, *A War for the Soul of America: A History of the Culture Wars* (Chicago: University of Chicago Press, 2015).
46. Cannon, *Governor Reagan*, 212; Brands, *Reagan*, 161–62.
47. Letter from Ronald Reagan to Charles M. Schulz, July 30, 1970, "Schul 952" folder, RRPL.
48. Cannon, *Governor Reagan*, 213; emphasis in the original.
49. *Sikeston Daily Standard* (Missouri), Oct. 25–30, 1971.
50. "Correspondence: Fan Letters re: specific strips" binder, CMSMRC.
51. Ibid.
52. Ibid.; U.S. Census Bureau, *1970 Census of the Population*, Volume 1, Part 1 (Washington, DC: Government Printing Office, 1973), 375.
53. "Correspondence: Fan Letters re: specific strips" binder, CMSMRC.
54. Ibid.; "Equal Rights for Women Clears the House, 354–23," *Washington Post*, Oct. 13, 1971. For more on the ensuing decade-long battle over the Equal Rights Amendment, see Donald T. Critchlow, *Phyllis Schlafly and the Conservative Grassroots: A Woman's Crusade* (Princeton, NJ: Princeton University Press, 2005).
55. "John Trubin, Political Insider and Aide to Javits, Dies at 83," *New York Times*, July 5, 2001; Correspondence: Fan Letters re: specific strips" binder, CMSMRC.
56. "John Trubin, Political Insider and Aide to Javits, Dies at 83"; Correspondence: Fan Letters re: specific strips" binder, CMSMRC.
57. "Correspondence: Fan Letters re: specific strips" binder, CMSMRC.
58. Amy Erdman Farrell, *Yours in Sisterhood:* Ms. *Magazine and the Promise of Popular Feminism* (Chapel Hill: University of North Carolina Press, 1998), 1. For the firsthand account of Steinem's journey as a feminist icon, see Gloria Steinem, *My Life on the Road* (New York: Random House, 2015).
59. Cover, *Ms.*, Apr. 1976.
60. "How to Start Your Own Business!" *Ms.*, Apr. 1976, 56–70.
61. Ibid.
62. Ibid.
63. For two good single volume treatments of the contours of the modern feminist movement, see Rosen, *The World Split Open* and Marjorie J. Spruill, *Divided We Stand: The Battle Over*

Women's Rights and Family Values That Polarized American Politics (New York: Bloomsbury Press, 2017).

64. "The ERA: What the Hell Happened in New York?" *Ms.*, Mar. 1976; "The 400,000 Vote Misunderstanding," *Ms.*, Mar. 1976; "Why Big Business is Trying to Defeat the ERA," *Ms.*, May 1976. For more on the anti-ERA movement see Critchlow, *Phyllis Schlafly and the Conservative Grassroots* and Spruill, *Divided We Stand.*
65. "Women in Sports," *Time*, June 26, 1978, 54–60; Susan Ware, *Game, Set, Match: Billie Jean King and the Revolution in Women's Sports* (Chapel Hill: University of North Carolina Press, 2011), 43–74.
66. "Women in Sports," *Time*, June 26, 1978, 54–60.
67. Ibid.
68. Ibid.
69. Ibid.
70. Ibid.
71. *Washington Post*, July 15, 1973; the best biography on Billie Jean King and her contributions to second-wave feminism is Ware, *Game, Set, Match*; for more on Schulz's relationship with King, see particularly Ware, *Game, Set, Match*, 93.
72. *Washington Post*, Oct. 1–2, 5–6, 1979. Marcie regularly refers to Peppermint Patty as "sir," despite the fact that Peppermint Patty continually insists that she stop. This title further demonstrates Peppermint Patty's tomboyish nature. In all of the television programs and films, she was voiced by a girl with a rough, gravelly voice. Schulz wanted it to be obvious that Peppermint Patty was a different sort of girl and that her difference in no way made her unacceptable to the other children, except perhaps when it came to romantic attraction.
73. Ware, *Game, Set, Match*, 93; Lucy Women's Sports Foundation poster, no date, 2004.189.001, Peanuts Licensing Archives, CMSMRC; "An Interview with Peppermint Patty," *womenSports*, Aug. 1977; U.S. Commission on Civil Rights, *More Hurdles to Clear: Women and Girls in Competitive Athletics*, No. 63 (Washington, DC: Clearinghouse Publishing, 1980); President's Award from the Women's Sports Foundation, c. 1985, 2002.118, Charles M. Schulz Awards Collection, CMSMRC.
74. *Time*, Nov. 24, 1986; *Washington Post*, Oct. 23, 1986.
75. *Time*, Nov. 24, 1986; Gallup/Phi Delta Kappa Poll of Public Attitudes Toward the Public Schools 1981, May 1981, iPOLL Databank, Roper Center for Public Opinion Research, University of Connecticut, ropercenter.uconn.edu.libdata.lib.ua.edu/data_access/ipoll/ipoll.html (Nov. 24, 2016); Life, Contemporary American Family Poll, Sep. 1981, iPOLL Databank, Roper Center for Public Opinion Research, University of Connecticut, ropercenter.uconn.edu.libdata.lib.ua.edu/data_access/ipoll/ipoll.html (Nov. 24, 2016); for more on the Reagan administration's handling of the AIDS epidemic, see Robert O. Self, *All in the Family: The Realignment of American Democracy since the 1960s* (New York: Hill and Wang, 2012), 367–98. For the best narrative of the fight against AIDS, see Victoria A. Hardin, *AIDS at 30: A History* (Washington, DC: Potomac Books, 2012). For the two best firsthand accounts of the political and social fight over AIDS in the 1980s, see C. Everett Koop, *Koop: The Memoirs of America's Family Doctor* (New York: Random House, 1991) and Randy Shilts, *And The Band Played On: Politics, People, and the AIDS Epidemic* (New York: St. Martin's Press, 1987).
76. *Time*, Nov. 24, 1986.
77. Ibid.

78. *Time*, Dec. 15, 1986.
79. Self, *All in the Family*, 115. For more on the unique challenges black women faced in the civil rights movement, see Danielle L. McGuire, *At the Dark End of the Street: Black Women, Rape and Resistance—a New History of the Civil Rights Movement from Rosa Parks to the Rise of Black Power* (New York: Vintage Books, 2011). For more on the manifestation of black feminism in 1970s material culture, see Tanisha C. Ford, *Liberated Threads: Black Women, Style, and the Global Politics of Soul* (Chapel Hill: University of North Carolina Press, 2015).

Epilogue

1. Kiron K. Skinner, Annelise Anderson, and Martin Anderson, eds., *Reagan: A Life in Letters* (New York: Free Press, 2003), 638.
2. Skinner, Anderson, and Anderson, *Reagan*, 638.
3. Stuart Elliott, "Will 'Peanuts' Characters Remain Effective Images, or Go the Way of Schmoo?" *New York Times*, Feb. 17, 2000, C8; Jared Gardner and Ian Gordon, eds., *The Comics of Charles Schulz: The Good Grief of Modern Life* (Jackson: University Press of Mississippi, 2017), 124.
4. James S. Granelli, "Knotts Agree to Sell Park," *Los Angeles Times*, Oct. 22, 1997. For more on the political history of Knott's Berry Farm, see Lisa McGirr, *Suburban Warriors: The Origins of the New American Right* (Princeton, NJ: Princeton University Press, 2001). Deloris Tarzan Ament, "Dog Days at Louvre," *Seattle Times*, Jan. 14, 1990.
5. Historian Andrew Hartman has recently argued that the culture wars were a conflict between "those who embraced the new America [of the 1960s]" and "those who viewed it ominously." This interpretation of the conflict characterizes the Left as a "progressive" movement, while charging that the Right was primarily engaged in "backlash." Perhaps a more positive understanding of the culture wars is found in Robert O. Self's *All in the Family* where he conceives of the battles between Left and Right as a national argument over what the American national "family" should look like. It is, in Self's conception, a war over social, cultural, and political citizenship, not progression and regression. For more on this debate, see Andrew Hartman, *A War for the Soul of America: A History of the Culture Wars* (Chicago: Chicago University Press, 2015) and Robert O. Self, *All in the Family: The Realignment of American Democracy since the 1960s* (New York: Hill and Wang, 2012). By the mid-1990s, there would be national battles over public school history curriculums that conservative critics argued overemphasized past tragedies like slavery and McCarthyism at the expense of slighting its perceived successes like the Constitution and victory in World War II. Most recently, this debate has been reignited through the publication of the *New York Times*'s Pulitzer-winning "1619 Project." For more on this and the larger context of the culture wars of the 1980s and 1990s, see James T. Patterson, *Restless Giant: The United States from Watergate to Bush v. Gore* (New York: Oxford University Press, 2005), 254–91; Adam Serwer, "The Fight Over the 1619 Project Is Not About the Facts," *The Atlantic*, Dec. 23, 2019; Allen C. Guelzo, "'The 1619 Project' Tells a False Story About Capitalism, Too," *Wall Street Journal*, May 8, 2020. Also see Sean Wilentz, *The Age of Reagan, 1974–2008* (New York: Harper, 2008).
6. David Larken, ed., *Peanuts: A Golden Celebration* (New York: HarperCollins, 1999), 122; "This Week's Picks," *Washington Post*, Oct. 16, 1988; Leonard Maltin, *Charlie Brown: A Boy*

for All Seasons (New York: Museum of Broadcasting, 1984), reprinted in M. Thomas Inge, ed., *Charles M. Schulz: A Conversation* (Jackson: University Press of Mississippi, 2000), 126.

7. "Good Grief! The *Peanuts* Gang and the Pilgrims are a Poor Match," *Los Angeles Times*, Oct. 21, 1988; "Peanuts Become Pilgrims," *New York Times*, Oct. 21, 1988.
8. Charles M. Schulz, "The Mayflower Voyagers," *This is America, Charlie Brown* (1988); "This Week's Picks," *Washington Post*, Oct. 16, 1988; "What's Up This Week," Baltimore *Sun*, Oct. 16, 1988; "Morning Report," *Los Angeles Times*, Oct. 13, 1988; "Good Grief! The *Peanuts* Gang and the Pilgrims are a Poor Match," *Los Angeles Times*, Oct. 21, 1988.
9. "Good Grief! The *Peanuts* Gang and the Pilgrims are a Poor Match"; "Peanuts Become Pilgrims."
10. "This is America?" *New York Amsterdam News*, June 2, 1990.
11. Reagan and his speechwriters actually borrowed the "shining city upon a hill" rhetoric from the nation's last Massachusetts president, John F. Kennedy. Recently scholars have found surprising ties between the Kennedy and Reagan administrations, most notably in their economic and tax philosophies. For more on these particular connections, see Lawrence Kudlow and Brian Domitrovic, *JFK and the Reagan Revolution: A Secret History of American Prosperity* (New York: Portfolio, 2016). "Ringing Rhetoric: The Return of Political Oratory," *New York Times*, Aug. 19, 1984. For more on evangelicalism and its rising influence in American culture in the last quarter of the twentieth century, see Steven P. Miller, *The Age of Evangelicalism: America's Born-Again Years* (Oxford: Oxford University Press, 2014) and Darren Dochuk, *From Bible Belt to Sunbelt: Plain-Folk Religion, Grassroots Politics, and the Rise of Evangelical Conservatism* (New York: Norton, 2011).
12. Charles M. Schulz, "The Birth of the Constitution," *This is America, Charlie Brown* (1988).
13. Charles M. Schulz, "The NASA Space Station," *This is America, Charlie Brown* (1988).
14. Charles M. Schulz, "The Building of the Transcontinental Railroad," *This is America, Charlie Brown* (1989).
15. Charles M. Schulz, "The Smithsonian and the Presidents," *This is America, Charlie Brown* (1989). Schulz's script notably dated slavery to 1620 in the colony of Virginia, not to 1619, as in the *New York Times Magazine*'s recent "1619 Project."
16. "An Animated '88 Awaits on the Drawing Board," *New York Times*, Dec. 27, 1987.
17. "Schulz at 3 O'clock in the Morning," *Comics Journal*, No. 200 (Dec. 1997), reprinted in Inge, *Charles M. Schulz*, 236–41.
18. Russell D. Moore, "Tragic Comic," *Touchstone*, Mar. 2008. For son Monte Schulz's rebuttal of Michaelis's biography and the thoughts of other *Peanuts* experts, see "Who Speaks for Sparky? The *Schulz and Peanuts* Roundtable," *The Comics Journal*, No. 290, May 2008, 26–111. For the most convincing argument that Schulz did not in fact fall away from his faith, see Stephen J. Lind, *A Charlie Brown Religion: Exploring the Spiritual Life and Work of Charles M. Schulz* (Jackson: University Press of Mississippi, 2015), 176–98.
19. "Retiring Schulz Has Ties to AU," *The Herald Bulletin*, Jan. 3, 2000, Anderson University Archives.
20. "You Were Good, Charlie Brown," *Chicago Tribune*, Apr. 29, 1993.
21. "Good Grief," *Wall Street Journal*, Oct. 22, 1999; "Charles Schulz Interview," *NEMO: The Classic Comics Library*, Jan. 1992, reprinted in Charles M. Schulz, *The Complete Peanuts, 1950 to 1952* (Seattle: Fantagraphics Books, 2004), 334.
22. "MetLife Grounds Snoopy. Curse You, Red Baron!" *New York Times*, Oct. 21, 2016.
23. *Toronto Star*, May 12, 2020.

Bibliography

Primary Sources

Manuscript Collections

Anderson University and Church of God Archives, Anderson, Indiana
Charles M. Schulz Museum and Research Center, Santa Rosa, CA
Gerald R. Ford Presidential Library, Ann Arbor, MI
J. Walter Thompson Company Papers, David M. Rubenstein Rare Books and Manuscript Collection, Duke University, Durham, NC
Lyndon B. Johnson Presidential Library, Austin, TX
Mort Walker Papers, Syracuse University Library, Syracuse, NY
Papers of Lorene Genevieve Byrnes and Roy David Burns, University Archives, University of Iowa Library, Iowa City, IA
Pauli Murray Papers, Arthur and Elizabeth Schlesinger Library on the History of Women in America, Radcliffe Institute for Advanced Study, Harvard University, Cambridge, MA
Richard Nixon Presidential Library, Yorba Linda, CA
Ronald Reagan Presidential Library, Simi Valley, CA
Vietnam Center and Sam Johnson Vietnam Archive, Texas Tech University, Lubbock, TX

Magazines

Advertising Age
Atlanta Weekly
Christian Century
Christianity Today
Coast Weekly
Collegiate Challenge
Dayton Daily News and Journal Herald Magazine
Decision
Editor & Publisher
Forbes
Life
Mainliner
Ms.
Nation's Business
New York Times Magazine
Newsday
Newsweek
Penthouse
Psychology Today
Saturday Evening Post
Slate
The Atlantic
Time

Variety
Vital Christianity
womenSports
Young Calvinist

Newspapers

Abilene Reporter News
Altoona Mirror
Appleton Post Crescent
Argus Leader
Arizona Republic
Athens Messenger
Atlanta Constitution
Atlanta Daily World
Baltimore Sun
Berkshire Eagle
Charleston Daily Mail
Charleston Gazette
Chicago Daily Defender
Chicago Daily Tribune
Christian Herald
Christian Science Monitor
Clearfield Progress
Corpus Christi Caller Times
Denver Post
Dothan Eagle
Farmington Daily Times
Florence Morning News
Glens Falls Times
Great Bend Daily Tribune
Hartford Courant
Huron Daily Plainsman
Independent Recorder
Joplin News Herald
Kingsport Times
Lake Charles American Press
Los Angeles Sentinel
Los Angeles Times
Lubbock Morning Avalanche
Middlesboro Daily News
Minneapolis Star Tribune
Morning Herald
New Journal and Guide
New York Herald Tribune
New York Times
Oneonta Star
Panama City News
Paris News
Pharos-Tribune and Press
Pioneer Press
Pittsburgh Courier

Playground Daily News
Salt Lake Tribune
Sandusky Register
Seattle Times
Sikeston Daily Standard
Somerset Daily American
Times Herald Record
Toledo Blade
Wall Street Journal
Washington Post
Wellsville Daily Reporter
Yale Daily News

Secondary Sources

Books

Altman, Rick. *Film/Genre*. London: British Film Institute, 1999.
Anderson, Terry. *The Sixties and the Movement*. New York: Oxford University Press, 1999.
Appy, Christian G. *American Reckoning: The Vietnam War and Our National Identity*. New York: Viking, 2015.
Appy, Christian G. *Patriots: The Vietnam War Remembered from All Sides*. New York: Penguin Books, 2003.
Appy, Christian G. *Working-Class War: American Combat Soldiers & Vietnam*. Chapel Hill: University of North Carolina Press, 1993.
Armstrong, Jennifer Keishin. *Mary and Lou and Rhoda and Ted: And All the Brilliant Minds Who Made the Mary Tyler Moore Show a Classic*. New York: Simon & Schuster, 2013.
Arsenault, Raymond. *Freedom Riders: 1961 and the Struggle for Racial Justice*. Oxford: Oxford University Press, 2011.
Bailey, Beth, and David Farber, eds. *America in the Seventies*. Lawrence: University Press of Kansas, 2004.
Balogh, Brian. *The Associational State: American Governance in the Twentieth Century*. Philadelphia: University of Philadelphia Press, 2015.
Bang, Derrick. *Charles M. Schulz: Li'l Beginnings*. Santa Rosa: Charles M. Schulz Museum and Research Center, 2003.
Barbour, Chad A. *From Daniel Boone to Captain America: Playing Indian in American Popular Culture*. Jackson: University Press of Mississippi, 2016.
Beidler, Philip D. *Scriptures for a Generation: What We Were Reading in the '60s*. Athens: University of Georgia Press, 1994.
Beito, David T. *From Mutual Aid to Welfare State: How Fraternal Societies Fought Poverty and Taught Character*. Washington, DC: Heritage Foundation, 2000.
Berkowitz, Edward D. *Something Happened: A Political and Cultural Overview of the Seventies*. New York: Columbia University Press, 2006.
Branch, Taylor. *At Canaan's Edge: America in the King Years, 1965–68*. New York: Simon & Schuster, 2006.
Brown, Kate. *Plutopia: Nuclear Families, Atomic Cities, and the Great Soviet and American Plutonium Disasters*. New York: Oxford University Press, 2013.
Brundage, W. Fitzhugh, ed. *Beyond Blackface: African Americans and the Creation of American Popular Culture, 1890–1930*. Chapel Hill: University of North Carolina Press, 2011.
Bruscoe, Elizabeth. *The Reformation of Machismo: Evangelical Conversion and Gender in Columbia*. Austin: University of Texas Press, 1995.
Cannon, Lou. *Governor Reagan: His Rise to Power*. New York: Public Affairs, 2003.

Carroll, Peter N. *It Seemed Like Nothing Happened: the Tragedy and Promise of America in the 1970s*. New York: Holt, Rinehart, and Winston, 1982.

Carson, Rachel. *Silent Spring*. Cambridge, MA: Riverside Press, 1962.

Carter, Dan T. *The Politics of Rage: George Wallace, the Origins of the New Conservatism, and the Transformation of Modern Politics*. Baton Rouge: Louisiana State University Press, 2000.

Cohen, Lizabeth. *A Consumers' Republic: The Politics of Mass Consumption in Postwar America*. New York: Vintage Books, 2003.

Coles, Robert. *The Middle Americans: Proud and Uncertain*. Boston: Little, Brown, 1971.

Connelly, Matthew. *Fatal Misconceptions: The Struggle to Control World Population*. Cambridge, MA: Harvard University Press, 2008.

Cooley, Angela Jill. *To Live and Dine in Dixie: The Evolution of Urban Food Culture in the Jim Crow South*. Athens: University of Georgia Press, 2015.

Costello, Matthew J. *Secret Identity Crisis: Comic Books & the Unmasking of Cold War America*. New York: Continuum, 2009.

Cowie, Jefferson R. *Stayin' Alive: the 1970s and the Last Days of the Working Class*. New York: The New Press, 2010.

Crespino, Joseph. *In Search of Another Country: Mississippi and the Conservative Counterrevolution*. Princeton, NJ: Princeton University Press, 2007.

Critchlow, Donald T. *Intended Consequences: Birth Control, Abortion, and the Federal Government in Modern America*. New York: Oxford University Press, 1999.

Critchlow, Donald T. *Phyllis Schlafly and Grassroots Conservatism: A Woman's Crusade*. Princeton, NJ: Princeton University Press, 2005.

Cronon, William. *Nature's Metropolis: Chicago and the Great West*. New York: Norton, 1991.

DeGroot, Gerard J. *The Sixties Unplugged: A Kaleidoscopic History of a Disorderly Decade*. Cambridge, MA: Harvard University Press, 2010.

Delmont, Matthew F. *Why Busing Failed: Race, Media, and the National Resistance to School Desegregation*. Oakland: University of California Press, 2016.

Deloria, Philip J. *Playing Indian*. New Haven, CT: Yale University Press, 1998.

DePastino, Todd. *Bill Mauldin: A Life Up Front*. New York: Norton, 2008.

Dochuk, Darren. *From Bible Belt to Sunbelt: Plain-Folk Religion, Grassroots Politics, and the Rise of Evangelical Conservatism*. New York: Norton, 2011.

Doherty, Thomas Patrick. *Cold War, Cool Medium: Television, McCarthyism, and American Culture*. New York: Columbia University Press, 2003.

Douglas, Susan J. *Where the Girls Are: Growing Up Female with the Mass Media*. New York: Three Rivers Press, 1994.

Dow, Bonnie J. *Watching Women's Liberation 1970: Feminism's Pivotal Year on the Network News*. Urbana: University of Illinois Press, 2014.

Drake, Brian Allen. *Loving Nature, Fearing the State: Environmentalism and Antigovernment Politics before Reagan*. Seattle: University of Washington Press, 2013.

Dunaway, Finis. *Seeing Green: The Use and Abuse of American Environmental Images*. Chicago: University of Chicago Press, 2015.

Eagles, Charles W. *The Price of Defiance: James Meredith and the Integration of Ole Miss*. Chapel Hill: University of North Carolina Press, 2014.

Elmore, Bartow J. *Citizen Coke: The Making of Coca-Cola Capitalism*. New York: Norton, 2015.

Engelhardt, Tom. *The End of Victory Culture: Cold War America and the Disillusioning of a Generation*. Amherst: University of Massachusetts Press, 1995.

Farber, David. *The Age of Great Dreams: America in the 1960s*. New York: Hill and Wang, 1994.

Farrell, Amy Erdman. *Yours in Sisterhood: Ms. Magazine and the Promise of Popular Feminism*. Chapel Hill: University of North Carolina Press, 1998.

Flippen, J. Brooks. *Nixon and the Environment*. Albuquerque: University of New Mexico Press, 2000.

Foley, Michael Stewart. *Confronting the War Machine: Draft Resistance during the Vietnam War*. Chapel Hill: University of North Carolina Press, 2003.

Foley, Michael Stewart. *Dear Dr. Spock: Letters about the Vietnam War to America's Favorite Baby Doctor*. New York: New York University Press, 2005.

Ford, Tanisha C. *Liberated Threads: Black Women, Style, and the Global Politics of Soul*. Chapel Hill: University of North Carolina Press, 2015.

Formisano, Ronald P. *Boston Against Busing: Race, Class, and Ethnicity in the 1960s and 1970s*. Chapel Hill: University of North Carolina Press, 1991.

Frum, David. *How We Got Here: The 70's: The Decade that Brought You Modern Life (For Better or Worse)*. New York: Basic Books, 2000.

Gallup, George. *The Gallup Poll: Public Opinion, 1935–1971, Vol. III*. New York: Random House, 1971.

Gardner, Jared, and Ian Gordon, eds. *The Comics of Charles Schulz: The Good Grief of Modern Life*. Jackson: University Press of Mississippi, 2018.

Gilbert, James Burkhart. *Men in the Middle: Searching for Masculinity in the 1950s*. Chicago: University of Chicago Press, 2005.

Gitlin, Todd. *The Sixties: Years of Hope, Days of Rage*. New York: Bantam Books, 1987.

Gordon, Ian. *Comic Strips and Consumer Culture, 1890–1945*. Washington, DC: Smithsonian Institution Press, 1998.

Gruening, Ernest. *Many Battles: The Autobiography of Ernest Gruening*. New York: Liveright, 1973.

Halberstam, David. *The Fifties*. New York: Random House, 1993.

Hale, Grace Elizabeth. *A Nation of Outsiders: How the White Middle Class Fell in Love with Rebellion in Postwar America*. New York: Oxford University Press, 2011.

Hale, Grace Elizabeth. *Making Whiteness: The Culture of Segregation in the South, 1890–1940*. New York: Pantheon Books, 1998.

Hall, Mitchell K. *Crossroads: American Popular Culture and the Vietnam Generation*. Lanham, MD: Rowman & Littlefield, 2005.

Hankins, Barry. *Francis Schaeffer and the Shaping of Evangelical America*. Grand Rapids, MI: William B. Eerdmans, 2008.

Hardin, Victoria A. *AIDs at 30: A History*. Washington, DC: Potomac Books, 2012.

Hartman, Andrew. *A War for the Soul of America: A History of the Culture Wars*. Chicago: University of Chicago Press, 2015.

Harvey, Robert C. *The Art of the Funnies: An Aesthetic History*. Jackson: University Press of Mississippi, 1994.

Hays, Samuel P. *Beauty, Health, and Permanence: Environmental Politics in the United States, 1955–1985*. Cambridge: Cambridge University Press, 1989.

Henriksen, Margot A. *Dr. Strangelove's America: Society and Culture in the Atomic Age*. Berkeley: University of California Press, 1997.

Herring, George C. *America's Longest War: The United States and Vietnam, 1950–1975*. Boston: McGraw-Hill, 2002.

Hoff, Derek S. *The State and the Stork: The Population Debate and Policy Making in US History*. Chicago: Chicago University Press, 2012.

Howard, Sheena C., and Ronald L. Jackson II, eds. *Black Comics: Politics of Race and Representation*. London: Bloomsbury, 2013.

Howe, Sean. *Marvel Comics: The Untold Story*. New York: Harper, 2012.

Huebner, Andrew J. *The Warrior Image: Soldiers in American Culture from the Second World War to the Vietnam Era*. Chapel Hill: University of North Carolina Press, 2008.

Hughes, Langston. *Vintage Hughes*. New York: Vintage Books, 2004.

Inge, M. Thomas, ed. *Charles M. Schulz: Conversations*. Jackson: University Press of Mississippi, 2000.

Inge, M. Thomas, ed. *My Life with Charlie Brown*. Jackson: University Press of Mississippi, 2010.

Isserman, Maurice and Michael Kazin. *America Divided: The Civil War of the 1960s*. New York: Oxford University Press, 2008.

Iverson, Kristen. *Full Body Burden: Growing Up in the Shadow of Rocky Flatts*. New York: Crown, 2012.

Jackson, Kenneth T. *Crabgrass Frontier: The Suburbanization of the United States*. New York: Oxford University Press, 1985.

Jacobs, Meg. *Panic at the Pump: The Energy Crisis and the Transformation of American Politics in the 1970s*. New York: Hill and Wang, 2016.

Jenkins, Philip. *Decade of Nightmares: The End of the Sixties and the Making of Eighties America*. New York: Oxford University Press, 2006.

Johnson, Rheta Grimsley. *Good Grief: The Story of Charles M. Schulz*. New York: Pharos Books, 1989.

Johnson, Robert David. *Ernest Gruening and the American Dissenting Tradition*. Cambridge, MA: Harvard University Press, 1998.

Jones, Daniel Stedman. *Masters of the Universe: Hayek, Friedman, and the Birth of Neoliberal Politics*. Princeton, NJ: Princeton University Press, 2012.

Klatch, Rebecca E. *A Generation Divided: The New Left, The New Right, and the 1960s*. Berkeley: University of California Press, 1999.

Koop, C. Everett. *Koop: The Memoirs of America's Family Doctor*. New York: Random House, 1991.

Kruse, Kevin M. *One Nation Under God: How Corporate America Invented Christian America*. New York: Basic Books, 2015.

Kudlow, Lawrence, and Brian Domitrovic, *JFK and the Reagan Revolution: A Secret History of American Prosperity*. New York: Portfolio, 2016.

Kuznick, Peter J., and James Gilbert, eds. *Rethinking Cold War Culture*. Washington, DC: Smithsonian Institution Press, 2001.

Landers, James. *The Weekly War: Newsmagazines and Vietnam*. Columbia: University of Missouri Press, 2004.

Lassiter, Matthew D. *The Silent Majority: Suburban Politics in the Sunbelt South*. Princeton, NJ: Princeton University Press, 2006.

Lee, Stan. *The Superhero Women*. New York: Simon & Schuster, 1977.

Lepore, Jill. *The Secret History of Wonder Woman*. New York: Knopf, 2014.

Lewis, Penny. *Hardhats, Hippies, and Hawks: The Vietnam Antiwar Movement as Myth and Memory*. Ithaca, NY: ILR Press, 2013.

Lind, Stephen J. *A Charlie Brown Religion: Exploring the Spiritual Life and Work of Charles M. Schulz*. Jackson: University Press of Mississippi, 2015.

Lockwood, George. *Peanuts, Pogo, and Hobbes: A Newspaper Editor's Journey through the World of Comics*. Syracuse, NY: Syracuse University Press, 2013.

Lyons, Paul. *New Left, New Right, and the Legacy of the Sixties*. Philadelphia: Temple University Press, 1996.

Lytle, Mark. *America's Uncivil Wars: The Sixties Era From Elvis to the Fall of Richard Nixon*. New York: Oxford University Press, 2006.

Mailer, Norman. *Miami and the Siege of Chicago: An Informal History of the Republican and Democratic Conventions of 1968*. New York: World Publishing, 1968.

Manseau, Peter. *One Nation, Under Gods: A New American History*. Boston: Little, Brown, 2015.

Marling, Karal Ann. *As Seen On TV: The Visual Culture of Everyday Life in the 1950s*. Cambridge, MA: Harvard University Press, 1994.

Martin, William. *A Prophet with Honor: The Billy Graham Story*. New York: Morrow, 1991.

Martini, Edwin A. *Agent Orange: History, Science, and the Politics of Uncertainty*. Amherst: University of Massachusetts Press, 2012.

Matusow, Allen J. *The Unraveling of America: A History of Liberalism in the 1960s*. Athens: University of Georgia Press, 2009.

May, Elaine Tyler. *Homeward Bound: American Families in the Cold War Era*. New York: Basic Books, 1988.

McGirr, Lisa. *Suburban Warriors: The Origins of the New Right*. Princeton, NJ: Princeton University Press, 2001.

McGuire, Danielle L. *At the Dark End of the Street: Black Women, Rape, and Resistance: A New History of the Civil Right Movement from Rosa Parks to the Rise of Black Power*. New York: Vintage Books, 2011.

Mendelson, Lee. *A Charlie Brown Christmas: The Making of a Tradition*. New York: HarperResource, 2000.

Mendelson, Lee. *Charlie Brown and Charlie Schulz*. New York: New American Library, 1971.

Michaelis, David. *Schulz and Peanuts: A Biography*. New York: Harper Perennial, 2007.

Miller, Steven P. *The Age of Evangelicalism: America's Born-Again Years*. New York: Oxford University Press, 2014.

Millett, Allan R. *The War for Korea, 1945–1950: A House Burning*. Lawrence: University of Kansas Press, 2005.

Millett, Allan R. *The War for Korea, 1950–1951: They Came from the North*. Lawrence: University of Kansas Press, 2010.

Moeller, Susan D. *Shooting War: Photography and the American Experience of Combat*. New York: Basic Books, 1989.

Moreton, Bethany. *To Serve God and Walmart: The Making of Christian Free Enterprise*. Cambridge, MA: Harvard University Press, 2009.

Nama, Adilifu. *Super Black: American Pop Culture and Black Superheroes*. Austin: University of Texas Press, 2011.

Naske, Claus-M. *Ernest Gruening: Alaska's Greatest Governor*. Fairbanks: University of Alaska Press, 2004.

Nickerson, Michelle M. *Mother of Conservatism: Women and the Postwar Right*. Princeton, NJ: Princeton University Press, 2012.

Nord, David Paul. *A History of the Book in America, Vol. 5: The Enduring Book: Print Culture in Postwar America*. Chapel Hill: University of North Carolina Press, 2009.

Norrell, Robert J. *The House I Live In: Race in the American Century*. New York: Oxford University Press, 2005.

Nyberg, Amy Kiste. *Seal of Approval: The History of the Comics Code*. Jackson: University Press of Mississippi, 1998.

Oakley, J. Ronald. *God's Country: America in the Fifties*. New York: Dembner Books, 1986.

Patterson, James T. *Brown v. Board of Education: A Civil Rights Milestone and Its Troubled Legacy*. New York: Oxford University Press, 2001.

Patterson, James T. *Grand Expectations: The United States, 1945–1974*. New York: Oxford University Press, 1996.

Patterson, James T. *Restless Giant: The United States from Watergate to Bush v. Gore*. New York: Oxford University Press, 2005.

Phillips-Fein, Kim. *Invisible Hands: The Businessman's Crusade Against the New Deal*. New York: Norton, 2009.

Rogers, Heather. *Gone Tomorrow: The Hidden Life of Garbage*. New York: The New Press, 2005.

Rome, Adam. *The Bulldozer in the Countryside: Suburban Sprawl and the Rise of American Environmentalism*. Cambridge: Cambridge University Press, 2001.

Rome, Adam. *The Genius of Earth Day: How a 1970 Teach-In Unexpectedly Made the First Green Generation*. New York: Hill and Wang, 2013.

Rosen, Ruth. *The World Split Open: How the Modern Women's Movement Changed America*. New York: Penguin Books, 2000.

Rothman, Hal K. *The Greening of a Nation?: Environmentalism in the United States since 1945*. Fort Worth: Harcourt Brace College Publishers, 1998.

Sabin, Paul. *The Bet: Paul Ehrlich, Julian Simon, and Our Gamble over Earth's Future*. New Haven, CT: Yale University Press, 2013.

Saguisag, Lara. *Incorrigibles and Innocents: Constructing Childhood and Citizenship in Progressive Era Comics*. New Brunswick, NJ: Rutgers University Press, 2019.

Sandbrook, Dominic. *Mad as Hell: The Crisis of the 1970s and the Rise of the Populist Right*. New York: Knopf, 2011.

Schmitz, David F. *The Tet Offensive: Politics, War and Public Opinion*. Lanham, MD: Rowman & Littlefield, 2005.

Schulman, Bruce J., and Julian E. Zelizer. *Rightward Bound: Making America Conservative in the 1970s*. Cambridge, MA: Harvard University Press, 2008.

Schulman, Bruce J. *The Seventies: The Great Shift in American Culture, Society, and Politics*. Cambridge, MA: Da Capo Press, 2002.

Schulz, Charles M. *Peanuts Jubilee: My Life and Art with Charlie Brown and Others*. New York: Rinehart and Winston, 1975.

Schulz, Charles M. *Peanuts: A Golden Celebration*. New York: HarperCollins, 1999.

Self, Robert O. *All in the Family: The Realignment of American Democracy since the 1960s*. New York: Hill and Wang, 2012.

Self, Robert O. *American Babylon: Race and the Struggle for Postwar Oakland*. Princeton, NJ: Princeton University Press, 2003.

Sherry, Michael S. *In the Shadow of War: The United States since the 1930s*. New Haven, CT: Yale University Press, 1995.

Shilts, Randy. *And the Band Played On: Politics, People, and the AIDs Epidemic*. New York: St. Martin's Press, 1987.

Short, Robert L. *The Gospel According to Peanuts*. Atlanta: J. Knox Press, 1965.

Skinner, Kiron K., Annelise Anderson, and Martin Anderson, eds. *Reagan: A Life in Letters*. New York: Free Press, 2003.

Slotkin, Richard. *Gunfighter Nation: The Myth of the Frontier in Twentieth Century America*. New York: Atheneum, 1992.

Small, Melvin. *Antiwarriors: The Vietnam War and the Battle for America's Hearts and Minds*. Lanham, MD: SR Books, 2002.

Smith, Sherry L. *Hippies, Indians, and the Fight for Red Power*. New York: Oxford University Press, 2014.

Solomon, Charles. *The Art and Making of Peanuts Animation: Celebrating Fifty Years of Television Specials*. San Francisco: Chronicle Books, 2012.

Soluri, John. *Banana Cultures: Agriculture, Consumption, and Environmental Change in Honduras and the United States*. Austin: University of Texas Press, 2005.

Soper, Kerry D. *We Go Pogo: Walt Kelly, Politics, and American Satire*. Jackson: University Press of Mississippi, 2012.

Souder, William. *On a Farther Shore: The Life and Legacy of Rachel Carson*. New York: Broadway Books, 2012.

Steinem, Gloria. *My Life on the Road*. New York: Random House, 2015.

Strömberg, Frederik. *Black Images in the Comics: A Visual History*. Seattle: Fantagraphics Books, 2003.
Sugrue, Thomas J. *The Origins of the Urban Crisis: Race and Inequality in Postwar Detroit*. Princeton, NJ: Princeton University Press, 1996.
Sutton, Matthew Avery. *American Apocalypse: A History of Modern Evangelicalism*. Cambridge, MA: The Belknap Press of Harvard University Press, 2014.
Tisserand, Michael. *Krazy: George Herriman, A Life in Black and White*. New York: Harper Perennial, 2016.
Tucker, Richard. *Insatiable Appetite: The United States and the Ecological Degradation of the Tropical World*. Berkeley: University of California Press, 2000.
Verney, Kevern. *African Americans and US Popular Culture*. London: Routledge, 2003.
Wacker, Grant. *America's Pastor: Billy Graham and the Shaping of a Nation*. Cambridge, MA: The Belknap Press of Harvard University, 2014.
Walker, Brian. *The Comics: The Complete Collection*. New York: Abrams ComicArts, 2011.
Ware, Susan. *Game, Set, Match: Billie Jean King and the Revolution in Women's Sports*. Chapel Hill: University of North Carolina Press, 2011.
Waterhouse, Benjamin C. *Lobbying America: The Politics of Business from Nixon to NAFTA*. Princeton, NJ: Princeton University Press, 2013.
Weisbrot, Robert, and G. Calvin Mackenzie, *The Liberal Hour: Washington and the Politics of Change in the 1960s*. New York: Penguin Press, 2008.
White, Theodore H. *The Making of the President 1960*. New York: Atheneum House, 1961.
Whitted, Qiana. *EC Comics: Race, Shock, & Social Protest*. New Brunswick: Rutgers University Press, 2019.
Whitfield, Stephen J. *The Culture of the Cold War*. Baltimore: Johns Hopkins University Press, 1996.
Wilentz, Sean. *The Age of Reagan, 1974–2008*. New York: Harper, 2008.
Williams, Daniel K. *Defenders of the Unborn: The Pro-Life Movement before Roe v. Wade*. New York: Oxford University Press, 2016.
Williams, Daniel K. *God's Own Party: The Making of the Christian Right*. New York: Oxford University Press.
Wright, Bradford W. *Comic Book Nation: The Transformation of Youth Culture in America*. Baltimore: Johns Hopkins University Press, 2001.
Young, Neil J. *We Gather Together: The Religious Right and the Problem of Interfaith Politics*. New York: Oxford University Press, 2016.
Zelizer, Julian. *The Fierce Urgency of Now: Lyndon Johnson, Congress, and the Battle for the Great Society*. New York: Penguin Books, 2015.
Zelko, Frank S. *Make It a Green Peace!: The Rise of Countercultural Environmentalism*. New York: Oxford University Press, 2013.

Articles

Foley, Michael Stewart. "A Politics of Empathy: Johnny Cash, the Vietnam War, and the 'Walking Contradiction' Myth Dismantled." *Popular Music and Society* 37, no. 3 (June 2013): 338–59.
Griffith, Robert. "The Selling of America: The Advertising Council and American Politics, 1942–1960." *Business History Review* 57, no. 3 (Autumn 1983): 388–412.
Kahrl, Andrew W. "Fear of an Open Beach: Public Rights and Private Interests in 1970s Coastal Connecticut." *Journal of American History* 102, no. 2 (Sep. 2015): 433–62.
Lind, Stephen J. "Christmas in the 1960s: *A Charlie Brown Christmas*, Religion, and the Conventions of the Television Genre." *Journal of Religion and Popular Culture* 26 (Spring 2014): 1–22.

O'Connor, Mike. "Liberals in Space: The 1960s Politics of Star Trek." *The Sixties* 5, no. 2 (2012): 185–203.

Ridgeway, Ann N. "Allen Saunders." *Journal of Popular Culture* 5 (Fall 1971): 385–420.

Smith, Jean K. "Christmas Seals 1978." *Art Education* 31, no. 7 (Nov. 1978): 4–5.

Tilley, Carol L. "Seducing the Innocent: Frederic Wertham and the Falsifications That Helped Condemn Comics." *Information & Culture* 47, no. 4 (2012): 383–414.

Index

For the benefit of digital users, indexed terms that span two pages (e.g., 52–53) may, on occasion, appear on only one of those pages.